The Healthy
COMPANY

Eight Strategies to Develop
People, Productivity, and Profits

Robert H. Rosen, Ph.D.
with Lisa Berger

Foreword by James A. Autry

JEREMY P. TARCHER/PERIGEE

TO JAY AND SUZANNE

Jeremy P. Tarcher/Perigee Books
are published by
The Putnam Publishing Group
200 Madison Avenue
New York, NY 10016

Library of Congress Cataloging-in-Publication Data

Rosen, Robert H.
    The healthy company : eight strategies to develop people,
  productivity, and profits / Robert H. Rosen with Lisa Berger ;
  foreword by James A. Autry.
        p.   cm.
    Includes bibliographical references and index.
    ISBN 0-87477-708-9
    1. Industrial management.   2. Personnel management.   3. Quality of
  work life.   4. Success in business.   I. Berger, Lisa.   II. Title.
  HD31.R723   1992
  658—dc20   92-28602 CIP

First Tarcher/Perigee edition 1992

Jeremy P. Tarcher, Inc.
5858 Wilshire Blvd., Suite 200
Los Angeles, CA 90036

A Tilden Press Book

Design by Mauna Eichner

To communicate with Robert Rosen, or for more information about
Healthy Companies, contact: Healthy Companies, 1420 16th Street, N.W.,
Washington, D.C. (202) 234-9288.

Manufactured in the United States of America
10   9   8   7   6   5   4   3   2   1

First Edition

This book is printed on acid-free paper.

Contents

Foreword

ALL OF US KNOW people in business who like to say, "Let's just skip to the bottom line." So okay, let's just skip to the bottom line of this book:

Healthy people make healthy companies. And healthy companies are more likely, more often, and over a longer period of time, to make healthy profits and to have healthy returns on their investments.

So healthy people and healthy relationships are at the very core of success in business, but for too long the old fear-based hierarchical paradigms of management and of management-employee relationships have driven the way business is done in America. I might add that those old paradigms also have just about driven business into the ground.

But the last chapters on management by fear are being written. They are being written by the workers who, in Max DePree's words, are increasingly "volunteer workers" and who are not afraid. They are not afraid because they know that they do not have to work for salary and benefits alone—or at least they do not have to do that for very long.

So the new question for managers, for leaders, is this: "Just what will these new workers work for if it's not for money and benefits and perks and status?"

Answer: They'll work for love.

This means that the new challenge for managers is to create a loving workplace, or if you're uneasy with that word, call it the caring workplace. Management and leadership in the nineties will be about creating a place in which people can feel good about what they do, can feel ennobled by it, and can be rewarded by it—not only with professional and financial growth but with personal and spiritual growth as the heart of those rewards.

Creating this kind of workplace is hard work. It requires full-time, everyday commitment and engagement with the job. It requires that we think of management as a calling, a helping profession, a sacred trust in which the well-being of people is put in the manager's hands for most of their waking hours.

It means letting go of ego, of the old concepts of control and supervision—not to mention manipulation—and embracing instead the equally old but in business rarely used concepts of honesty and trust, which lead ultimately to the empowerment of every employee.

It means being honest with how we feel as well as with what we say.

It means having the courage to represent the employees to higher management and representing higher management to the employees.

It means giving people special treatment, not because we like them or they belong to a certain club or have skin of a certain color or are of a certain gender, but because they have special human needs.

It means understanding that authority and power and influence are not the same, and that influence is more important than the other two.

It means depending on *who you are* and not on what title you hold in order to build relationships, to create a community of work, to achieve the goals which you have envisioned.

It means asking instead of telling.

It means serving and being a resource and a helper instead of an overseer.

Easy stuff to say. Hard stuff to do.

That's where Bob Rosen's work can help. He has put together in *The Healthy Company* an enormously useful compendium of observations, research, case histories, and wisdom. He establishes a philosophical and theoretical thesis as well as practical guidelines. There is material here that defines in lucid terms exactly what makes a company healthy, which allows managers to assess themselves and their potential, helps them address the physical *and* emotional needs of employees, and defines the most fundamental management-employee goal of all: healthy relationships.

The truth of this book is that it lays out for all who will read it exactly what managers will have to do to heal themselves, their relationships, and their companies in order to succeed in the nineties. This brings us right back to the bottom line: Healthy people, and nothing else, make healthy companies.

JAMES A. AUTRY
President of Magazine Group,
Meredith Corporation and
author of *Love and Profit*

Acknowledgments

THE HEALTHY COMPANY is the product of a large family. I would like to extend my deepest thanks and appreciation to a number of those who have made a special contribution to this project:

To Jay and Suzanne, who loved, inspired, and believed in me and taught me all about values and possibilities.

To my family—Barbara, Dick, Randi, Beatrice, Harry, Joe, Rick, Christopher, Ryan, Dorothy, John, Margot, Jerry, Lynne, Mark, Erin, Amanda, Michael, Paul, Nancy, and Snapper—for surrounding me with love and encouragement.

To my special friend and business partner, Sarah Bullard Steck, who is always a source of insight and support; and to my colleagues at Healthy Companies, especially Janet Moyer, Mary Boylen, Jill Klobucar-Logan, Ellen Nash, Virginia Dickey, and Verna Cauley for their commitment and hard work on this project.

To Lisa Berger, a true journalist in every sense of the word, and Joel Makower, for his creativity and keen sense of humor.

To my family of friends: Amy Cunningham, Marshall Singer, Tom Mader, Susan Blake, Phil Polakoff, John Burnim, Jared Falek, Mark Grayson, Sam Paschall, Leslie Scallet, Stanley and Karlyn Robinson, Bob Steck, Jim Mathews, and Gary Hasza, whom I love and admire.

To the MacArthur Foundation, who believed in me and in the value of healthy companies. To my dear colleague and friend Denis Prager and his staff, and to the many people who study human and organization development and provide a true catalyst for change.

To my colleagues and friends at the Washington Business Group on Health, who provided me with constant stretching and support: Miriam Jacobson, Roni Vacarro, Don Galvin, Gail Schwartz, Robert Levin, Anne Kiefhaber, Carol Cronin, Rick Lee, Cathy Certner, Ellen Menton, Ruth Behrens, Barbara Armstrong, Kathy Doherty, and the many others along the way. Special thanks to all the WBGH members who taught me about life in corporate America. My warmest thoughts go to Bill Goldbeck, founder of the WBGH, as a friend, colleague, mentor and source of inspiration.

To my terrific business colleagues, who continue to challenge me: Dennis Jaffe, Cynthia Scott, Alan Westin, Diana Chapman Walsh, Robert Levering, Ernie Savoie, Ian Browde, Chris Bisgard, Bob Beck, Brad Googins, Kirk Hanson, Michele Hunt, Leon Warshaw, Douglas LaBier, Josh Mailman, John Kao, Rick Bellingham, Gillian Rudd, Carey Horwitz, Elsa Porter, Marilyn Puder-York, Andrew Sherman, John Sauer, Hal Tragash, Elaine Willis, and Burt Brim.

To my clinical colleagues, who inspired me over the years with their deepest insight and sensitivity: Stuart Sotsky, David Glass, Ron Kurz, Bruce Copeland, Fred Strassburger, Rebecca Reiger, and my friends at Children's Hospital and the George Washington University Medical Center.

To the organizations who have made a commitment to building healthy organizations: Business Enterprise Trust, Social Venture Network, World Business Academy, National Association of Women Business Owners, European Council for Health, Human Resource Network, Council on Economic Priorities, National Institute on Mental Health, National Institute for Occupational Safety and Health, and the DHHS Office of Disease Prevention and Health Promotion.

To those who helped create the MacArthur Foundation program: Joseph Bevan, Larry Bushmaker, Harold Davis, Barbara Feuer, Robert Fischer, John Fleming, James Francek, Ellen Frank, Axel Goetz, Jack Hanley, Willis Harmon, Ted Hearne, Jeanne Kardos, Richard Kilburg, Salvadore Maddi, William May, David Me-

Kardos, Richard Kilburg, Salvadore Maddi, William May, David Mechanic, Nancy Merritt, Meredith Miller, Tom Pasco, Jim Renier, Morton Silverman, John Simmons, John Sweeney, Loring Wood, and Walter Wriston.

To those who shared their insights during the writing of this book: Sarah Hardesty Bray, Juanita Weaver, Mitchell Marks, Laura Henderson, Charito Kruvant, Lyman G. Bullard, Jack Smith, Pete Massochi, Edward Brethaeur, Nate Karch, Sandra Spangenberg, Nancy Taylor, Bryan Lawton, Lennie Copeland, Lewis Griggs, Jan Van Meter, Eileen Sweeney, Mary Bruxelles, Ken Barry, David R. Johnston, Gerald Ledford, Don Jalpert, Scott Panick, Jim Anderson, Mark Battle, Barbara Sloan, Bill O'Brien, Richard Kotz, and Aimee Toth.

To those who came before me and carved a path: Warren Bennis, Michael Maccoby, Harry Levinson, Max DePree, Bob Haas, Edgar Schein, Tom Peters, Larry Hirschorn, Edward Lawlor, Peter Senge, John Fielding, Ken Pelletier, Ian Mitroff, Peter Drucker, Milton Moskowitz, Rosabeth Moss Kanter, and Manfred Kets deFries.

To the hundreds of healthy companies and their partners who sharpen my ideas, expand my perceptions, and provide boundless inspiration for my work.

And finally to my publisher, Jeremy Tarcher, and editor, Rick Benzel, who pushed me to discover a healthy company inside me that I would never have imagined.

Bob Rosen

TO: THE READER

FROM: BOB ROSEN

RE: THE HEALTHY COMPANY

SEVERAL YEARS AGO ON a business trip to Chicago, I met two successful entrepreneurs at O'Hare Airport while waiting out a thunderstorm on a Friday afternoon. We covered all the bases, from domestic politics and interest rates to reforms in the Soviet Union. The conversation eventually turned to my work and I told them I was writing a book called *The Healthy Company.* At this, one of the men looked at me and asked, "Oh, is it a novel?"

I am often confronted with this kind of skepticism when I talk about the subject, but I have never believed that healthy companies are figments of my imagination. It *is* possible for people to get what they need and want from work at the same time companies get what they most desire from people. Healthy companies are not only possible but are crucial for staying alive and competitive in the twenty-first century.

This book is about building healthy companies. Its ideas and ideals are a natural progression of thinking, blending years of expertise from the management and health sciences. From Frederick Taylor's scientific management to Tom Peters' evangelical excellence, these ideas bridge the academic and business worlds, combining research findings with real-life business examples. This book is not meant to be an exhaustive scholarly review, nor is it a comprehensive compendium of healthy company practices. Others in the field have already done this. My perspective is more of an eclectic one, integrating disciplines and taking a holistic view of people and their organizations.

Some business leaders have already built successful companies based on these principles. Harry Heinz, founder of the great company of fifty-seven varieties, is such a leader, who instituted a number of forward-looking policies under the vision of *heartpower*. An employee cafeteria, emergency room on the premises, gym with swimming pool, and classroom training—all at the company's expense—were just a few of his innovations. Heinz knew these programs benefited his employees and the company.

There have also been periods in history when we paid special attention to humanistic principles at work. In the 1960s, for example, the human potential movement led business to examine the psyche of its workers and work groups. However, there was never any solid connection made between humanistic principles and economics.

In the 1990s, no longer are these ideas simply the nice ways to conduct business. They are not just perks, short-term frills, or the inventions of a few socially responsible companies in the heartland of America. Now more than ever, they are the requirements of running a successful business.

I learned about heartpower early in my career as a psychologist treating troubled teenage sons and daughters of successful business people. In working with these families, I saw firsthand the effects of Type-A personalities with their controlling, distant, and driven demeanors. These people were in no way bad men or women; they were not deliberately making life difficult for their spouses, families, employees, or themselves. They just knew no other way to be successful, and they thought there was no room in the competitive world for feelings of empathy, nurturing, openness, and spontaneity.

Over the next ten years, I had the opportunity to consult with the Washington Business Group on Health, a membership organization of two hundred Fortune 500 companies providing leadership on human-resource policy concerns. There I coordinated several task forces and conducted research, surveys, and hundreds of interviews with business and health leaders across the country. In 1987, with the help of the MacArthur Foundation, I began a three-year development project to examine the intersection of human and economic concerns. What I found was both frustrating and discouraging.

For one thing, it didn't take long to discover what many of you know very well. If American business is not yet in the coronary care unit, it certainly suffers from a severe case of structural arteriosclerosis. You know the signs as well as I do—productivity decline, inadequately trained workers, constant job hopping, and employees who complain about unfairness and bad management.

What surprised me most was that there was little top-down appreciation for how people contribute to a company's bottom line. The link between people, principles, and profits was consistently shockingly underestimated. Many of the human capital experts responsible for managing these issues—human resource, medical, training, and benefits professionals—were out of the mainstream of their company's operations. They had little influence in decision making and limited data to make a solid case for the importance of people. In many cases, the operating managers rarely paid much attention to their suggestions. I wanted to know why, given all the knowledge available about the interrelationship of human development, motivation, and productivity.

I well remember a conversation I had with the senior manager of an investment bank during the Wall Street boom of the 1980s. His company was raking in money at a dizzying rate, his professionals were working practically around the clock, and employee compensation and turnover rates were both at stratospheric levels. I asked how he dealt with employee burnout. "We don't," he said dismissively. "We know damn well that when our traders and M&A [mergers and acquisition] boys get to around the age of forty, they're pretty burned out . . . not much use to us anymore. Maybe a drug or alcohol problem, probably a divorce or two in the background." He shrugged. "But what the hell? They've made a lot of money for us. And they've made enough money for themselves to afford to stay at a drying-out clinic and then go sail their yachts for the rest of their lives."

With examples like that in too great an abundance, where financially strong companies seem to get that way in part by using their employees like oranges to be sucked dry and discarded, I knew my work would be an uphill battle. So I set out to find a different model to replace what I saw as the outmoded and dysfunctional paradigm, the malignant model of leadership.

Since then, I have been seeking out and consulting managers and executives, examining what's inside America's business people and their companies. From start-up entrepreneurs to mid-level managers to Fortune 500 CEOs, I've listened to the daily traumas, the career struggles, and the inner pain that come with managing workers in the late twentieth century. I've also talked with employees and heard their frustrations and dissatisfactions. But most importantly I've observed the most progressive, people-oriented companies in America. From this grew the concept of healthy companies.

My point of view is that many people and organizations sell themselves short, operating well below full potential. Instead of striving for health and productivity, they accept stress and mediocrity as the norm. As a result, they lead unhealthy lives and build unhealthy organizations, both of which undermine the success of the other.

This book is about doing it better. It's about becoming an architect of your own healthy company. Whether you are president of a multibillion-dollar communications company, the product manager of a consumer products firm, the loan officer at a bank, a warehouse supervisor of twenty employees, head of a data processing department, or the owner of a fledgling restaurant, this book is written for you. No organization is exempt. The concept of a healthy company is relevant to all work sites and across all industries.

The book is designed as a coursebook. Following the introduction the eight chapters reveal the eight principles of the healthy company. In them, you will find abundant practical tips and advice, personal questionnaires, state-of-the-art research, hundreds of company examples, and voices from the leaders of healthy companies across the country.

Each chapter usually includes three sections. The first section, "Inside Out," is designed as a journey of self-examination. It begins with a personal questionnaire assessing your attitudes, prejudices, and sabotaging behaviors, followed by a series of action steps. Though this questionnaire is not statistically valid, it will provide a score to help you get started. The second section, "What Managers Can Do," incorporates these insights into practical advice for managing the human side of business. The final section, "Corporate Policies and Strategies," illustrates the most effective healthy company practices. There are well over two hundred organizations cited in this book, not all of which are healthy from top to bottom. In fact, there may be companies mentioned that you personally know are unhealthy places to work. In those cases, the company may have been healthy in the past or somewhere in the organization an enlightened manager was willing to stand up for what he or she believed was right. Nonetheless the practices listed do represent some of the best policies available in each of the areas.

You may already work for a healthy company and need only a simple refresher course; your bosses and colleagues may understand and support your values, in which case you probably use many of these suggestions.

However, I find many people aren't so fortunate. Their company is not as healthy and they must learn to navigate through difficult circumstances. Some healthy managers choose to work in unhealthy companies, where they are considered mavericks and are cajoled for their lack of business acumen. They deal daily with the resistance of insecure, cynical bosses and passive, suspicious employees. Other managers are unhealthy themselves and end up sabotaging their own dealings with employees. In either case, you must be honest with your barriers and resistances.

Regardless of your starting point, I suggest you open yourself up to a fresh perspective on organizational life. The success of these suggestions depends on you being your own CEO—taking charge of your life—first personalizing, then institutionalizing the ideas of healthy companies. Working in and growing a healthy company is hard work. It requires full-time commitment, patience, and persistence. It is a long-term process of continuous improvement in which all workers—employees, managers, and executives—must examine their own attitudes and values, their relationships with others, and finally the quality of the work environment.

My hope is that on completion of the book you will have enhanced your leadership skills and become a better manager of human capital. You will have improved your own self-awareness, learned to manage in healthier ways, and created a work environment that optimizes the human resources of your firm.

The Anatomy of a Healthy Company

IMAGINE GOING TO WORK, walking into your office or plant, and encountering a vibrant, stimulating atmosphere. In talking to employees about an upcoming deadline or project, you hear only enthusiasm and commitment. They are eager to work hard, listen to your vision and strategy, and graciously share ideas. Some of the employees brainstorm about possible glitches and how to boost sales and profits. They banter with you and among themselves, their easy humor showing that they enjoy their work and that they like and respect you.

As the day progresses, they are on the phone, meeting among themselves, or intent at the computer, sometimes coming to you with creative ideas or special requests. Each assignment is approached with a sense of urgency. These diligent employees are continuously looking for ways to improve their product or service, to deliver it faster and better, and to upgrade their skills.

When someone volunteers to take charge, others are quick to join in to help. They know that on another project, they may be the leader and need support. They are confident that you value their input: you listen to their suggestions and are flexible enough to accommodate each of them. The atmosphere is charged by employee voices that are sincere and remarkably human and personal. There are no awkward silences when

A healthy company is immediately noticeable. Employees "bounce" into work, they are interested in their jobs, they speak in the first person rather than the third person ("my responsibility" or "our job" rather than "their fault"), and they go home feeling good about themselves and their accomplishments.

ROBERT W. REED
Vice-President, Intel Corp.

1

bosses pass by, nor is there secretive scribbling of self-protective memos or sullen hostility between employees competing for bigger budgets and more attention. The usual me-versus-you antagonism has been replaced by a sharing of responsibilities and a feeling that all are working together. Teamwork and partnerships, rather than the old rigid ladders, make up the company structure.

Perhaps most remarkable about this new atmosphere is a feeling of respect. From the flexible schedules to the fair salaries and benefits to the sharing of vital information, the company shows that it truly cares about people, and employees reciprocate this trust with loyalty.

This is a sketch of what I call a healthy company. This kind of organization may sound far-fetched—a corporate utopia that only dreamers or the very naive would believe in. For many companies, it is. But among the millions of businesses in this country, some are quietly, decisively transforming themselves into healthy companies. They are driven by an unshakable conviction that only a healthy company will be alive and competitive in the coming years.

POTENT PRESSURES

Why is it imperative that we encourage the growth of healthy companies? As I travel around the country visiting organizations, I see them struggling with five potent forces that are redefining the nature of American business. A handful of companies have already recognized and capitalized on these forces; others feel the pressures but do not know how to channel them into future plans. Still others do not even see them, and if and when they do, it may be too late. Companies that ignore these forces or underestimate their impact do so at their peril. These are the forces at work:

The Power of People

The power of people is perhaps the most potent force, for it reaches into all facets of all kinds of businesses, touching every stage of operations and every strategy, goal, or vision. All companies are affected, regardless of how many employees they have—from the five-person ad agency to the ten-thousand-plus manufacturing firm. In its simplest form, the power of people is replacing traditional assumptions that other tangibles, such as financing, markets, or technology, determine the course of a company. The new reality is that how people work, think, and feel dictates the direction and success of a business.

Several demographic shifts are further magnifying the power of people. The shrinking work force; the demand for smart, skilled, motivated workers who have more mental than manual skills and can process information quickly; and the growing service economy, which stresses quality, teamwork, and attention to customers, all are underscoring the importance of the individual. The 1990s labor market is a seller's market—where employees are the sellers and their employers are the buyers. In this people-oriented, relationship-driven workplace, profit is generated through the hearts and minds of all employees—through their competence, capacity, and commitment. Competitive advantage will go to the companies that understand this.

Because individuals are contributing more and more to the lifeblood of companies, the costs of mismanaging them can only drain those companies. Management can choose either to treat people as valuable human assets to be maintained and improved on or to continue the hemorrhaging, treating them as costly liabilities that increasingly demand more money for health claims, accidents, mediocrity, and replacement.

White male corporate culture is disappearing, and the workplace is becoming less a melting pot than a mosaic. The white male share of the labor force will drop to 39.4% by the year 2000 from 48.9% in 1976, according to the U.S. Labor Department, while the share of women and people of African, Hispanic, Asian, and Native American origin will rise.

Quoted in the *Wall Street Journal*

A Company of Strangers

The changing complexion of the workplace is the second force. Soon typical American workers will not be white, middle-aged men but a collage of people—women, blacks, Hispanics, Asians, older workers, and the disabled. Although ethnically rich, this diverse work force confronts years of singular thinking, opening up potential conflicts and misunderstandings. Old assumptions about people's training, schooling, values, and cultural backgrounds are no longer operative and must be discarded for a new openness and flexibility. In a company of strangers, both management and coworkers need to learn about each other and strive to meld everyone into a unified and multitalented work force.

The Dynamic Blender

I call the third force the dynamic blender. In a word, it is high-pressure, lightninglike *change*. From the suddenly omnipresent fax machine to the marketing opportunities created by the economic revolution in Eastern Europe, in some companies the accelerating and never-ending pace of change is little understood and therefore badly managed.

Most of us are struggling to understand, accommodate, and benefit from change; but in the process, we can become easily burned out, stretched beyond limits, and overstressed. The companies and managers who see the opportunities in this so-called blender—who learn how to work with different kinds of employees, navigate the human side of change, and take advantage of technological and competitive breakthroughs—will escape the suffering of misjudging and mismanaging the consequences of this force.

Only the strongest and healthiest survive and thrive in a rapidly changing work environment . . . we need a more resilient work force, better able to take the stresses and strains of change.

JAMES HENDERSON
Director, Human
Resources, Pacific Bell

The New Psychological Contract

Another subtle but powerful force is a new psychological contract between employee and company that is redefining traditional understandings about promises, loyalties, working relationships, and roles. From the corporate view, this new contract recognizes that employers can no longer offer lifetime jobs, guaranteed advancement, or kindly paternalism. Economic survival demands that they be able to expand and contract quickly and be flexible enough to respond to changing markets and emerging opportunities.

But companies need committed employees in order to react quickly to the marketplace, and they need these fast reflexes at a time when employee criticism, mistrust, and self-interest are ubiquitous. So employers must offer a new contract that gives the company this flexibility, but at the same time presents employees with more chances for personal and professional growth. Employees will accept the new contract only with the provisos that their employers are honest, open, and fair with them and that they have a larger say in their jobs.

The Human Crisis

This force refers to the need for a dramatic expansion of companies' roles and responsibilities to incorporate the whole employee, not simply the person who works eight hours a day. This crisis demands that companies begin to pay attention to employees' minds, bodies, relationships, and families. Companies that ignore the total person will receive a very painful lesson in terms of the costs of employing a person who has physical and/or mental ailments or whose family life is a source of stress.

Some companies are trying to address this crisis through expanded benefit programs. The old, narrowly defined health insurance and pension packages are now considered entitlements, so employers are developing a broader set of work-life benefits. For instance, employee health plans have exploded beyond a group policy with a large insurance carrier to encompass complete wellness programs, fitness centers, employee assistance plans, and support for dependents and family members.

While this trend certainly increases a company's attractiveness to new employees, it marks just the beginning of confronting the crisis. Employees also want more compassion and opportunity at work, more enlightened attitudes and behavior—in short, a corporate mentality that recognizes and appreciates the human side of its business as much as the financial side.

Being competitive on quality, price, and service will increasingly demand employees who are more productive, skilled, flexible, creative, conscientious, and committed than ever before.

DICK NEUMANN
Vice-President, Bechtel
Group, Inc.

THE PAIN OF MISMANAGEMENT

These five pressures are inevitable and inexorable. While they could be cause for celebration and opportunity, people and companies alike are fumbling in their attempts to master them. Instead of coming to grips with these forces, employees and employers too often refuse to change, focus on the short term, grow more cynical, and concentrate on personal interests and maintaining their power.

Ultimately, people and organizations are not working well together. Like the aftermath of an earthquake, workplaces are becoming a jumble of friction, miscommunication, and steadily deteriorating relationships. Workers are more stressed and dissatisfied with work; organizations are unhealthy, unproductive

There can be little growth and development for employees at any level in a sick and stagnant organization. It is in the best interests of both the individual and the organization to have a healthy organization that can provide opportunities for growth.

EDGAR SCHEIN,
Professor of Management,
Sloan School of Management, MIT

Some Facts on Mismanagement

- An MIT Commission on Industrial Productivity found that "U.S. industry is not producing as well as industries of other nations." In 1974, we developed 70 percent of the world's advanced technology; by 1984, our share was 50 percent; by 1994, it will be 30 percent.

- According to the National Commission on Productivity, only two of every ten employees work at full potential. Nearly half the work force expends only the minimum effort needed to get by.

- The average Fortune 500 company spends nearly one-fourth of its after-tax profits on medical bills. At Control Data Corporation, an unhealthy employee cost the company $509 more a year than a healthy one.

- An International Survey Research Study of 112,000 workers at 28 U.S. companies found that just 50% felt that benefit programs met their needs in 1989–1990, versus 83% in 1982–1983.

- Recent studies indicate that nearly 15 percent of all U.S. workers now abuse alcohol and/or drugs. Nearly a third report excessive stress and burnout.

- The National Council on Compensation Insurance warns that the growing number of stress-related worker compensation claims will soon strangle an already swelled liability system.

- Since 1950, industrial injuries have tripled. Each injury results in seventeen days lost from work, with an average accident cost of about $10,000. According to the National Safety Council, these injuries came to a staggering $35 billion.

- A 1990 Towers Perrin/Hudson Institute report indicates that already 65 percent of companies are experiencing labor shortages and that the new ethnic and racial mix of employees is a significant concern to management.

- In a survey of Fortune 500 companies, 58 percent reported difficulties finding employees who possessed basic arithmetic and reading skills. Only 12 percent of managers receive any job training from their employers when they start work and only 17 percent receive formal training for job advancement.

- A 1990 Gallup/New York Business Group on Health survey indicates that stress, anxiety, and depression are pervasive in many workplaces and lead to high levels of absenteeism and impaired productivity.

places of employment; and their relationship is more fragile and less predictable than ever before.

When I talk to both CEOs and employees, I hear a litany of complaints, suspicion, and pain. By and large, employees feel alienated, shut out of the company loop and its corporate mission and disenfranchised by employers who demand more, impose dehumanizing bureaucracies, and operate according to capricious rules and regulations. Their psychological needs for self-esteem, growth, and well-being are not being met. Employees deeply believe that their personal values are at odds with what is important and worthwhile to their employers. They hear CEOs make speeches about fairness and equality, then learn about astronomical executive pay packages. They hear about a company's invigorating spirit of competitiveness, then find that office politics, not professional excellence, reap the biggest promotions.

For managers, the pain is twofold: it comes from above—from senior executives who insist that they show results immediately while simultaneously cutting back, and from below—from employees who lack a sense of urgency and responsibility, shirk their duties, and are apathetic about their work. Managers are caught in between, grappling with the limitations of unskilled employees and dysfunctional teams while trying to tame the tensions generated by rapid change. To cope and survive, many of them feel forced into hoarding their power and looking out only for themselves. Thus, despite their conviction that they are good people managers, the management style of many managers is controlling and self-centered.

The company pain is most obvious. You can see it in escalating costs of labor and benefits eating away at profits and operating budgets; in declining productivity and morale; in high turnover rates and poor recruiting results; and in a lagging ability to innovate and compete internationally. This pain is also apparent in the inability of companies to check our social problems, from AIDS to illiteracy, many of which have invaded the workplace and undermined the work force.

Each of these participants—employees, managers, and companies—suffers from inertia and resistance. All dislike the status quo but balk at changing their ways. Encircling this situation is an ever-widening gap between what people say they believe and value and how they behave.

Jobs and coworkers are replacing family and neighborhood as central influences in many people's lives. Increasingly, business sets the tone for what is—and what is not—acceptable behavior. . . . Corporations must have commitments beyond their income statements.

JAMES T. LYNN
Chairman of the Board and CEO, Aetna Life and Casualty Company

Based on current trends, our health-related costs could reach $2 billion by year 2000! That's almost twice our annual budget for all capital expenditures today.

SAM GINN
CEO, Pacific Bell

Short-term thinking is the societal disease of our time . . . it's asking what the poll is saying, not what's great for the country and what's best for the future, but what do I say in the short term to get me from here to there.

NORMAN LEAR
(quoted in *On Becoming a Leader* by Warren Bennis)

Employees say they want a voice to influence decisions, yet often do only what is asked of them and blame problems on management. Managers say they value employees who are open and suggest new ideas, yet they often refuse to listen, maintaining, "This is the way we've always done it" and "It's worked so far— why fix it if it isn't broken?" And companies that issue policy statements declaring that people are their most important asset and that "Quality First" is their motto may skimp on wages, heap huge bonuses on upper management, and push employees to shortcut quality to boost short-term production.

In short, one might say that employees, managers, and companies have colluded in shortsighted, superficial thinking about the best way to manage people and organizations. Values, emotions, and relationships are viewed as soft and unbusinesslike. Accounting systems measure current costs, not the value of long-term human assets. Legal obstacles retard instituting better practices we know would improve the quality of work-life. "Return on investment" and "debt to equity" exclude the value of human capital. And a malignant model of management prevents everyone from honest self-examination.

This unpleasant picture raises an obvious question. Why have we allowed ourselves, our employees, and our companies to become this way? The whys reach back to antiquated attitudes about people and management. For decades, companies have operated on the belief that immediate productivity and profits were more important than people, that shareholders were more important than employees. They pushed for instant, transitory rewards and ignored the potential of seasoned development of people and products.

In this environment, employees have been regarded as costly liabilities that were constantly depleting and had to be pushed and shoved for maximum output. If the past decade had a motto, it was "Profits at Any Price," and the price it paid was a slipshod work force, defective goods and services, and a faltering future.

But the future begins today, and if all of us—individuals and institutions—do not invest in our work force now, this short-sightedness will haunt us for decades to come. Our workplaces will become even more painful places to work, and American business will shrivel away.

Consequences of an Unhealthy Company	
job dissatisfaction	extended lunches
poor morale	grievances
decreased commitment	tense work relations
diminished work quality	poor judgment
diminished work quantity	excessive medical costs
work slowdowns	EEO complaints
accidents	fatigue
disciplinary actions	mental blocks
indecisiveness	career stagnation
unnecessary turnover	poor communication
tampering and sabotage	unscheduled downtime
workers' compensation	absenteeism
decreased motivation	reduced productivity
burnout	excessive health costs
lateness	disability

What drives and organizes people is values, not strategy or quantitative rewards. If I can organize people around purpose, that is the most powerful form of leadership.

TOM CHAPPELL
CEO, Tom's of Maine

WHAT IS A HEALTHY COMPANY?

By now you probably have a pretty good picture of what a healthy company is not—the mismanaged personal and business pressures, coupled with the consequences they have inflicted, offer a graphic illustration of the guts of an unhealthy company.

A healthy company, on the other hand, is much more than simply the absence of these forces and feelings. Just like a fine athlete is more than someone who isn't weak, a healthy company embodies people and practices that combine and coordinate to produce an exceptional performance.

I have consulted with a number of healthy companies, and while as a group they were very diverse, they all possess and emanate a certain vitality and spirit. This spirit is not a religious fervor or a mindless cheerleader enthusiasm but a deep feeling of shared humanistic values at the core of the company. They are the glue that binds healthy, successful employees with healthy, productive workplaces. These values influence the way people act and think at all levels of the company and form the

What we've learned is that the soft stuff and the hard stuff are becoming increasingly intertwined. A company's values—what it stands for, what its people believe in—are crucial to its competitive success. Indeed, values drive the business.

ROBERT D. HAAS
Chairman, CEO,
Levi Strauss & Co.

Consequences of a Healthy Company

healthy leaders	clarity of mission and purpose
quality service	flexibility
employee loyalty and commitment	customer care
	proactive thinking
creativity and innovation	sense of urgency
people-skilled managers	reliable, accountable employees
attraction and retention of the best	low turnover
	manageable human capital costs
efficiency	vitality and energy
reduced waste and accidents	job satisfaction
	open, direct communication
alignment of personal and company rules	healthy, safe jobs
	sense of resilience
high performance	reduced crises
collaboration	self-managing teams
healthy employees	cost control
continuous learners	

foundation for corporate policies and practices. They define roles and responsibilities and dictate how business decisions are made. These principles are expressed and applied to workers at all levels, from receptionists and loading dock workers, through managers and executives, and into the board of directors.

Each value can be defined, and I will do that in the remainder of this book. But before exploring specifics, I want to emphasize their organic nature—these values are perpetually interacting, expanding, and contracting like a living entity. Each value depends on and determines the health of the others; sickness or disease that undermines one weakens all; robustness in one value strengthens all. The values at the heart of a healthy company enable it to continuously grow, evolve, and renew itself, reinforcing what is productive and positive while sloughing off the unhealthy and unworkable. In short, the causes and effects among values, people, and companies are not linear but circular. Values *are* the center of the enterprise; they circulate through every cell and artery of a company, and a company and its employees either reinforce healthy values or bring about their decline.

Healthy company values bind people to their organizations. By creating a language of common aspirations and appealing to principles of dignity, commitment, and growth, these values help to create an identity that connects thousands of people around a shared mission. Suddenly, the traditional hard values of business success and the nontraditional soft values of human development merge into one dream.

This convergence generates a synergy, producing something greater than the sum of its parts: a vital business that lives and breathes a healthy philosophy, that treats people as more than profit-producers, views relationships as more than simply financial contracts, and regards the workplace as not just a setting for business but as a holistic environment that nurtures, stretches, and empowers people. The result is an organization that optimizes people, principles, and profits. The values people hold in the healthy company are listed on the following two pages.

What's important about a great workplace is that profits are not something to be achieved at the expense of the people responsible for creating them. A great workplace suggests that it's possible to achieve that success while enriching the lives of the people who work there.

ROBERT LEVERING
A Great Place to Work

Commitment to Self-Knowledge and Development

This value is a commitment to one's own personal growth and understanding. On a personal level, people with this value are introspective, principle-driven, and constantly learning about themselves. Managers translate this learning into leadership that inspires both personal and professional development in employees.

Organizations dedicated to self-knowledge are learning institutions. Their value of people as appreciating assets, not costly liabilities, overshadows all other decisions. Through a broad, caring human-capital investment strategy, executives make large investments in training, managers cultivate employee effectiveness and their successors, and employees learn to innovate and take risks. For these companies, managing learning is a full-time job, and for their companies to grow each year, every employee must grow and develop.

Firm Belief in Decency

The basic precept here is decency: instinctively treating others as would any feeling, thinking human being and as one would like to be treated oneself. This value is founded on the conviction that people work best when they are respected—when they are genuinely appreciated for what they bring to a company.

In healthy companies, actions speak louder than words, promises are kept, discrepancies between what managers say and what they do rarely surface, and half-truths, prevarications, or deceptions are not tolerated. Managers are honest with employees, sharing their knowledge and even feelings; and they are fair, apportioning rewards and criticism according to accomplishments and deeds. Openness is a ground rule for all relationships. Regardless of the forum, the feedback is always candid, helpful, fair, and constant.

The Economics of a Healthy Company

Healthy companies enhance the development of people and add value to the bottom line. As measured by a variety of financial indicators, they perform better than their unhealthy competitors.

Employees of healthy companies contribute value, instead of draining off operating budgets, because they have less absenteeism, fewer costly accidents, and lower health-care costs. They are more dependable and productive: they lose less time to interpersonal or family problems or to worrying about what their employer is thinking; they devote less mental time to figuring out how to get even or to maneuver politically; and they don't limit their output to a narrow range of responsibilities. Consequently, the company reduces unnecessary human capital costs; identifies the untapped talent of the work force; cultivates people managers who learn to appreciate employees; builds relationships that weather crisis and change; and inspires vital, energetic employees who care about the company and its success.

These savings to company performance and financial health have been quantified. The studies show that people-oriented companies are the strongest in their industries:

■ Companies that have "progressive management styles . . . and a people-oriented culture" had 64-percent higher annualized sales growth over a five-year period than those without this culture, according to a study by human-resources consultant Dennis J.

Respect for Individual Differences

People who respect individual differences know that an office is populated by individuals who look different, act different, and grew up in different cultures but who are equally capable and worthwhile. Rather than insisting that everyone conform to a white, middle-class norm, employees and managers value the richness, diversity, and imaginative ideas dissimilar people bring to their jobs.

Companies show their respect by not promoting policies or tacit standards that imply a homogeneous work force. For example, promotions are equally available to women and minorities;

First you have to have an environment of mutual trust and respect. You need to have an environment that taps everyone's creative potential. It's terribly important that you not turn bright, able people into robots by giving them procedure books and checklists.

ROSS PEROT
Chairman, Electronic Data Systems

Kravetz. Highly progressive companies had profit margins averaging 5.3 percent compared with 3.3 percent for less progressive companies.

- The companies identified in the 1984 book *The 100 Best Companies to Work for in America* are more than twice as profitable as the average for the Standard & Poor's 500, based on their earnings per share and stock appreciation. According to Dean Witter, the publicly traded companies on this list earned 17.69 percent more for investors than S&P 500 companies.

- A study of 101 industrial firms found that those using participative-management techniques outscored other firms on thirteen of the fourteen Value Line Investors Survey measurements, including financial strength, earnings per share, and net profits. The survey also found that the participative companies showed lower employee turnover and absenteeism and fewer grievances.

- A survey by economists at the New York Stock Exchange of 1,158 companies found that three-fourths of the firms reported that human-resource programs improved productivity and lowered costs.

- A comparison of the twenty-year performance of progressive companies (those with a variety of human-resource programs) and nonprogressive companies found that the former had significantly higher long-term profitability and financial growth, according to Harvard Business School professor Rosabeth Moss Kanter.

work schedules are flexible enough to accommodate all kinds of families; and employees are encouraged to express their personal differences. There are no second-class citizens, only human beings of equal worth with special roles and responsibilities.

Spirit of Partnership

This value is a strong belief in community, in the strength of shared effort, the value of teamwork, and the satisfaction of partnership. Though personally capable, both manager and employee truly believe that two minds are better than one and that many minds are best. They make great team players and form strong relationships, because they understand the dynamics of giving and taking, leading and following.

Together, responsible employees and empowering managers form a special team—an entrepreneurial partnership of adults dedicated to mobilizing each others' talents and producing results. This group is not a collection of so-called "Indians and one chief" but a collaboration of co-equals, with individuals stepping forward to take the lead when they have more experience, specialized knowledge, or unique creative talents in a given area than others. This partnership's motto is "Everyone Is a Leader, Everyone Is a Follower."

High Priority for Health and Well-Being

Healthy employees are a company's most valuable asset. Like a well-crafted piece of precision equipment, employees must be maintained and polished—from reducing the level of their cholesterol to giving them time for family matters.

Inherent in this value is the certainty that work can either make people sick or improve their health. The physical and psychological climate at work—including the size of the computer screen, the interior air, the level of boredom in a job, and the attitudes of supervisors—plays an enormous role in well-being and performance.

At the company level, health and well-being are emphasized through adequate health and disability coverage, wellness and employee-assistance programs, flexible scheduling, family-leave policies, competitive and equitable pay, and profit sharing. Safety

Many executives touch and influence the lives of thousands of people, both inside and outside the company. Their touch can be a blight or a blessing. Their influence can build up a person or tear him down.

WILLIAM WALTON
Cofounder, Holiday Inn
Hotels

According to a Gallup Poll, one in four workers suffers from stress-related problems; absentee rates among these employees are three times those of their coworkers. Business Week *estimates that the cost to business of stress-related problems and mental illness is $150 billion annually in health insurance, disability claims, lost productivity and other expenses.*

too is a concern, and healthy companies do more than tout its importance—they institute practical, vital safeguards in every corner of the workplace.

Appreciation for Flexibility and Resilience

This value is founded on the inevitability of change and the necessity of taking charge of any natural evolution, be it financial, technological, or personal. Resilient employees exhibit this value in their attitude toward new situations and obstacles. They ask plenty of questions and are not easily discouraged. Rich with capability, not conformity, they don't avoid the tough jobs or duck responsibility. When they do get overwhelmed, their spirit, vitality, and winning attitude guide them through the hard times.

Managers with this value know that regardless of what an employee actually does every day, whether it is mundane or unique, manual or mental, people need variety, flexibility, and a sense of completion and ownership. The healthy company reinforces this value through a variety of offerings: they give employees the tools to cope with change; they provide advance notice of layoffs and relocations; and they make the transitions as smooth as possible.

Passion for Products and Process

With a clear mission and plan of action, people with a passion for products are active, effective doers. They set goals, benchmarks, and timetables and know where they are going and why. These people *care* what happens to their company—they feel personally involved and responsible for its successes and failures.

However, their passion for outcome does not interfere with their respect for process. Although persistent and competitive, they care as much about how they produce something as the product itself; as driven as they are, they know they must take into account the interests and needs of all their constituents.

That is why patience and persistence are essential—a natural outcome of their strong belief in people, their respect for relationships, and their commitment to the company's long-term mission. Experience has shown these people that even if they

America is not and has never been a static society. Our national character and our unique strengths have grown out of the diversity of our people and our special abilities to adapt to change and rise to challenge.

OWEN B. BUTLER
retired Chairman and
CEO, Procter & Gamble

As time goes by, talking about values will be regarded as absolutely essential . . . just as essential as marketing or logistics or strategic planning or thinking or decision-making.

RICHARD ZIMMERMAN
Chairman and CEO,
Hershey Food Corp.

achieve quick results, these results are often transitory and often undermine personal and economic success.

Ultimately, the healthy company views products and profits not as its immediate goal, but rather as the result of doing everything else right. Its economic success, improved quality, better service, and competitive advantage are the by-products of shared values and collective effort.

These values are the lifeblood of a healthy company—they flow through the arteries of the organization. Each employee, manager, and executive must decide how to put them to work. Regardless of the size of your work group or your location on the corporate ladder, what happens to these values is in your hands.

Incorporating values entails bringing about a metamorphosis, beginning with yourself, then applying the values to your immediate work surroundings, and ultimately spreading them throughout your company. Thus, as you read each chapter, you will find that the insights and suggestions originate on the personal level, then grow larger and outward to include your role as a manager, and finally encompass your entire company's beliefs and activities.

If you assimilate these values as your own, and live and work by them as practical, sensible guidelines, you will be healthy and so will the company you lead. The following chapters evolve directly from these core values and represent the eight principles of the healthy company.

As long as our reserves remain hidden, we doom ourselves, collectively, to a more fearful, less productive and far less optimal future. . . . But the U.S. workplace of the 1990s and beyond can be pro-child, pro-worker empowerment, pro-family, and as a result be increasingly profitable.

WILLIS B. GOLDBECK,
Founder, Washington
Business Group on Health

INSIDE OUT

Do You Work in a Healthy Company?

This is a list of common features found in a healthy company. Consider to what degree you feel each statement is true for your company. Use your current work group as a reference.

1 Never	3 Sometimes	5 Always
2 Rarely	4 Often	

1. Employees have a voice in decisions.

2. People enjoy coming to work.

3. Company communications are clear and timely.

4. Employees are treated fairly.

5. Workers get the resources they need to do their jobs.

6. Employees are noticed and appreciated for performing well.

7. People are kept informed about what is going on in the company.

8. Employees manage the pressure of their work.

9. The company cares about quality and service.

10. Employees are satisfied with company benefits.

11. Policies are flexible enough to take into account personal and family needs.

12. Individual and team efforts are rewarded.

13. Employees spend more time producing than complaining.

14. The company manages change and crisis well.

15. Individual differences in lifestyle and culture are appreciated.

16. There are opportunities for learning and career advancement.

17. There is a spirit of vitality and camaraderie at work.

18. Problems are shared openly and solved in teams.

19. Health and safety is a top priority.

20. The company considers human resources an investment, not a cost.

What Your Answers Mean

If you scored between 85 and 100, you are fortunate to work for a healthy company. Scores from 50 to 85 indicate that there are both healthy and unhealthy practices in your organization, with plenty of room for improvement. If you rated your company below 50, you are undermining your most valued asset, and it is time to take an honest look at your approach to leading people.

The Power of Respect Is Greater Than the Power of Money

AS YOU WALK THROUGH the doors at Herman Miller, Inc., an atmosphere of respect emanates from the company like a warm light. It radiates from people's attitudes and actions, from the president down to the night watchman, and is detectable in such small signs as friendly, informative notices on bulletin boards to more significant indications, including the absence of special perks for executives. Respect at Herman Miller is a feeling encountered at every junction and evidenced in every activity.

Herman Miller, Inc., is an office-furniture designer and manufacturer, headquartered in Zeeland, Michigan. Established in 1923, the company is the source of major innovations in the design of residential and office environments. But its most noteworthy achievement may be its healthy-company approach to managing people. This approach has produced remarkable results. Recent sales for the company stand around $765 million and net profits have reached $48 million. Since 1975, its compound annual growth rate has been 41 percent. An annual employee turnover of 7 percent is less than half the American average. Much of the company's financial success can be laid at the feet of its highly productive work force, which totals about 5,400.

In my experience, there are two great motivators in life. One is fear. The other is love. You can manage an organization by fear, but if you do you will ensure that people don't perform up to their real capabilities.

JAN CARLZON
Chairman and CEO,
Scandinavian Airlines

◢◣ **herman miller**

Retired company chairman Max DePree deserves a large share of the credit. Says DePree, "Our people and our values—these are exactly the things most fragile and important in our corporation . . . people want to trust the CEO, that is why we should be more involved in principles and relationships than in numbers."

Many companies preach a philosophy of respect and responsibility, but at Herman Miller, this belief represents more than words. DePree related a story to me that vividly illustrates his commitment to these principles. He tells of an assembly-line worker showing up at his office annoyed and insisting on speaking with him. When shown into the chairman's office, the young woman demanded, "Do you know that two production managers were just fired?" DePree investigated the firing, agreed that the managers should not have been dismissed, brought them back, and then demanded that the impulsive vice-president who fired them resign. In the end, DePree was pleased about the woman's outburst—pleased that she felt secure enough to test his open-door policy and involved enough that she would come see him. "I consider it an enormous honor that I was approached with some expectation of fair play," he says.

This incident exemplifies how respect flows through the organization and emerges in a host of policies and practices that revolve around honesty and open communication. Respect at Herman Miller is a two-way street: the company respects the intelligence and integrity of each employee, and employees respect the company's decisions, judgment, and corporate mission. Right from the hiring of new employees, when managers focus more on character and the ability to get along with people than traditional milestones of experience and qualifications, to the participative, team atmosphere ingrained into the business environment, ideas and words flow among and between all levels of management and hourly workers. In addition to monthly business reviews on the corporate financial performance, employees are kept informed about what is happening everywhere in the company. Other ways this firm regularly communicates respect are through team meetings, caucuses, councils, department meetings, and the Suggestion System Office.

Herman Miller operates a plan called "Our Own Share," a system for rewarding employees for contributions and ideas that produce financial and productivity benefits. Employees learn about the company's performance every month, and these results, plus customer reactions and return on assets, determine bonuses. In short, employees are laboring for very real and very regular pay incentives on top of their wages.

Employees' worth and contributions are acknowledged in other ways. Every worker receives stock after one year at the company. The company has created "People Services" in place of Personnel, dedicated to ensuring that employees are treated fairly and honestly. For instance, during the era of hostile takeovers, the furniture maker instituted silver parachutes for all employees with more than two years' service. If the company were bought by an outsider, fired employees would have a very comfortable cushion.

Max DePree has explained the Herman Miller philosophy in his book *Leadership Is an Art:*

I perceive one immense omission in my psychology—the deepest principle of human nature is craving to be appreciated.

WILLIAM JAMES
Harvard psychologist and father of modern psychology

> What is it most of us want from work? We would like to find the most effective, most productive, most rewarding way of working together . . . we would like a work process and relationships that meet our personal needs for belonging, for contributing, for meaningful work, for the opportunity to make a commitment, for the opportunity to grow and be at least reasonably in control of our own destinies. Finally, we'd like someone to say "Thank you."

No wonder Herman Miller is one of the new icons of business management.

RESPECT: LIP SERVICE OR CORPORATE TRUTH

The subject of respect comes up often in conversations I have with executives, usually in the context of discussing formal company policies. Everyone agrees that respect is enormously important in the workplace, and typically people tell me that in their company, "We all respect one another." At this point I become skeptical, because I know that while the power of respect may be acknowledged, few managers and businesses are truly using it.

One reason genuine respect is not more prevalent is that business talks and writes about it but rarely acts on it. Respect is given much lip service, but in the daily workings of a company it is largely ignored; at best it is prominently displayed in slogans. Just as flag-waving is no substitute for patriotism, so, too, are company pronouncements about the importance of respect no substitute for relationships based on respect. The lip service given to respect comes in many forms:

- A company promoting slogans like "Employees are our greatest asset," while it makes plans—sometimes involving restructuring and layoffs—in secret.
- Touting opportunities for women, while skimping on maternity benefits or not promoting women on the same basis as men.
- Announcing an austerity program and budget cuts while continuing executive perks and bonuses.
- Circulating a strict code of ethics, while allowing expensive gifts from clients to be accepted by high-level executives.
- Asking for employee opinions, then never opening the suggestion box or giving suggestions scant attention.
- Voicing a loud commitment to service and quality, while pressuring people to work faster and cut corners.

Admittedly, beneath this lip service often lies a strong belief, not necessarily deliberate deception. Many companies are sincere about their pronouncements and confident that their workplaces are imbued with respect although, in truth, disrespect reigns.

Both individuals and companies suffer when the human element of the workplace is ignored or devalued. When relationships are dishonest, people spend more time protecting their turf than promoting their ideas or forming productive partnerships. When work practices are unfair, employees do all they can to compensate for the injustice by always attending to their own needs first. When communications are closed, secrets prevail and stress follows closely behind. When their efforts go unappreciated, employees feel little attachment to their companies.

A survey of 400 managers by Robert Kelly, business professor at Carnegie Mellon University, shows that one-third distrust their bosses and 55 percent do not believe top management.

Like jilted lovers, workers and managers become more cautious after they have been burned once. Relationships are severed, deceptions allowed, manipulations accepted. Lies are excused under the rationale of the way we do business.

ROBERT REICH
Professor, Harvard
University

Business pays a high price for all this disrespect. The most blatant costs are poor morale, high turnover, and a company's inability to attract quality employees. But other costs are not so obvious: employees that stay with a company devoid of respect become disinterested, passive, and inefficient; workdays typically are characterized by late arrival, constant socializing, personal phone calls, long lunches and coffee breaks, and early departure. Some disaffected employees use company time and resources to operate another business. Resentful employees show high rates of absenteeism and belligerently claim regular mental-health days. Other pieces of fallout among the disrespected are drug abuse, employee sabotage, employee theft, moonlighting, claims for workmen's compensation, and higher health-care expenses. Clearly, the price of disrespect is not only a higher cost of doing business but also smaller profits.

Building respect in the workplace is a two-step task. The first is personal: you must look inside yourself to discover the opinions and beliefs that influence your attitude toward people at work. You need to explore the values, experiences, and assumptions that you bring to work every day and apply to your co-workers and bosses. Only when you know the substance and even the origins of your values can you begin to understand how they affect your work attitudes and the level of respect you grant other people.

The word *respect* is derived from the Latin *respectare,* which means "to see." Respect is a special kind of vision. First you must turn this vision inward—into the source of your own self-esteem —to learn what makes you feel valued, motivated, and respected. Then you must focus this insight outward to try to understand the emotions, feelings, needs, and aspirations of your employees.

The second step toward building respect is creating an environment of relationships and business practices that support your newfound insights. Perceptive executives liken a respectful relationship to a close bond. Fel-Pro chief executive Lewis Weinberg likens the employee-company relationship to a marriage: "If you don't pay attention to the important things, you won't have a good thing going. But if you bend over backward, you will." This means you must examine your relationships and work activities and explore ways they can contribute to and enhance a living, breathing spirit of respect. Doing this, as you probably know, is

The cynicism out there is frightening. Middle managers have become insecure, and they feel unbelievably hurt. They feel like slaves on an auction block.

PETER DRUCKER

more complicated than simply believing in respect, because respect is composed of a number of elements that, like a chemical mixture, interact and bond together. These elements are:

- *trust* made tangible
- *appreciation* of the human elements
- *communication* that is clear and candid
- *ethics* that are unequivocal

It is in developing each of these four areas that you make respect come alive.

TRANSLATE TRUST INTO THE TANGIBLE

Trust is the first essential ingredient of respect. Trust can take a long time to earn and be lost in a moment's thoughtlessness. We all need it yet rarely talk about it; we know in our hearts and minds when we have it and when we do not. Trust is a kind of maturity: it is the trademark of those who have grown beyond the childish insecurity of constantly protecting and worrying about themselves and confidently knowing that other people's interests often complement, not conflict with, their own.

An intangible, sometimes elusive quality, trust has a dual nature, because it comprises both the ability to trust others and the quality of being trustworthy ourselves. And both facets of trust are essential in a trusting relationship; trust breaks down if only half of it is present. The existence or absence of both sides of trust is apparent in our attitudes and actions, including our thoughts about and reactions to coworkers.

Although trust sounds like a collection of nebulous feelings, it can be broken into five clear qualities:

Credibility. At its most basic, this quality is about truth—the believability of your spoken and written words. If credible, when you announce that the company wants to promote from within, employees know this is true. When you promise support for a risky venture, employees know you won't abandon them without their consultation. Unfortunately, many business people have learned over time to make all the right promises, regardless of

The bottom line follows everything else. We say in our company that profit is like breathing, it's required. So we don't pay a hell of a lot of attention to it. What we pay attention to is creating an environment, setting up the circumstances and the goals, so that people can do the work that produces the bottom line.

JAMES AUTRY
President, Magazine
Group, Meredith
Corporation

how believable or true they may be. These are often casual, verbal commitments, as in statements like "I'll back you up on this one," or "I'll look into it," or "Sure, I want your opinion." Loose promises like these raise expectations, so when they are forgotten, they torpedo any trust that has been cultivated. Spoken words should be as believable as a notarized statement.

People can become tangled up by credibility, because they believe that if they do not know the truth or cannot share it, they must say something rather than stopping at saying nothing or admitting ignorance and so preserving credibility. So they utter partial truths, not recognizing the border between these and lies. Inevitably, lesser degrees of credibility reach the slippery slope of deceit.

Dependability. The dependable person makes good on promises, whether they are declared, implied, or even assumed by others. Any expression of commitment extends beyond mere words or pieces of paper and is backed foursquare by actions. If you promise to help out on a project deadline, do not disappear at four-thirty under the guise of having a business appointment. The absence of dependability is indifference. When there is no connection between your promises and what you do, people stop listening, believing, or taking you seriously.

Predictability. This means not springing unpleasant surprises on people, which could be anything from sudden shifts in mood or temper to overnight changes in positions and opinions. People are wary of working with someone who is unpredictable, for nothing is worse than the stress of uncertainty, which makes us tense, defensive, and fearful.

Valuing the common good. Trust demands that sometimes a person put aside self-interest and strive for the good of the group. James Autry, head of the publishing group at Meredith Corporation, notes that this issue is one of the toughest in business: "I think we're always walking on the edge between the good of the group and the good of the individual. It's the most difficult challenge in business." Moreover, a person's recognition of mutual gain must move him or her beyond only personal concerns to understand that self-interest and the common good can be the same.

At work, for instance, this person must not be constantly self-promoting but promoting team efforts. Without this value, one is a pure opportunist.

Emotional safety. With this quality, you do not abuse people's health, feelings, self-image, or values. Rather, you take their concerns seriously and their interests to heart. Without safety, people feel uneasy and vulnerable, never knowing from which direction they may be attacked. People who feel safe at work know, for instance, that their boss will not ask them to work where it is dangerous and that they will not be subject to humiliation or public criticism.

Another layer of emotional safety is voicing confidence and belief in your employees. Telling people who work for you that you will back them—that you trust their word and their judgment—makes them feel comfortable and secure. It also means you shield them from office politics and unnecessary criticism, giving them the freedom to perform.

The High Price of Distrust

A few years back, I was consultant to a medium-sized paper manufacturer that was moving offices to larger, more attractive quarters thirty miles down the road. When the company first announced the move, its 300-plus employees were anxious and uncertain—they did not know what the move meant personally in terms of their jobs. They were concerned about commuting, work schedules, office space, and expanding or shrinking responsibilities. The company promised to move in six months, yet the deadline passed and nothing happened. Silence poured from the executive office—no explanation, no new deadline, no information. When rumors began to circulate about the company being in financial difficulty and for sale, the chief executive responded with denials, renewed declarations about the move, and announced a new deadline.

This charade went on for almost a year, as employees grew fearful and uncertain about their jobs and angry at their bosses, while management persisted in its story about moving. When the charade finally ended and the company announced that it was not moving and hinted that a sale had fallen through, any rem-

The competitive work ethic, so prevalent in society, is actually the poorest preparation for the kind of trust-building that healthy relationships require. It is antithetical to some of the most important relationship issues: the ability to open up and become known to another person, the willingness to be vulnerable to another, the valuing of equality, the commitment to collaborating rather than competing.

Business executive

nants of credibility and trust between the company and its employees had vanished. In the following year, the company lost 35 percent of its employees and, given its two-faced reputation, had a hard time recruiting comparable replacements.

As this example illustrates, trust as a business quality has enormous clout, but executives and managers are often unaware of how they influence it. Generally, at the beginning of a relationship, both company and employees trust each other and have high expectations. Yet whenever this trust is tested and found to be flawed, it deteriorates rapidly. For example, if employees see obvious signs of distrust—such as hidden microphones in an office, video spy cameras, or capricious searches through desks and lockers—they know their trust is misplaced. As with the paper-company employees, even when there is low-level behind-the-scenes distrust, people will become frustrated and disappointed, then grow angry and feel deceived and betrayed.

Trust either feeds on itself and grows or fades faster and faster until it disappears. Ignoring how your actions affect trust or procrastinating paying attention to it in the hope that somehow people will feel more trusting on their own merely allows distrust to mushroom and take over, or worse. "One responds to betrayal with bitterness and cynicism, and with willing and stoic isolation," says author and philosopher Peter Koestenbaum. "One builds a fortress and lives in it. One creates a moat and remains contained inside. One becomes armored like a turtle, protected like a cactus, and defended like a porcupine."

Distrust destroys employee morale and productivity, and it costs a company in a variety of ways: multimillion-dollar golden parachutes; legal fees to enforce employee contracts; employee polygraph tests; office politics; and elaborate employee manuals. Less obvious costs are destructive rumors, backstabbing, or a work slowdown.

If people feel somehow that their side of the scale isn't balanced with yours, they may go to extremes to balance it. If management is arrogant, if it keeps all the perks to itself [when] the company does well, [or] pushes all the disaster downhill [when] times are bad, then there are certain collateral behaviors you can expect to see.

MICHAEL CRINO
Professor of Management,
Clemson University

INSIDE OUT

How Trusting are You?

Building trust may be harder to create than any other quality of respect, because it requires a personal search and an emotional leap. You must take the first step. In the early stages, building trust is not necessarily a reciprocal relationship. You must extend your trust before it is returned. To do that, you must look within yourself for those values and attitudes that make it easy—or hard—for you to trust. Here are some questions to get you started and a scale for scoring them:

People have unerring detection systems for fakes, and they won't put up with them. They won't put values into practice if you're not.

ROBERT HAAS
Chairman and CEO,
Levi Strauss & Co.

1 Never	3 Sometimes	5 Always
2 Seldom	4 Often	

1. When you first meet someone, are you wary of his or her motives?

2. Do you believe that self-interest—"looking out for Number One"—is essential to professional survival?

3. Do you check up on people after asking them to do something?

4. Do you believe most people are strictly motivated by money or power?

5. Do you frequently ask, "What's in it for me?"?

6. Do you mistrust people's word and need a commitment in writing?

7. Do you consider a commitment flexible depending on changing circumstances?

8. Is it easy for you to tell half-truths to smooth things over or to motivate someone?

9. Do friends tease you or complain that you are not consistent?

10. Do you feel that in some circumstances, people's feelings don't matter?

11. When criticized or called to account for doing something, is your first reaction to justify yourself, regardless of whether you were right or wrong?

12. Are you a naturally suspicious person?

What Your Answers Mean

If you scored between 40 and 60, you are not naturally trusting—your instincts compel you to be suspicious or to leap to judgments until you are shown a reason to trust; a 20-to-40 score indicates a moderate level of trust that still harbors a residue of suspicion and distrust; a score of less than 20 indicates that you are generally trusting and trustworthy.

You may not have answers to all these questions. Trust does not exist in a vacuum—it takes two, so share these questions with someone who knows you well and solicit that person's opinion on how much or little you trust others.

If you are more suspicious and mistrustful than not, you may want to think about some even tougher questions, questions about your early family experiences and relationships that affected your attitude toward all people. Your mistrust may be due to ancient family relationships, old bosses, past disappointments, or rejection. How did you react in the past? How valid are your early experiences now? You may discover that you are still creating the kinds of relationships you fear most. Surely, some of these attitudes may be based in reality, but it may be time to give some others up.

Remember that if you do not trust people, they probably know that from your reactions and words. Constantly checking up on employees signals that you do not trust them. And if you try to cover up your uncertainties about them with half-truths or obfuscation, your distrust becomes even more transparent and the cycle of distrust between people will keep feeding on itself and growing. If you view people as unreliable and undependable, they will assume that about you. If you are quick to judge people's motives, you may judge wrongly and cause problems that do not exist or create ill will by putting people on the defensive. People resent others who are solely out for themselves, but when we are around such individuals, we become more self-interested ourselves, and the destructive cycle continues.

A recent Harris Poll shows that 65 percent of middle managers sampled in Business Week's top 1000 companies believe salaried employees are less loyal to their companies today than ten years ago.

The Steps to Trust

Instilling trust is a slow, cumulative process that takes many small acts that may look trivial but are not to employees around you. Here are six first steps, some small, others large, you can take to begin to cultivate trust in your workplace.

1. SET THE TONE; SET THE EXAMPLES. Open the door to trust by talking about it with employees and explaining how it affects the office atmosphere. Start by talking about your personal capacity for trust or suspicion. If you were once betrayed by a boss who claimed your work, tell employees about the experience and how it affected you. Then scrutinize your behavior for inadvertent actions that might signal distrust: are you credible, dependable, and after the common good? Remember that it is up to you to establish the first steps.

I've always made myself available. Anyone who has a problem, I told them not to hesitate and come and sit down with me and see if we could figure out what the answer was. I think it's important to encourage people on the one hand to go out and do their own thing, but on the other hand to say, "I'm always your backstop."

IAN MACGREGOR
retired Chairman and
CEO, Amax

SCHERER
BROTHERS
LUMBER
COMPANY

2. SURVEY THE LEVEL OF TRUST IN YOUR OFFICE. Is there a high level of gossip in your company? Are people trusted to manage their own time, or are there strict rules for lunch hours and for when people arrive and leave, as well as multiple interim deadlines for projects? How often do directions or verbal understandings have to be put in writing? How much information is shared with the entire staff? Do employees typically learn about company changes through the grapevine? Are bathrooms the most productive meeting spots? Take a walk around your office and ask yourself these questions. You will most likely get a clearer picture of the level of trust in your company.

3. SHARE INFORMATION. This suggestion means spreading good news, sharing bad news, and explaining situations that may not reflect well on you. For example, you may have to inform an employee that his promotion is stalled, reveal that a sudden drop in sales is going to cut someone's budget, or disclose why one employee received a bigger bonus than another. This step also includes not making meaningless promises, such as assuring people that you will call them back, then forgetting, or declaring that you will attend a meeting for which you are too busy. Talk openly with employees about the health of the company—its finances, market position, and competitors. Be honest about benefits, perks, and upcoming job opportunities. Do not be afraid to give away previously privileged information, within reason.

4. LOOK FOR OPPORTUNITIES TO EXPLAIN YOUR PERSONAL MOTIVES. This is one of those difficult first steps—exposing a personal side and hoping that people don't ridicule or reject it. By sharing your personal motives and explaining the reasons behind decisions, you are opening the door to mutual acknowledgment that you are all working toward the same goals. When you keep personal motives to yourself, you invite misunderstandings or misinterpretation of your actions.

5. SCRUPULOUSLY AVOID PERSONAL CRITICISMS AND PERSONAL FAVORS. Maligning or mocking others for personal reasons, whether you are belittling them for how they dress or for how they spend their weekends, reveals prejudices and biases that make a person untrustworthy. On the other hand, befriending special employees sends the message that you have favorites and cannot be trusted to treat everyone equally.

6. HAND OUT SINCERE REWARDS AND PENALTIES. Publicly recognize people who are trusting or trustworthy and reprimand sneaky, deceitful, cover-up behavior. If someone in the office defers personal praise in order to credit the whole group, that person deserves recognition. However, do not use praise, attention, or kindness to manipulate, because people know when they deserve attention and if they receive it when they do not feel deserving, your rewards become meaningless.

Workers are becoming very cynical, according to Boston University management professors Donald Kanter and Phillip Mirvis. In a national survey of the working population, they found that 60 percent will tell a lie if they can gain by it; 58 percent pretend to care more than they really do; nearly 30 percent are dissatisfied with where they work; and 72 percent believe basic trust and faith are disappearing.

SHOW APPRECIATION FOR THE HUMAN ELEMENT

Appreciation seems simple and obvious, composed usually of paychecks and formal, public gestures such as awarding plaques and making thank-you speeches at recognition dinners. But it is more complex than money and gestures; it is a kind of corporate body language used to illustrate how much a company cares about its employees.

In most companies, true appreciation is more noticeable in its absence. There is an enormous gap these days between what companies think they are doing and what employees want and are actually getting. Many companies do not know how to show appreciation because they are out of touch with how employees feel. They think their employees only want more money and better benefits, bonuses, and job security. The truth is miles from this. If employees were to write a Bill of Rights, this is what it would contain:

- Respect our thoughts, feelings, values, and fears.
- Respect our desire to lead and follow.
- Respect our unique strengths and differences.

■ Respect our desire to participate and contribute.

■ Respect our need to feel like a winner.

■ Respect our desire to learn and develop.

■ Respect our desire for a healthy workplace.

■ Respect our personal and family life.

Studies confirm that most people feel they are paid fairly. What is missing, say employees, is appreciation at work. People need to feel valued for their skills and talents and for what they contribute to a company. The bottom line for this kind of appreciation is showing people that you recognize and value their special worth as human beings.

In many workplaces, however, employees feel like losers. Because management does not appreciate their efforts, they feel their employers are indifferent to them. And indifference is awful —it's not quite a slap in the face but more like a dismissive shove to the side. I see this indifference in all types and sizes of companies: people forgetting such simple courtesies as saying "thank you" and "please"; bosses ignoring individual employees' personal talents and interests; company policies that try to motivate and reward everyone the same way; and a preoccupation with productivity quotas rather than the people behind them. Explains former Unisys Corp chief executive Michael Blumenthal: "People want a sense of belonging. The cynical, look-out-for-yourself approach is uncomfortable for a lot of people. They don't want to apply it; they want to have a flag under which they fly. They want to be loyal to the organization."

Underlying indifference is often a manager's myopia or tunnel vision, an inability to see beyond one's own bubble with all its personal preoccupations. Some managers have never learned how to appreciate others, having grown up in an atmosphere where people are stingy with compliments. Other managers may withhold recognition because they believe employees already receive sufficient attention in their paycheck, or that they will use the appreciation shown them to make demands, or that those employees not recognized will feel slighted or resentful.

A simple personal reason some managers may avoid giving recognition is that they themselves feel ignored and unappreciated and cannot find the wherewithal to share what they do

When Louis Harris & Associates polled office workers and managers, they found a growing perception gap between what employees really want and what top management thinks they want. Managers assume that job security is of paramount importance to employees. Among workers, however, it ranks far below desire for respect, a higher standard of management ethics, increased recognition of employee contributions, and closer, more honest communications between employees and senior management.

Executive recruiters Challenger, Gray & Christmas, in Chicago, report that personal recognition is four times more important than salary among people looking for a new job.

not feel. Selfishness, perhaps even with a touch of narcissism, makes them preoccupied with themselves, and the toiling of others is simply backdrop—business as usual. They don't see the struggles and accomplishments of employees around them.

Indifference and myopia affect employees in unexpected ways. They may act angry or resentful, or they may return indifference with indifference and look elsewhere for appreciation. They may plow their energies and aspirations into activities outside the office, being numb, passive, and disinterested from nine to five, then emerging from the office vigorous and enthusiastic, whether tackling hobbies, sports, or a moonlight business. And their newfound energy is their employer's loss.

INSIDE OUT

How Well Do You Appreciate Others?

No one is free of a certain amount of shortsightedness and selfishness. Even the healthiest ego and smartest business person has blind spots and temporary lapses in failing to acknowledge the value of others. However, being able to compensate for these personal shortcomings and show coworkers appropriate appreciation will strengthen your business relationships.

Here are questions to help widen your field of vision—to discern what in your thinking may be getting in the way of feeling and expressing appreciation. Score them:

1 Never	3 Sometimes	5 Always
2 Seldom	4 Often	

1. Do you believe most people are basically lazy and need a push for motivation?
2. Do you believe most people value money as a reward above all else?
3. Do you believe that symbolic gestures such as thank-you notes or acknowledgments in a company publication are less meaningful to people than other kinds of appreciation?
4. Do you see little value in building up someone's ego?

Getting people to chase money . . . produces nothing except people chasing money. Using money as a motivator leads to a progressive degradation in the quality of everything produced.

PHILIP SLATER
Wealth Addiction

A survey of 5,000 employees by Wyatt Company found that fewer than 50 percent of them feel their bosses properly motivate them, provide regular performance feedback, or solve people problems.

5. Do you think feeling superior to others is healthy?

6. Do you believe competition or pitting people against each other makes things happen?

7. Do you believe in Andy Warhol's maxim "It's not enough that I should win—you should lose"?

8. Are you uncomfortable complimenting others for fear of what it may say about you or that the recipient will misunderstand your intentions or take advantage of you?

9. When getting to know someone, do you look first for his or her weaknesses?

10. At work, do you tend not to consider people's feelings and personal motives?

What Your Answers Mean

If you score between 40 and 50, you tend to be self-absorbed and find it difficult to show appreciation; a score between 20 and 40 indicates that you are quite capable of showing appreciation but that sometimes thoughtlessness gets in the way; and a score of below 20 indicates that you are perceptive about others' needs and show appreciation readily.

These questions probe unspoken assumptions you may harbor about people, silent feelings that might be coloring your attitude toward the people you work with. Many managers pride themselves on their refined people skills and their quick judge of character but often misread people's intentions or impose their own motivations on others. Their rewards may be someone else's punishment, as in the case of a senior partner in a Washington, D.C. law firm.

The partner came to me for advice: he was in charge of supervising the firm's pool of word processors, people on call twenty-four hours a day to crank out motions, briefs, and letters, and these employees were on the brink of rebellion. He didn't understand why they were unhappy or what they wanted—they were paid extraordinarily well and although they had to work strenuous hours and on short notice, their paychecks sometimes exceeded those of associates. In describing his predicament, the lawyer always referred to the employees as processors and ex-

The Hay Group, a Philadelphia consulting firm, concluded in a 1988 study that attitudes of middle managers and professionals toward work are becoming more like those of hourly workers, the most disaffected class of workers.

plained that they worked fastest when he gave two people the same document and a bonus to whoever out-typed the other.

This lawyer was obsessed with competing, winning, and making money, and he assumed everyone around him was too. He had never even considered that some employees hated competing and that they valued their relationships with each other more than they wanted to win. Nor had he ever contemplated showing his appreciation any other way than with a checkbook. Ultimately, he could not avert the rebellion and midnight walkout; too much damage had been done. But when the employees returned, he was able to rebuild bridges by eliminating his abusive, insensitive motivation techniques, recognizing that his processors were people and gradually applying intangible signs of appreciation and recognition.

The 1990s promise to be a time when American companies will place heavier demands on their managers —and that means the problem of how to keep valuable talents motivated will pose the most important management challenges of the decade.

Business Week

Learning to Show Appreciation

Individuals and organizations have to learn how to show appreciation. In the early days of transforming your company, you will probably need to take deliberate, calculated actions, but after a while it will come naturally.

Appreciation comes in two kinds of packages: intangible recognition in gestures and words, and tangible rewards such as financial incentives tied to performance. Both are essential. Words of support and encouragement are great for self-esteem but sound hollow if a company does not share its success and back it up with hard currency. Money alone skews people's thinking and goals; it can preoccupy people and become more important than anything else in the company. True appreciation is a balance between the two. The following suggestions are some new habits you can begin to practice.

Ask Your Employees What Excites Them

Conduct regular, informal interviews or discussions with employees, either individually or in small groups, about what motivates and excites them. One of the predictable, typical answers will be money, and you should be prepared to deal with it directly, honestly, and specifically. After you have laid bare the money question, talk about what else inspires your people to work enthusiastically. For instance, some employees may say they need a lot of figurative hand-holding and regular reviews, whereas others prefer independence and bristle at the thought of constant grading. Still others are at their best when they are learning on the job.

Discovering what motivates employees should be ongoing, because people's motivation changes as they age, develop in their job, or encounter different life experiences. If you recall stages of your own working life, you will probably note that at one point a high salary was essential while at another time, a word of praise from a senior vice-president you respected was like gold. So keep asking people what excites and moves them.

Sometimes, however, you will not be able to give people what excites them, even when their requests are reasonable. You may

Chief executives of America's largest companies made 160 times as much as the average blue-collar worker in 1989. American CEOs typically make two or three times as much as their counterparts in Canada, Europe and Japan. And top executive pay rose 12–15 percent in 1990 while profits of the Fortune 500 fell 12 percent.

Time magazine

How to Be Happy at Hanna

At Hanna Andersson, a direct-mail children's clothing firm in Portland, Oregon, CEO Gun Denhart asks her employees to follow these ten principles:

1. Enjoy your work. If you feel you don't, let's talk about it.
2. Don't dabble in office politics. Politics takes energy away from important work.
3. Get behind your task no matter how big or small. If it needs doing, it needs doing well.
4. Keep a balance between work and play. Too much of either is not wholesome.
5. Bring energy to your work. If you can't, it may mean you are in the wrong job.
6. Have no fear, we don't shoot the messenger at Hanna. We are all in this together.
7. Rest assured that success will reward us all. When success means profit, we'll share that as well.
8. Be kind and intelligent with others. Fairness and respect make good things happen.
9. Never stop growing. You're always encouraged to learn as much as you can about your job.
10. Apply love and respect in all you do. Love for your work, respect for others. It works wonders.

be under budget constraints or hamstrung by company policy. When this happens, explain your limitations to employees, then together try to fashion an acceptable alternative that gives them part of what they need and shows your concern. Most important in arriving at this compromise is truthfulness—your being honest with the employees about your powers and limitations, rather than trying to finesse their needs and pretending that what you have to offer matches what they need.

Get to Know Someone's Job

There is no better way to appreciate another than by walking in that person's shoes. By taking their perspective and experiencing their trials and tribulations, you can learn a lot about what motivates and infuriates other people. Managers at Lincoln Electric learn firsthand employees' perspectives and how their work affects them. All new MBAs at this company are required to toil on the welding line for eight weeks. "We want them to understand the difficulty of the factory environment and to have respect for the people out there," says president Donald Hastings.

No one can accuse Hyatt Hotels president Darryl Hartley-Leonard of not appreciating the grit it takes to run a hotel. He and his entire headquarters staff in Chicago devote one day a year to all jobs that make a hotel function. They work as housemaids, check-in desk receptionists, and telephone operators. President Hartley-Leonard has spent a long day with a whistle around his neck, working as a doorman. He recalls: "It was the damndest thing—employees came up to me and shook my hand. We didn't goof around at it, and it wasn't play-acting. You forget how trapped you are in a line job."

Show Your Appreciation Publicly

Every company benefits from employees who feel good about themselves, so don't be hesitant to celebrate their personal successes. ZEBCO, a fishing-tackle manufacturer in Tulsa, Oklahoma, is something of a master of appreciative gestures. Its employees can earn recognition from a long shopping list of symbolic thank-yous. One possibility is receiving the Trailblazer Award, given every month to an employee who makes the greatest contribution toward improving quality. The recipient is honored with a fishing reel with his or her name engraved on it, reserved parking for a month, a free meal in the cafeteria, a pin, and a Trailblazer patch. The employee's contribution isn't forgotten—the company hangs a photo of the person in a display area, and ZEBCO sends a letter home to let his or her family know about the achievement.

Give Paychecks for Perspiration

Financial incentives are arguably one of the best ways to show appreciation, and more and more companies are using them to link paychecks to perspiration and give employees a chance to earn money based on financial and production goals. However, most companies don't realize the tremendous opportunities available for using financial incentives to promote healthy company values.

A Wyatt Company survey found that 46 percent of employees think there is little connection between pay and performance.

Employees say they want to share in the success of their companies, and healthy companies are getting the hint, devising and publicizing incentive plans that are fair and objective and that involve a combination of cash and ownership. These plans include an array of choices for exercising the options: rewarding individuals for team success, paying for learning new skills, and giving employees a piece of the business. Here are various strategies companies use to tie paychecks to perspiration:

> *Link contributions to product revenues.* Computer manufacturers, such as Apple Computer and IBM, use this method to give specialists who develop software 10- to 20-percent royalties on sales.

> *Offer stock options.* Employees of America West Airlines are required to buy company stock equivalent to 20 percent of the first year's base pay and at a 15-percent discount. Once employees are shareholders, they receive annual stock-option incentives.

> *Tie bonuses to performance and profitability.* In Holland, Michigan, auto-parts manufacturer Prince Corporation distributes bonuses to employees once a year based on the corporation's overall profitability; each division's profitability; and employee's work performance. Workers are evaluated on attendance, quality and quantity of work, and their teamwork skills.

> *Share profits.* Employees at Allied Plywood Corporation, a wholesaler of building materials in Alexandria, Virginia,

receive monthly cash bonuses based on profits. While monthly bonuses are the same amount for everyone, annual bonuses depend on contributions to total profit, days worked, and performance.

Offer surprises. American Express Company thanked employees for three years of superior performance and two years of $1 billion-plus earnings by handing out company shares. Chairman James Robinson gave twenty-five shares each (trading around $30) to more than 50,000 employees.

A 1991 Industry Week survey found that nearly half of those surveyed said they do not have fun at work and that a dog-eat-dog climate prevailed in their firm.

Mind Your Manners

All of us aren't perfect when it comes to manners. After working with someone month in and month out, it is easy to take things for granted. Rather than remembering simple courtesies and consideration—asking for input, saying thank you, acknowledging employees' presence, and showing interest in them as people—we plow through our days with rarely a kind word to those around us. This, however, does not show appreciation. Broaden your manners beyond words and show your thoughtfulness by being on time to meetings (making people wait on you announces that you think their time is worth less than yours), not interrupting conversations or telephone calls, and making sure that casual conversations with employees involve give and take. Often, employees feel they must be solicitous and engaging with someone of higher rank, while the other person barely utters a word. If someone in the elevator asks about your weekend, answer, then find out about his or hers.

Blame the Process, Not the Person

When something goes wrong—you lose a client, a shipment is missed, or perhaps a paper is lost—everyone's first instinct may be to blame whoever is closest to the foul-up. This is a knee-jerk reaction for most people, because anger needs an object. But blowing up at the nearest warm body is counterproductive, because it makes people fearful and tentative.

If we make a mistake and know it, we tend to blame circumstances—such as not enough sleep, family pressures, not having enough facts, or incomplete instructions—but when someone else errs, we place the blame on the person's character, not on the circumstances. All of us lack this perspective in trying to under-

Bank of America

stand and correct mistakes. Therefore, why not first examine the circumstances around the blunder? Maybe the client left because of financial concerns. Maybe a shipment was missed because a truck broke down. Maybe a paper was lost because you need more file cabinets. Scrutinizing the situation before blaming people shows you understand the pressures and demands made on them and appreciate their efforts to adapt, cope, and be resourceful.

How Companies Show Their Appreciation

- Xerox Corporation recognizes people through its "You Deserve an 'X' Today" program. Any employee can give anyone else in the company a certificate, redeemable for $25, for excellent support, service, work, or cooperation.

- Burroughs Company posts a regular "Brag Sheet" at the employee entrance of its Canadian factory about individual workers' outstanding efforts.

- Holiday Inn Hotels ask guests to fill out a coupon praising an employee and to give that coupon to managers, who use it to single out the employee for recognition.

- American Airlines supervisors hand out coupons to employees for superior effort; employees then trade these in for gifts or free vacations.

- Diamond Fiber Products Company honors employees by making them members of The 100 Club, named for the points employees earn for perfect attendance records and accident-free diligence. In the first year, productivity soared more than 14 percent and the once disgruntled employees said the company made them feel valued.

- Bank of America recognizes outstanding employees by printing an eagle emblem on their business cards, thus announcing to associates that the person has received the CEO's Eagle Award for exceptional achievement.

- Scandinavian Airlines president Jan Carlzon sends personally written thank-you notes to employees when they excel.

- Phoenix Textiles, Inc., St. Louis, gives its employee of the month a reserved parking space at the front door, beside the president's space.

DEVELOP CLEAR, CANDID COMMUNICATION

Communication is basic to any business. Words, memos, and even unwritten and unspoken messages shape the substance of our jobs and the quality of our relationships. We all communicate, but exactly how clearly, how candidly, and how much all affects our health and company success.

Clear, candid communication is also a pivotal point of respect. It tells people they are important and have a right to know what you are thinking and feeling. Executives frequently ask me, "I know the importance of respect and trust and appreciation, but how do I *show* it? What do I do?" One sure sign of respect is communicating openly, honestly, and completely with employees.

DuPont, for instance, has maintained exceptionally high worker loyalty and confidence, despite cutting 37,000 jobs in the 1980s to reach its current 140,000 work force, through clear communications, specifically telling employees about impending layoffs and giving them as much as two years' warning.

A deliberately fuzzy message—lip service, obfuscation, or even silence—not only garbles communication but also sends what linguist Deborah Tannen calls a *metamessage,* an implied and more significant message. With poor communication, the metamessage is a low opinion of employees.

Good communications do more than enhance the feeling of respect around your office; they also boost motivation and productivity. Good communications includes listening intently to what people want from work, not your own personal agenda; verbalizing your own expectations, feelings, and intentions; providing feedback all the time; and talking to solve conflicts.

At times this communication may be simple and sound, almost trite, but if done sincerely, it works. SAS, the Scandinavian airline, used this technique effectively in the early 1980s when it was making major organizational changes. To explain this upheaval to employees—the change in operations, organization, and responsibilities—it distributed to all 20,000 employees a booklet entitled "Let's Get in There and Fight." Through slogans, cartoons, and simple statements of vision and purpose, it inspired employees to take responsibility and push the airline to new levels of service. The booklet, known as the "Little Red Book," became standard reading among SAS workers.

In a Foster Higgins survey, 97 percent of CEOs believe communicating with employees has a positive effect on job satisfaction, 79 percent believes it helps the bottom line, and 22 percent do it weekly or more often.

*When Opinion Research Cor-
poration of Chicago surveyed
100,000 managers and
workers of Fortune 500 companies in 1988, it found lines
of communication fraying.
Employees at all levels
reported that their com-
panies treated them with less
respect and consideration
than in years past.*

In an office with open and direct communication, employees know their responsibilities, what is expected of them, and how they stand with coworkers and supervisors. People feel secure and confident, and secure employees do not spend a lot of time wondering what the boss is thinking or whether a layoff is coming. Instead, they devote themselves to their jobs.

Unfortunately, many offices foster a system of communication where information and feedback are sparsely meted out. Closed-door meetings, confidential memos, tightly held financial statements, once-a-year performance evaluations, and a rare word of encouragement are the norm. Everybody loves secrets (they give us special knowledge, maybe even special power) and companies adore secrecy, from the names of people being considered for promotion to confidential plans for down-sizing. Companies nurture secrets like hothouse orchids.

In contrast, feedback at Dana Corporation criss-crosses virtually every office and factory through its "What Do YOU Think" program. Each facility displays one or more posters with letter forms addressed directly to J. Woody Morcott, company chairman. Says chairman Morcott, "If you have something that you want me to know about, write me a letter. I'll write back." He receives up to fifteen confidential letters each week and replies to each one in writing.

While companies may institutionalize secretiveness, individual managers can open up or shut down lines of communication. You are the keeper of the hothouse key—you determine whether office communications are open, clear, and candid. Rubbermaid CEO Stanley Gault goes to extraordinary lengths to be accessible and in touch with employees. When an employee badly needed to talk to him after his shift ended at five A.M., Gault gave up an hour's sleep and was there to greet him.

INSIDE OUT

How Well Do You Communicate?

Being direct and open with employees and coworkers takes insight and courage. You need insight into yourself to understand the particular experiences and attitudes that hinder your being frank and forthright, and you need courage to speak your mind and not be afraid of being direct. These questions will start you on the path to acquiring this insight and courage. Score them:

1 Never	3 Sometimes	5 Always
2 Seldom	4 Often	

1. Are you uncomfortable with people who talk about feelings like anger, love, jealousy, grief, or rejection?

2. Do you fear that people will react to your honesty with retaliation, rejection, or harsh judgment?

3. Do you think that being direct and open is a waste of time—that people are uninterested, too busy, see no point, or, worse yet, will take advantage of you?

4. Do you assume that people automatically know what you are thinking and feeling?

5. Do you make quick judgments about people's feelings and intentions?

6. Do you tell people what they want to hear in order to avoid confrontation or win approval?

7. Do you often interrupt people?

8. Do you find yourself often confronting people and giving unsolicited advice?

9. Do you consider yourself a very private person?

10. Do you relish secrets and knowing things other people don't?

11. Do you tend to avoid criticizing people because you feel nervous, guilty, or unfair?

12. Do you not praise people because you think it may make them complacent?

A Towers Perrin study of Fortune 500 companies of various communication techniques—surveys, telephone hotlines, quality circles, suggestion programs, and exit interviews—found that open-door communications are only "slightly ajar."

What Your Answers Mean

If you score between 40 and 60, you tend to be closed, judgmental, and generally uncommunicative; a score between 20 and 40 indicates that you are moderately open and candid; and a

Research shows that poor communication and inadequate supervision are associated with higher rates of coronary heart disease, ulcers, alcohol abuse, and stress. Employees who receive unclear messages from supervisors report higher blood pressure and depression.

score of less than 20 indicates that you are a very open person who speaks his or her mind about personal as well as professional matters.

Many people find it hard to talk about their feelings or to listen to others express theirs, especially at work, where many people believe personal emotions have no place. Such talk makes all of us feel vulnerable, as if we will lose face or control if we reveal human needs and weaknesses. One exception is James Autry of the Des Moines-based Meredith Corporation. Listen to how he communicates: "I use language that isn't considered real business language. I use a vocabulary some would consider mushy or soft. I say things like, 'You know we don't have to love each other but we do have to care about each other.' And I say things like, 'We have to take our work seriously but let's not take ourselves so seriously.' It's not a traditional business attitude."

It is easy to fabricate rationalizations to avoid direct connection with others. We may believe that nobody cares how we feel or that talking about feelings isn't professional. As a personal style, being unemotional, cool, and remote can work for some, but in business, an unreadable facade mostly creates hazards for people around you. Like it or not, we all bring our emotions to the office. Pretending as if you do not, or that they don't matter, forces those around you to guess what you are thinking and how you are feeling and to act on those often inaccurate guesses.

This behavior not only eats away at morale but also affects your company's financial health. Avoiding open, direct communication means that personnel clashes do not get resolved. It means employees never know as much as they should and therefore spend too much or too little time on assignments, and it means misunderstanding and resentment filter through every office and every relationship. It is the sign of an unhealthy company.

I once was called in to work with a senior vice-president of a major manufacturing company who was so uncomfortable with direct communication that he devised a host of tricks to avoid relationships in the office. He would sit for hours behind closed doors, issuing instructions through memos and the computer mail system. He considered face-to-face communication too risky—people might ask questions, raise objections, get into arguments, or become emotional. When he did speak with employees, he was impatient and controlling, keeping all conversation in a small, prescribed box: no small talk, wandering off the subject, or personal topics were allowed. Despite his uncommunicative style, he saw himself as a quick reader of people and had concluded long ago that employees work best when you keep them guessing. Not surprisingly, his employees felt isolated and bewildered, and I wasn't amazed when I heard that he had lost his job. After all, part of his job was communication and he had already lost his ability to communicate.

Learning How to Communicate

Recall a situation when you were ignored or not given any feedback—when you completed a big project without its being acknowledged, when personnel changes were made in your division without your notification, or when no one responded to a memo you had diligently written. You probably felt shut out, devalued, and angry. Remembering those feelings and how you reacted when confronted with little or no genuine exchange is the first step to establishing clear, candid communication. The following are direct steps you can take to open up the channels of communication around you.

Open Your Eyes and Ears

Good listening is essential to communicating. We all listen to each other in the sense that we hear voices and noise, but good listening is actually quite rare. It entails listening to the entire person—the words as well as the body language and the subliminal personal issues that float below the surface. How a person gestures; the tone, pitch, and loudness of the voice; and how close or far away someone stands in a conversation all signal messages about enthusiasm, confidence, agreement or disagreement, friendliness, or skepticism. Even the content of the words has many possible interpretations. For instance, an employee complaining about a deadline may really be saying he needs to spend more time with his children rather than criticizing how a project is being managed.

Avoid listening with half an ear, or, worse, half a mind. Eliminate obvious physical distractions such as phone calls, interruptions or contrived crises, or mental distractions such as

Researchers at the University of Toledo and Pennsylvania State University, interviewing upper-level managers to determine how well they gave subordinates feedback, discovered that most of the senior managers were more interested in talking about their own lack of feedback from their bosses.

impatience, an emotional reaction to the speaker, or being defensive. It is easy to allow or even encourage distractions because we do not want to listen for whatever reason, so scrutinize the distractions that divide your attention.

Another part of listening is asking questions—peeling back the layers of what people mean and want to say. Sometimes simply asking someone, "What do you mean?" or "Could you explain that a little more?" will extract a fuller communication. Don't be a passive listener; extract the information, elaborations, motivations, and feelings that you should know. At this juncture, it is often a temptation to jump in with a solution or suggestion rather than to question and analyze. Squelch that impatience, that desire to resolve immediately. Pause, listen, and ask.

Say What You Want, Say What You Mean

The norm in many business communications swings between tacit understandings and corporate doublespeak. People either say too little or speak and write in depersonalized, bureaucratic jargon. They use *synergy* to mean working together, *economic shortfalls* to mean losing money, and *appropriate professional conduct* to mean getting to the office on time.

Although these examples may sound trivial, they point to a basic obstacle in business communication: people rarely verbalize what they truly mean and want. Many people are better at indirect than direct communication, employing a variety of techniques, including humor, changing the subject, or answering a question with a question. Intentions and desires are couched in code language. The unfortunate results of these cryptic utterances are vague or lost messages. Employees must guess or assume the meaning, and their assumptions are usually off the mark.

Say directly what you mean or want. If you want employees to take more initiative, don't talk about the importance of creativity. If you want them to follow through better on customer requests, don't talk about paperwork procedures. If you want to tell an employee to get counseling for alcoholism, don't talk about vacation time.

The same directness should be applied to your written communications. Too often, memos, business letters, and written policies become an exercise of someone's formal, academic vocabulary, not a way to communicate plainly and clearly. Don't let your true meaning become obscured by stilted, pedantic words and dense sentences and paragraphs that ramble and dance around the issue.

Hoarding information—financial details, bad news, or coming changes in the company—is another way to avoid communication. Sometimes the hoarding is a deliberate dispensing of information on your subjective assessment of who needs to know. Other times it is unconscious—it simply does not occur to you to disseminate facts, figures, or explanations outside an immediate, small group of people.

But when it comes to communication, more is better and much more is best. Michael H. Walsh, chairman of Union Pacific Railroad, is a good example of this motto. Instead of communicating with his far-flung employees through impersonal memos or newsletters, he holds so-called town meetings with local UP employees. At last count, he had met with almost 10,000 workers, answering questions and talking about job security, management style, relationships with employees, union relations, personal incentives, executive pay, and trust. Says Walsh, "A CEO must be visible, vulnerable, and willing to tell the truth and demonstrate that you share employee concerns, even when you can't do much about them."

Smith & Hawken, an importer and marketer of quality garden tools, virtually insists on clear communication through its "5-15 reports," so named because they require no more than fifteen minutes to write and five minutes to read. Each report, submitted every Friday by most employees, is divided into three parts: a simple account of what the employee did during the week, a blunt description of the employee's morale, and one idea for improving the job or the company.

Elliot Hoffman, president and cofounder of Just Desserts, Inc., a San Francisco bakery, hosts an annual dinner for all employees where he gives a complete report on the company, from finances to future prospects, and opens the company books. Another feature of this dinner is the Hot Seat, where Hoffman and other executives must sit and answer any questions from any employees.

At a minimum, hold a staff meeting once a month. This is an excellent time to celebrate your victories, dissect your mistakes, and fine-tune future plans.

If there's going to be a downside, you should share it. . . . When we were experiencing hard times two years ago, I went to the board and told them I wanted to cut my salary.

HERB KELLEHER
CEO, Southwest Airlines

Feed the Feedback

In one sentence Ed Koch, the former mayor of New York, captured the essence of feedback. "How am I doing?" he would ask a crowd of citizens. Indeed, we all want to know how we're doing—what our bosses, coworkers, and even employees think of our performance.

On a personal, human level, our need for feedback stems from the insecurities most all of us possess. Few of us are so confident that we do not want the respect and good wishes of others. Our desire for feedback is, in part, a desire for positive affirmation of our abilities, efforts, and judgment.

At work, our desire for feedback takes on even more import, because it spurs performance and productivity. Regular feedback, in both formal evaluations and informal opinions, clarifies roles, responsibilities, and expectations and ultimately motivates people by making goals clearer and so more reachable.

All employees need feedback, regardless of how well or how badly they are performing and regardless of how low or high they are on the company totem pole. A manager interviewed by *Sloan Management Review* articulates what happens when feedback is handed out to a limited few: "A lot of people at the top don't think they have a responsibility to provide direction and supervision once people are past a certain level in the organization. You just let people go [until] they screw up and then you get out the big stick or axe depending on how big the screw-up and you get them back on track rather violently."

Regardless of whether the feedback is a formal performance evaluation or an informal reaction, it should be dispensed with these guidelines in mind:

> *Provide constant feedback, not simply an annual performance review or sporadic pats on the back.* This is not to say that you need to tell *each* employee *every* day what a wonderful job he or she is doing, but you should make a conscious effort to recognize and comment on good and poor performance.
>
> *Be sincere and honest in your feedback.* It loses currency if it is always in the form of a pep talk. Do not hesitate to disapprove, criticize, or say no. You will earn the right to do this if, at the same time, you are liberal with appreciation and gratitude.

A survey of sixty senior managers about company feedback found, "Although over 90 percent of all organizations in the United States employ some type of appraisal system, it has been estimated that less than 20 percent of performance appraisals are done effectively."

CLINTON O. LONGENECKER
and DENNIS GIOIA
Sloan Management
Review

Never criticize or reprimand in public. Heaping embarrassment on top of your negative reaction complicates the goal of changing or correcting a behavior you want to change.

Direct feedback at professional business actions. Avoid comments on personality issues, such as an employee's obsessiveness or laziness. Words like these are emotionally provocative and far too general. Focus your feedback on behavior and performance.

Tailor the feedback to the individual. Some people are simply more defensive than others. Navigate around their defensiveness by allowing them plenty of time to vent their feelings, then continue your feedback.

Resuscitate the performance review. Most employers conduct annual performance reviews that are usually one-sided exchanges. Do these reviews more often and make them interactive.

Tame Office Conflict

Conflict, disagreements, and even heated arguments are a natural part of business, but when conflict turns to resentment and competitive one-upmanship, it usually signals the breakdown of clear, candid communications. Something goes awry when there are missed meanings, misunderstandings, and mis-assumptions; messages get skewed and conflict erupts. Yet though conflicts are inevitable, they do not have to be destructive and harmful.

At Johnson & Johnson, retired CEO Jim Burke cultivated an atmosphere for what he calls constructive conflict. He describes it this way: "We have some very tough meetings, very open and often emotion-filled. By putting a lot of contention into our system, we get better results. [But] we try hard to be fair. It has a positive effect, as long as people understand that you're really not personalizing any of it. We have that kind of contentious environment, but it is not an ulcer-producing one."

Many people prefer to pretend as if a conflict does not exist and to hope that it will simply go away. The prospect of confronting conflict and anger is frightening. At first glance, these emotions seem much easier to ignore than to risk the unpredictable outcomes of confrontation, such as loss of control, loss of face, or loss of respect.

More often, though, many of us disguise conflict and express

Because we value open and direct communication, we give people permission to disagree. They can tell a manager, "It doesn't seem aspirational to be working with that contractor because from what we've seen, that company really mistreats its workers." . . . Those are very challenging discussions for peers to have—let alone for somebody to have with his/her boss.

ROBERT D. HAAS
Chairman and CEO,
Levi Strauss & Co.

our anger in various ways, some more transparent than others. We may be the avoider, who bottles up his or her anger and is passive, stoic, or uninvolved; the sidestepper, who channels his or her anger into irritability, complaining, or psychosomatic illness or is aggressive in unrelated matters; and the aggressor, who uses his or her anger as a weapon to attack, control, and manipulate.

At Claris Corporation, a software manufacturer in Santa Clara, California, conflict and dissent are seen as positive reactions, because employees are encouraged to contribute and discuss their differing views and to use them as a catalyst for new ideas. The company has even issued guidelines for people on how to respond to disagreements; among its suggestions are "Recognize that if you can feel free to disagree with others, they can also feel free to disagree with you" and "Strive to be less sensitive to constructive criticisms and more sensitive when providing criticism to others."

Identifying the source or recognizing someone who is angry or feels hurt is the beginning of solving a conflict. Then you have to step forward and come to grips with it. Here are some ways you can wrestle that conflict into submission and reestablish communication:

> *Admit to yourself and others that a problem exists.* Denial is seductive and easy, especially if the evidence is intangible or simply a hunch. If you sense a conflict exists, it probably does, so bring it out into the open. Give it a name, describe it, and define it.

> *Declare your intention to find a solution.* Put people on notice that you and they are going to talk about the conflict and take an active role in resolving it. You might say, "I know there's a problem between us; my commitment is to figure out what's wrong and to make amends."

> *Break the conflict into issues or smaller parts,* and one by one find areas where people agree or disagree. This way, you narrow the problem and begin to establish common ground between the warring parties.

> *Don't let immediate emotions escalate the conflict.* Sometimes people's emotional reactions to the act of talking about a problem overtake discussion of the conflict that started it all. Be wary of these emotional side trips and do not lose sight of the initial conflict.

EXCELLENCE IN ETHICS

Imagine a garden with ethics being bright flowers and respect being rich soil. Ethics cannot grow in rock or survive on weak potting mixtures. They need personal attention and cultivation in a place that assigns a higher value to people than to profits.

Entire books and college courses are devoted to the study of business ethics. Companies appear to know much about ethics, too: a survey of 2,000 corporations by the Ethics Resource Center found that 92 percent have codes of ethics on insider trading, bribery, and conflicts of interest. However, another survey reveals that between 1975 and 1984, more than three hundred Fortune 500 companies were involved in one or more illegal acts. Perhaps companies know less about ethics than they think.

Ethics is a twisting, turning subject blending economics, law, management science, and metaphysics with plenty of psychology. And business ethics are becoming even more complicated as different cultures and nationalities bring together contrasting ideas of right and wrong. For some, ethics is largely a theoretical, labyrinthine subject best left to philosophers or business-school professors, while others consider ethics a real and daily concern, as tangible and immediate as the weather.

For me, ethics is basically an issue of fairness: fair treatment of people (fair promotions, fair benefits, and fair hearings). For an organization to be fair, it must balance its priorities, giving as much weight to people concerns as it does to economic ones. Overall, to be fair means balancing your natural self-interest with the interests of others. The ethical person knows when to put aside selfish, personal needs and act on the behalf of the welfare of many people.

Cynics insist that *business ethics* is an oxymoron and that any commercial venture must emphasize survival even at the occasional expense of fair play. This thinking reasons that the pressures of competition, short-term profits, and constant change create an atmosphere where the ends justify the means.

I do not believe, however, that profits must be sacrificed in order to be ethical. Some companies known for their high ethical standards are also highly profitable. In a study of twenty-five corporations with established reputations for strong ethics and healthy finances (among them Cadbury Schweppes, Corning Glass Works, Diamond Shamrock, Digital Equipment Corpora-

The most destructive thing that I know about in enterprises is unfairness—perceived unfairness. People can forgive mistakes if there's a sincere effort to try to be fair. But deliberate unfairness destroys the communication, the cooperation, and all of the things that are necessary for successful teamwork.

BILL GORE
W. L. Gore & Associates

Employee theft costs businesses $75 billion annually, compared with $16 billion just 15 years ago. Surveys indicate that more than half the workers in the country take supplies, materials and equipment from their employers.

ROBERT REICH
Professor of Government,
Harvard University

tion, IBM, Jaguar, Motorola, 3M, and Southwestern Bell), ethics researcher Mark Pastin identified three traits common to all: fairness, personal responsibility, and purpose.

Like the high price of distrust, unethical behavior exacts a hefty fee. From small daily incidents to gross illegalities, shoddy ethics are costly. Deteriorating ethics present very real bottom-line ramifications. The ultimate consequences of unethical behavior are lower revenues and profits and damaged future earning capacity for individual companies and entire industries.

Unfortunately, shallow ethics are becoming more widespread. Figures show an alarming rise in impropriety, questionable practices, and fraud. Recent scandals among the savings-and-loan industry, defense contractors, and commodity traders point to dramatic increases in conflicts of interest, paying or accepting bribes, misuse of confidential or proprietary information, violating antitrust laws, price fixing, and personal enrichment through expense accounts.

These are the unethical acts that receive news attention. But on a smaller, personal level, you probably encounter dozens of unfair, unethical instances every day. Commonplace events such as sexual harassment, the boss taking long lunches, or small lies to clients about why a job is not completed—these too are issues of ethics.

Many companies have instituted codes of conduct to address these problems. However, some of these do's and don'ts read like a superficial public-relations device that ends up doing more to satisfy the conscience than to add value to the company. Gary Edwards of the Ethics Research Center in Washington, D.C. has concluded that "A majority of the ethics codes in place today read like a text from a business law class, spelling out what is legal and what is not, rather than addressing the morals, values and ethics that should exist between a company, its employees, customers and suppliers." People familiar with company practices know whether such codes have any real bite and force or are simply window dressing. Ultimately, relationships and day-to-day dealings tell the real story about a company's code of ethics.

For example, the ice-cream maker Ben & Jerry's scrutinizes the ethics of its business every year and issues a social-performance annual report that evaluates how the company has integrated its stated social goals with the way it conducts business. Union Carbide was obviously concerned about unfairness when it moved its headquarters to Danbury, Connecticut and eliminated unequal perks. Every one of its 2,350 private offices were configured to be the same size and furnished with the same items, and the company did away with the executive dining room and executive parking. And Volvo is apparently aware of this problem, because it offers managers an annual seminar on culture and values, covering such topics as individual and collective freedom, civil disobedience, property and power, and classical philosophy.

INSIDE OUT

How Ethical Are You?

Some of our personal values are in a perpetual state of flux, while others are very fixed. But whether fluid or not, our ethics guide us through peaks and valleys of the day. Here are questions to help you unearth your personal code and shed light on how your personal ethics color your work relationships.

Score them:

1 Never	3 Sometimes	5 Always
2 Seldom	4 Often	

1. Do you apply different values or standards to situations depending on whom you talk to?

2. Do you judge and value people according to how much money they earn? Where they went to school? Who they know?

3. Do you consider a verbal commitment—your word— less binding than a legal contract?

4. Do you believe there are degrees of honesty and that a little dishonesty is acceptable?

5. Have you ever stolen anything? What were the circumstances?

6. Do you believe in using the harmless, white lie?

7. Do you use threats as a kind of motivation?

The Business Roundtable Task Force on Corporate Responsibility and the Ethics Resource Center examined twenty-six companies with codified principles announcing public service as a company priority. "What we found," reports Johnson & Johnson retired CEO James Burke, who chaired the study, "was that those companies with a written commitment to be socially responsible recorded an average 10.7 percent [annual] growth in profits compounded over 30 years. This was 1.34 times better than the growth of the gross national product over the same period."

*My belief is that organiza-
tional ethics is dependent on
personal ethics . . . we must
become better people if we
are to have better organizational governance. Good
systems do not produce good
people; rather, good people
produce good systems.*

ROBERT BECK
Executive Vice-President,
Bank of America

8. Do you believe that everyone has a price—that loyalty and commitment can be bought?

9. Are there some things you would do only if you were paid enough?

10. Do you believe ethics is not something that can be taught but that people must acquire through experience?

What Your Answers Mean

A score of 40 to 50 indicates that you do not have a strong code of ethics but tend to adjust your opinions and reactions to the individual situation; a score of 20 to 40 indicates that your ethics are more-or-less fixed but may be modified depending on a situation; and a score of less than 20 indicates a firm code of ethics that holds true in almost all situations.

None of us possesses pristine ethics that have never been challenged or relaxed. Yet I have met a number of business people who seem to have abandoned ethical considerations in most of their daily decisions, spending more time thinking about what to do rather than figuring out how to be. When this happens, ambition, self-interest, and manipulation take precedence over fairness and integrity, and this cloud of questionable ethics affects everyone, especially employees, who respond with feelings of fear, resentment, and betrayal. A group of business executives who have banded together to fight this trend have formed an organization called the Business Enterprise Trust. Led by James Burke, former CEO of Johnson & Johnson, the Trust makes annual awards to business people for acts of courage, integrity, and social vision.

Find Your Personal Code

Everyone has a personal code of ethics—a collection of values and beliefs that form the underpinning of how we think, react to others, and conduct our lives. Usually our ethics are so ingrained, so much a part of who we are, that we are not aware of them as a code, per se. Unethical behavior can be eradicated, but it requires insight and action. The following two pointers offer a strategy and step-by-step blueprint for instilling ethics and fairness into your working life.

Align Your Personal and Business Ethics

People tend to compartmentalize their lives, separating business values and personal values; we somehow assume there is a difference between loving and parenting and working and spending. Every morning on the way to our job, we make an unconscious readjustment and slip into slightly different values and ethics; we believe what works at home with our loved ones doesn't necessarily apply to decisions at the office.

In the healthy company, there is no sharp distinction between personal and business ethics; there is a single concrete code of ethics for all situations. A strong connection exists between one's personal, deeply held values and the ways those values play out in practice.

However, business is a constant test of conflicts and compromises. This terrain is marked by quicksand, where ethics may briefly sink or even disappear; the best way to navigate it is to compare your personal ethics with your assumptions and actions at work. Examine situations and potential compromises to see whether your personal values endure.

One company that helps employees confront this issue is the aerospace firm Boeing, which has established a permanent position, Corporate Director of Business Practices, for scrutinizing ethical behavior. Employees can call the director toll free, and he frequently shares with them this ethical rule of thumb: "If you wouldn't want to explain it to your family or see it in the paper, question whether it's right." Boeing also distributes to its employees an extensive list of Business Conduct Guidelines. Here are questions Boeing asks its employees to help them evaluate their ethics:

- Could any of the statements you make to a customer be misleading?

- Would any of your marketing techniques cause embarrassment either to your company or a customer?

- Are there any restrictions on the type of courtesies you can extend to a customer?

- Do you use any time, materials, equipment, or information that belong to the company in your outside business?

Public companies present challenging ethical problems. What is proper conduct for an ethical manager who controls the resources of absentee owners? Should his behavior differ from that of the owner-manager who is spending his own money? Should he undertake non-required activities that have a pro-social potential but that impose real economic costs on the owners he has been hired to represent?

WARREN BUFFETT
Chairman and CEO,
Berkshire Hathaway

- Do you ever justify accepting business gifts or courtesies with arguments like "Everybody does it," "I deserve a reward," or "No one will know"?
- Because of business travel, the airline awards you a free ticket. Should you use it for your vacation?
- Do you turn a blind eye to obvious sexual harassment?
- Do you cover up for a fellow worker who is an alcoholic or drug abuser?

We talk continually about management of one's career but we neglect to talk about the management of one's character. Strength of character is shaped throughout life by many small decisions, and by precautionary measures that give one resources to fall back on in times of temptation.

KIRK HANSON
President, Business
Enterprise Trust

Levi Strauss & Co.

Since its founding in 1850, this San Francisco-based apparel manufacturer has combined strong commercial success with a commitment to healthy company values. In 1989, company sales were a record $3.6 billion with profits of $272 million. While the full rainbow of respect, colored with trust, appreciation, communication, and ethics is a rare sight, it is a cornerstone of Levi Strauss's philosophy and operations. The company's most important asset is its 31,000 employees' aspirations.

ASPIRATIONS STATEMENT

We all want a Company that our people are proud of and committed to, where all employees have an opportunity to contribute, learn, grow and advance based on merit, no politics or background. We want all our people to feel respected, treated fairly, listened to and involved. Above all, we want satisfaction from accomplishments and friendships, balanced personal and professional lives, and to have fun in our endeavors.

When we describe the kind of Company we want in the future, what we are talking about is building on the foundation we have inherited: affirming the best of our Company's traditions, closing gaps that may exist between principles and practices, and updating some of our values to reflect contemporary circumstances.

What Type of Leadership is Necessary to Make Our Aspirations a Reality?

New Behaviors. Leadership that exemplifies directness, openness to influence, commitment to the success of others, willingness to acknowledge our own contributions to problems, personal accountability, teamwork and trust. Not only must we model these behaviors but we must coach others to adopt them.

- Do you insist on employee loyalty while ignoring or attacking employees who criticize and suggest changes?
- Do you gloss over problems or shortcomings in your reports to superiors?
- Would you speak out against a company policy that was harmful to other employees or outsiders?
- Are resources and promotions distributed equally? What about training and travel perks?

Diversity. Leadership that values a diverse work force (age, sex, ethnic group, etc.) at all levels of the organization, diversity in experience, and a diversity in perspectives. We have committed to taking full advantage of the rich backgrounds and abilities of all our people and to promote a greater diversity in positions of influence. Differing points of view will be sought; diversity will be valued and honesty rewarded, not suppressed.

Recognition. Leadership that provides greater recognition—both financial and psychic—for individuals and teams that contribute to our success. Recognition must be given to all who contribute: those who create and innovate and also those who continually support the day-to-day business requirements.

Ethical Management Practices. Leadership that epitomizes the stated standards of ethical behavior. We must provide clarity about our expectations and must enforce these standards through the corporation.

Communications. Leadership that is clear about Company, unit, and individual goals and performance. People must know what is expected of them and receive timely, honest feedback on their performance and career aspirations.

Empowerment. Leadership that increases the authority and responsibility of those closest to our products and customers. By actively pushing responsibility, trust and recognition into the organization, we can harness and release the capabilities of all our people.

Another economic theorem is that unethical behavior rises in a profit squeeze. Actually, the implication that ethics is bad for business is simplistic. Unethical behavior tarnishes an industry's reputation and drives out customers. Also, transaction costs are higher, the more unethical the market. The less people trust one another, the greater is the need for accountants, inspectors, lawyers and regulatory agencies.

AMITAI ETZIONI
Professor of Business,
George Washington
University

Business finds it easiest to talk about ethics, but there is no agreement on what the word means. It is more difficult to talk about moral principles; more difficult still to talk about spirituality and love; and most difficult to talk about the shadow side of human character—our inevitable transgressions and failures. . . .

Project on Moral
Character and
Development at Work

Set Your Ethical Climate

Regardless of how large your company or how many employees you supervise, you have the power to create an atmosphere in which people treat each other fairly and with integrity. You establish this climate a number of ways: through actions, communication, rewards, and written guidelines. Here are several specific ways to do this:

Draft a code of ethics for your immediate work group. To do this, you need to talk with employees about the kinds of ethical dilemmas they encounter, how they are handling them, and how they can adjust their reactions.

Identify ethical conflicts or potential conflicts as early as possible. Kirk Hanson, Stanford University ethics expert, suggests you address these questions: Which action produces the greatest net benefit to all parties? Does the proposed action violate any party's rights or any key ethical principles? Are the benefits and burdens conferred by the action fairly distributed?

Reward and discipline ethical and unethical behavior. Include a category for ethics in annual performance evaluations and publicly honor employees for principled behavior. Also make clear the consequences of filing false reports, marketing dangerous or defective products, and failing to report such conduct to others.

Institute safe channels for employees to address unfair work practices. One approach might be to create a policy and support mechanism for handling complaints and issues raised by whistle-blowers. An arbitration system that is fair and accessible should be part of this policy.

Remember to ask prospective employees about their ethics.

Another company pursuing excellence in ethics is Federal Express, with its Guaranteed Fair Treatment Procedure (GFT). Believing all employees have a right to fairness in a workplace free of intimidation, this formal process for handling employee grievances consists of three steps: (1) Management Review—complaint and review by management committee within seven days; (2) Officer Review—review by vice-president or senior vice-president of the division; and (3) Executive Review—review by an appeals board consisting of the CEO, COO, and chief personnel officer. GFT plaques are found in offices throughout the company, and summaries of important cases appear in the FedEx newsletter. Federal Express employees endorse the program almost unanimously and CEO Fred Smith says, "It's the glue that holds this company together."

Exactly how a company blends the four elements of respect into its culture and daily routine depends on the individuals inside the company. The leadership by managers and employees dictates whether the power of respect is put into practice. As this chapter illustrates, respect is both a right and a responsibility. Turning these healthy relationships into tangible results is the subject of the next chapter, which examines issues of power and partnerships and how they can determine the character and course of a company.

Wise Leaders Know How to Follow

FOR DECADES, IT WAS the duty of workers to do, managers and executives to think. That attitude was found at nearly every level in nearly every sector of the economy, from Fortune 500 corporations to small family start-up businesses. Given the climate of the times, companies were managed in conservative, conforming, and traditional ways. In this atmosphere of top-down management, management distrusted employees, and vice versa, and hoarded authority, power, and control, while workers avoided responsibility and personal involvement in their jobs.

In the late 1970s, the situation at Ford Motor Company was typical of the times: labor and management clashed constantly, and profits and quality were declining. Employee feelings were reflected in their work, and their attitude was notorious. Even the public knew better than to buy a car made on either Monday or Friday, when widespread absenteeism at Ford plants made its automobiles rattle and shake. Sales of Ford cars and trucks plummeted 49 percent between 1978 and 1982. In three years, Ford lost more than $3 billion. It closed eleven plants and laid off half its blue-collar workers, as well as hundreds of managers. The company's plight was exacerbated by the economic downturn,

Think of the thousands of companies that achieve adequate performance and lackluster profits with employees they treat like second-class citizens. Then imagine for a moment the power of an organization blessed with fully engaged, fully energized, fully appreciated followers.

ROBERT KELLY
Professor, Carnegie
Mellon University

the oil crisis, and America's sudden love affair with small, high-mileage Japanese cars.

Chairman Donald E. Petersen, who retired in 1990, recognized that the problem did not lie with oil prices, outdated technology, or foreign competitors. The problem—and the solution—were inside the Ford plants, with the people who worked at and ran the company. "We needed to change the 'now-hear-this' mentality, the notion that an employee should listen carefully and not think too much," he recalls.

But how do you turn around decades of heavy-handed management and thousands of apathetic employees? Ford's solution went to the heart of an unhealthy company: the quality of its leadership and the level of employee commitment.

THE CRISES OF COMMITMENT AND LEADERSHIP

Ford is an extraordinary company, but crises like the ones it faced have become ordinary among many American businesses—and not just companies with thousands of employees or with rows of impersonal production lines. In small offices and shops alike, employees are caught in a downward spiral of sinking commitment. The spiral begins with employees being treated like second-class citizens or simple-minded laborers who must be constantly goaded into working. This leads employees to react to the lack of control over their jobs and management's low expectations by feeling annoyed, rebellious, and disinclined to exert themselves or care about their work. Finally, their lack of motivation—and at times irresponsible behavior—makes management think even less of them, push harder, and allow them even less say over their jobs. Any commitment employees possessed disappears into a black hole of apathy.

At the same time, executives and managers faced with such disinterested, lethargic employees set in motion their own crisis, a crisis of leadership. They try to curb the negative attitudes and halt the damage by exerting stronger controls, dispensing less information, and manipulating behavior. In short, they tighten their management but in the process forsake the kind of leadership needed to redress the situation. Instead of sharing with employees a vision and common goals, they impose unilateral standards; instead of relinquishing authority and spreading responsibility, they curtail people's freedom to make meaningful decisions; instead of inspiring enthusiasm and spirit, they insist on conformity and agreement.

Jack Stack, chief executive of a Missouri manufacturing company, describes the crises this way: "I can't stand going into factories and businesses and seeing all these faceless people around. They don't look healthy, and they don't act healthy, and they're a big problem for corporate America . . . you can't have high productivity with faceless people. They're not happy with themselves, they're not happy with their jobs, they bring you down."

Everyone and No One Is to Blame

Employees, managers, and companies did not become this way overnight. This double crisis evolved slowly, invisibly, and in a conspiracy of silence, with few people taking responsibility for what was happening. Whether a company made housewares or sold houses, no one asked, "Why do people hate their jobs?" or "Why are people underperforming?" And most assuredly, few people talked about what they really wanted from work and what they needed to perform best. Instead, employees and management seemed to be pretending that someone else was the cause of their problems and responsible for the solutions.

On the one hand, employees say they want more responsibility, more participation, and more meaning in their jobs, but at the same time, they often behave like indifferent teenagers—avoiding extra chores, not showing good judgment or good sense, and testing the limits of employers' tolerance and authority. On the other, managers push for accountability by telling employees to act like adults and take responsibility and initiative, but then do little to encourage this behavior. Instead, they treat employees like children, closely monitoring them, holding tight reins on authority, and hoarding vital information that would add sense and meaning to employees' work. Furthermore, many company policies reflect the same, if not a stronger, crisis of leadership. They construct rigid hierarchies and a class society that relegate employees to the rank of serf.

The best analogy for describing this behavior and attitude is a family metaphor, with employees behaving like unruly adolescents, managers like first-time parents afraid of showing

I really believe that individuals are capable of doing a lot more than they believe they can do. Given the right environment, you can get surprising results. I believe all of us can do ten, twenty, thirty times more than we might think.

JAMES BURKE
retired CEO,
Johnson & Johnson

weakness or losing control, and companies like strict, omnipotent grandparents. Though companies may like to think of themselves as one big, happy family, in reality, many operate like

---

The Commitment Continuum

In my seminars on healthy companies, I have asked managers to rate the level of commitment among their employees. They see about 20 percent of employees operating at full capacity, who are enthusiastic and committed team players and who care about their jobs, customers, and company. The remaining 80 percent fits a range of types, from conservative and conforming to apathetic and antagonistic. Yet these people are not lost causes—they are capable of remarkable commitment and of making major contributions to a company—and in truth, they can and must be rescued. American business cannot run on so many dead cylinders. The job of resuscitating these employees begins with understanding the nature of commitment and its continuum of behavior and attitudes.

STAGE ONE: HOSTILE AND ANGRY

- always complains and blames others
- is prone to sabotaging, tampering, and lying
- feels taken advantage of by the company
- antagonizes and alienates coworkers and customers
- consistently performs badly
- requires constant supervision
- files excessive disability and worker's-compensation claims
- constantly criticizes the company

STAGE TWO: ANXIOUS AND FEARFUL

- is uncooperative, always finding fault
- finds ways to get around company policies
- is chronically absent and tardy
- doesn't get along with coworkers
- uses health and disability claims excessively
- is mistrustful; lacks loyalty
- drags feet; never takes initiative
- is overwhelmed by changes

dysfunctional families, with individual members each suffering from an arrested development.

This chapter is about how to break out of these traditional,

STAGE THREE: APATHETIC AND DEPENDENT

- provides average performance
- is tardy, as well as error and accident prone
- is not interested in learning new skills
- is indecisive
- is demanding and complaining
- is uninvolved in company goals
- shows little concern for property and safety
- does just enough to get by

STAGE FOUR: CONSERVATIVE AND CONFORMING

- provides above-average performance
- is undermotivated, with untapped potential
- has good people skills
- is reactive; waits for problems to happen
- is not always accountable or reliable
- takes long lunches; misses deadlines
- abuses company perks
- lacks a sense of urgency

STAGE FIVE: ENTHUSIASTIC AND COMMITTED

- cares about customers and results
- is flexible and adaptive; embraces change
- learns constantly
- is open, honest, direct, and trustworthy
- is responsible and accountable
- knows how to lead and follow
- is people-sensitive and people-skilled
- is a cooperative team player

Most organizations are not doing a good job of seeing that their employees understand the business they are part of, get information about how it is performing, having the power to influence its results, and get rewarded on the basis of how well it operates.

Employee Involvement in America, American Productivity and Quality Center

Leadership means to reach people, to inspire them, not in their 5 percent of logical intelligence, nor their 10 percent of ignorance, greed, and fear, but in their 85 percent of feelings and emotions, of unreason and of heart.

PETER KOESTENBAUM
philosopher and author,
The Heart of Business

The moment they [workers] walk into the factory, the company transforms them into adolescents. They have to wear badges and name tags, arrive at a certain time, stand in line to punch the clock or eat their lunch, get permission to go to the bathroom, give lengthy explanations every time they're five minutes late, and follow instructions without asking a lot of questions.

RICARDO SEMLER
President, Semco S.A.

counterproductive roles and create a new family—a healthy company—in which rigid control is replaced by empowering leadership and in which responsibility and authority are shared by all members. In the healthy company, there are no controlling parents, dependent adolescents, or manipulative grandparents. Rather, such a company is composed of teams of committed employees who share power and who assume and pass around leadership as business situations demand. Employees are given the freedom to act, to try out their own ideas, and to be responsible for producing results. This company goes beyond traditional participatory management practices to put together a new configuration of complementary leaders and followers. Exactly how to assemble these partnerships and encourage leadership is the meat of this chapter, which shows the corporate family how to grow up.

THE ADOLESCENT EMPLOYEE

Adolescence is a time of internal turmoil, acculturation, and identity formation that starts around age twelve and ends in the late teens. Yet some employees, regardless of their real age or position in a company, do not act as if they have outgrown this period. Here is how employees—be they new clerical workers or seasoned managers—exhibit these adolescent qualities at work.

Identity Conflicts

The most profound question of adolescence revolves around the dilemma of whether one is a child dependent on authoritative parents or an independent, young adult responsible for his or her well-being and livelihood. Adolescents naturally feel conflicts about dependence and independence; they want the comfort of someone caring for them as well as the freedom that comes with having total control over their lives. The adolescent is eager to try out new experiences and test newly developed abilities, yet needs approval and reassurance.

In adolescent employees, an equivalent identity conflict is acted out daily as they wrestle with their role and responsibilities. Adolescent employees are never sure from one situation to another how much responsibility they want or can handle and whether they are a boss or a worker, a leader or a follower. A typical situation is an employee asking for total responsibility for a project, such as handling a client or producing a report, but then refusing to accept unanticipated consequences, such as missing deadlines or going over budget.

Ego Conflicts

Like teenagers, adolescent employees see the world through narrow eyes, rarely considering the entire landscape or the other people around. They see themselves as the center of the universe and comprehend only immediate gains, personal conveniences, and nearby vistas. The notion of the corporate good or collective benefits is either vague or unpalatable. This enlarged ego also blinds them to personal shortcomings: nothing is ever their fault; they blame everyone else for their problems or failures. Ego-conflicted employees rarely understand how their jobs relate to the larger business perspective. The consequences of decisions involving strategic planning, competitive pressures, and corporate finances are beyond their range. These employees do not grasp the importance, for instance, of retaining earnings instead of funneling all profits back to employees. Although some of their problem is immaturity, a good deal is rooted in ignorance. They do not know how their company lives and operates, because no one has shared this information and they have not pressed to know it.

Most people who work in companies don't understand business. They have all kinds of misconceptions. They think profit is a dirty word. They think the owners just slip it into their bank accounts at night. They have no idea that 46 percent of business profits goes to taxes. They've never heard of retained earnings. And there's a good reason for all this ignorance. No one teaches them how a business works.

JACK STACK
CEO, Springfield
Remanufacturing Corp.

Authority Conflicts

People conflicted about authority reveal this dilemma daily: they simultaneously resent directions and oversight, and yet refuse to take initiative; they insist on doing things their way, then perform carelessly; and they bristle at constant monitoring but are notorious for not following through on projects and finishing the last, vital 5 percent.

Paradoxically, such a person often idealizes authority in distant hero figures or in the mythical perfect boss. Stuck in the maturation process, the employee constantly tests the limits of management's authority and patience. Ultimately, this testing

becomes a game of power and control. To the adolescent employee, authority is a weapon someone else has and an obstacle he or she must resist, rather than a source of inspiration or a form of leadership.

MANAGERS AS MALFUNCTIONING PARENTS

Managers contribute to the twin crises of commitment and leadership by mishandling their power and misperceiving their roles. Just as no one is really taught how to be a parent, few of us are taught the art of leading; instead, we learn by watching and imitating others. Unfortunately, this does not make for the most enlightened or proficient manager.

Typically, when managers rise through employee ranks to reach that corner office, they react in two ways. First, they abandon common sense and the memories of powerlessness of employee life, and they copy managers who have preceded them, thus repeating their sins and shortcomings. Second, fearful of losing their precious gains or worried that they may be in over their heads, they hoard control and manipulate their power or they shirk the responsibility altogether. They either behave like ultrastrict parents who refuse to give their kids any freedom or responsibility, or throw up their hands in helplessness and declare they cannot control their kids.

These parental or managerial reactions can be traced to two internal conflicts: the struggle for control and the rise of narcissism.

The Struggle for Control

Managers are often torn by the exercise of power, because they do not understand the nature of control. They regard it as a single powerful tool, a weapon to be grasped as tightly as possible. In their minds, control is the machine by which they get things done and more control means they can accomplish more; control in anyone else's hands hinders or derails accomplishments. In many businesses, says business author Peter Block, control is a *sine qua non*. "To live in an organizational pyramid is to pay great attention to control. At times it seems we value control above all else. Whole departments and whole levels of man-

Look at management as a function, not a class. If you go into the role thinking that management is a class, you'll be sorely disappointed when you find that people rebel against you.

MIKE BUSCH
Director of Training,
Herman Miller Co.

agement are created simply for the purpose of keeping control. It is as though if we lose control, we've lost everything," Block writes in *The Empowered Manager.*

As with any valuable commodity, managers seek to acquire control, trade on it, and strengthen it or avoid dealing in it at all. A study of 18,000 managers by Teleometrics, Inc., a Texas consulting firm, concluded that managers generally fall into two categories: those who are fearful of power and its effects on employees, and so avoid using it, and those who wield it like a great club.

Teleometrics reports that about 30 percent of managers fall into the first group, which it characterizes this way: "They consider work an onerous task and wind up protecting people from work because they fear they won't be liked if they seem too demanding." But the other 70 percent are what Teleometrics calls John Wayne Managers. These people "plan, direct, control and coordinate, and frequently find their own sleeves rolled up in order to get the job done right."

Most managers devote a large portion of their working lives to maintaining control, regardless of whether it is limited, such as with supervision over a shift of waiters, or extensive, such as with supervision of an entire construction job. Not only do they maneuver and scheme in their own activities, but they fiercely prevent control from slipping into employees' hands.

Adding to the dilemma are managers' inadequate leadership skills. They have seldom learned the softer side of management—how to empower, guide, teach, or liberate. They may try these techniques out, but whenever an effort falters, they regress to the traditional ways—pushing employees, making demands, and becoming more manipulative and controlling. Under the stress of possible failure, they become even more demanding and controlling or absolve themselves of responsibility and give up.

The Rise of Narcissism

In many companies, the corporate ladder encourages managers to misconstrue their identity and their position. Like the Greek demigod Narcissus, managers fall in love with their own reflection. Once elevated in a company, they begin believing that not only are they better than employees, but smarter, quicker, more perceptive, and more knowledgeable.

People get to the top by believing in themselves and by working hard. But once at the pinnacle, they sometimes forget that they don't have all the answers within themselves and that it's not a crime or shame to admit it. . . . the executive attitude toward managerial power that wins worker loyalty esteems authority as a privilege, not a right. Responsible executives see themselves as trustees, not tyrants.

WILLIAM WALTON
Cofounder, Holiday Inns

We have an idea of individualism—rugged individualism—embedded in our culture, and it is truly a wonderful thing. . . . But rugged individualism has a downside, in that this same person tends to take the work of defining and solving problems on his own shoulders. He is inclined to see himself as the Atlas who can hold up the world by himself.

RONALD HEIFETZ
Professor, Harvard Kennedy School of Government

This self-aggrandizement is not just obnoxious, it is harmful to a business. It leads managers to discount employees' ideas, to be blind to what they need to work better. Narcissistic managers lose insight an̶ a thick wall between themselves and er̶ g shadows on efficiency, innovation, co̶ ̶vity.

T̶ ̶R

̶ny organizations—a rigid, impervious con- ̶ment bunker—reinforces and perpetuates both ̶ment and leadership problems and creates corollary ̶which I call architecture, access, and incentives.

A Crisis of Architecture

Many companies are built wrong: they are constructed like totem poles. Some totem poles are larger and more ornate than others, but the basic order is the same—a vertical configuration with limited lines of communication and a better view and more perks the higher you climb. People are in touch only with those directly above or below them, and those higher up generally overestimate the importance of their position. This top-down arrangement does not encourage cooperation and a feeling of belonging but rather reinforces feelings of dependency, nearsighted self-interest, and risk aversion. Companies promote this inflexible hierarchy through words and deeds: precise ordering of titles, rigid roles and responsibilities, stifling rules and regulations, value-laden symbols such as the size of offices, and chain-of-command directives.

When the architecture is suffocating, people can't breathe. Passive and powerless, they give up trying or actively search for ways to retaliate.

A Crisis of Access

This predicament is grounded in long-standing corporate tradition—a paternalistic assumption that a select few in a company know what is best for all employees. Many companies deliberately keep employees in the dark, handing out only scraps of information. They believe that secrecy serves their purpose and that employees need to know only what directly affects their jobs. The secrecy is for self-protection, because knowledge is power; and if employees knew, for instance, what executives earn or how to manage cash-flow cycles, they might rival their bosses.

The crisis of access is like a drought, a scarcity of nourishing information and communication. The result is a small-minded company that does not get the best work out of its employees.

A Crisis of Incentives

Companies typically reward the wrong people—the politicians, not the producers. They reward the appearance of productivity and enthusiasm or immediate success, not actual effort, genuine commitment, or long-term investments of time and thought. Managers who are adept manipulators—avoiding responsibility for negative consequences, stealing thunder and ideas from others, and seeking to please rather than performing —receive the attention and rewards. The quiet, competent manager who is more concerned with collaborative relationships than with self-protection is invariably overlooked. Only a rare executive, such as Ross Perot, chairman of Electronic Data Systems, Inc., recognizes the value of this kind of manager. "If we have the best of the best employees," Perot declares, "then we will succeed. I don't want any corporate politicians, any upwardly mobile corporate gypsies, I don't want some guy that wants to move ahead at the expense of others. I want someone who gets to the top because he's better than anyone else."

Pyramids emphasize power, promote insecurity, distort communications, hobble interaction, and make it very difficult for people who plan and the people who execute to move in the same direction.

RICARDO SEMLER
President, Semco S.A.

THE FORD SOLUTION

Executives at Ford had to do something radical to pull the company out of its free-fall. While forced for economic reasons to apply the usual remedies—layoffs, budget cuts, plant closings, and rushing new models into production—they sensed that different kinds of change were also required. The company needed to retool its entire culture—its attitudes about leadership and the interaction between employees and management.

"The only solution for Ford, we determined, was a total transformation of our company . . . to accomplish it, we had to earn

True involvement takes more than just pushing any one, two, or three of the four features—power, information, knowledge, and rewards—to all levels of the organization. All four of these features must be moved to the lowest level of the organization.

EDWARD LAWLOR
Professor of Management,
University of Southern
California

Data Bank
A survey of 390 large companies reveals these reasons behind their implementing employee involvement programs:

*To improve productivity—
70 percent*

*To improve quality—
72 percent*

To improve employee motivation—58 percent

To improve employee morale—54 percent

the commitment of all Ford people. And to acquire that commitment, we had to change the way we managed people. We had to create a new sense and understanding of cooperation and teamwork," explains Ernest J. Savoie, director of Ford's Employee Development Office.

The company began with small steps, holding meetings with groups of employees and asking for their candid thoughts and suggestions. Managers polled employees individually. Pipefitter Jim Bradley remembers being astounded when a manager he rarely saw came up to him on the factory floor and asked, "What can I do to help you?"

The commitment to cooperation and shared responsibility was dubbed the Employee Involvement (EI) program, and each plant established its own Employee Involvement process, usually starting with problem-solving groups composed of mostly hourly workers to attack a single snag. For instance, assembly-line workers suggested making all bolts the same size, thus saving employee time from rummaging through bins of different-size bolts and changing wrenches. Another suggestion was to cut a larger hole in a panel so that employees could tighten a bolt more easily and without fear of dropping it into an inaccessible cavity.

The company not only listened and responded; it also encouraged employees to manage and lead, taking over tasks routinely handled by managers, such as scheduling work or stopping the assembly line if quality was falling. Employees were given a powerful voice in making decisions and determining how their workplace functioned.

The EI process offered only half a solution; it needed a managerial component to be complete, and so Ford inaugurated another radical program, Participative Management (PM), to teach managers how to lead in this new environment. The magnitude of instituting a major change in management was revealed through a survey of 3,000 Ford managers. The survey found that the overwhelming majority were traditionalists dedicated to protecting the status quo.

The company inaugurated the EI/PM programs together through a series of leadership development conferences to teach the ideas behind both concepts and how to implement them. The guiding principle for these programs was to involve employees in every facet of the business, from product design to customer orientation. Ford declared its new cultural values in a statement called Mission, Values and Guiding Principles (MVGP). It states that "people are the source of our strength. They provide our corporate intelligence and determine our reputation and vitality. Involvement and teamwork are our core human values."

On the factory floor, this philosophy translated into teamwork, attention to quality, and involving everyone to improve efficiency. Employees are learning new skills, sharing tasks, and communicating better with each other and managers.

As we all know, Ford turned itself around. It launched the Taurus and Probe in 1985, which became symbols of the company's sleek new image, efficient production, and employee satisfaction. That year, its new-car market share was just under 19 percent; four years later it had risen to over 23 percent. In 1979, 400 out of 1,000 cars had to be pulled aside for repairs; today that number is down to about 20. The production of 75,000 workers in 1979 equaled the production of 49,000 workers ten years later.

Employee attitudes mirror the production improvements. In a survey of salaried employees, almost half say they are highly involved in the decisions affecting their jobs. Among all employees, about 80 percent agree that Ford's statements about the importance of quality are backed up by its deeds. Given these attitudes, it is significant but not surprising that Ford's contract with the United Auto Workers is negotiated without acrimony or problems.

Ford has not found the miracle cure for flagging employee commitment. The Employee Involvement/Participative Management process is not perfect; not all employees believe in or actively join in the process. Yet given Ford's condition before and after the changes were implemented, its EI/PM process is one of the most dramatic employee and company turnarounds in corporate history. Its solution, which extended even beyond EI/PM to open, cooperative labor relations and a new commitment to education, training, and quality, offers lessons for all companies.

> *The way employees treat customers reflects the manner in which they're being treated by management.*
>
> JAMES A. PERKINS
> Senior Vice-President,
> Personnel, Federal Express

LEADERSHIP AT EVERY LEVEL

As Ford Motors learned, a healthy company cannot afford to shelter unruly adolescents, insecure managers, or a corporate culture that stifles involvement and innovation. Inadequacies at every level need to be replaced by leadership at every level: employees who lead with enthusiasm and commitment, managers who lead by involving and motivating employees, and companies that lead by fostering a business environment that is open and empowering.

To achieve leadership at every level, organizations must rely on two principles: participation and psychological ownership.

The Power of Participation and Ownership

Participation is the lubricant in tomorrow's workplace—people sharing responsibility and working together to accomplish mutual business goals. With true participation, all workers have a right and a responsibility to contribute, to stay informed, and to share the fruits of their labor. Whether their work is as mundane as directing traffic or as exotic as researching rare viruses, participation makes people feel validated because their work has meaning, because they can influence the outcome, and because they can have a positive impact on others. Real participa-

The very structure of the human brain seems to press individuals toward a sense of completion or closure with respect to perceptions, tasks and activities. It is not surprising, then, that the problem of meaningless work is alleviated when workers engage participatively in solving problems and creating changes.

MARSHALL SASHKIN
Organizational Dynamics

Participation at Milcare

Milcare, a Grand Rapids, Michigan, company known for innovative solutions in health-care furniture, offers these 10 guidelines for effective participation.

1. Participation is a right and responsibility.
2. Everyone must be "literate" on business realities.
3. Participation is neither paternalistic nor permissive.
4. Everyone must accept "problem ownership."
5. Management is open to competent influence.
6. Participation is the means to become more competitive.
7. Decisions are made at the most appropriate levels.
8. Employees have access to all the necessary resources.
9. Everyone must adhere to a system of accountability and commitment.
10. Participation is a process that is managed and continually renewed.

tion makes people feel as though they are in control and ultimately in charge of their own destiny.

Psychological ownership is the consequence of true participation; it is feeling committed to an ideal, an activity, or even a person. Ownership arises when people see that their efforts *can* make a difference, that they are an integral part of the process. It is a feeling of pride, a sense that you own the experience, with all its accompanying successes and failures.

The degree of participation and ownership among employees defines their levels of commitment to a job. With no emotional connection, there is indifference, perhaps even hostility

We believe in the potential competence of every individual and their enormous potential . . . everyone has an enormous appetite to achieve happiness, which is the fulfillment of one's talent and potential.

BILL O'BRIEN
CEO, Hanover Insurance
Company

Improve Your Health with More Participation

Remember the rat experiments in psychology class? Put a rat inside a cage, introduce some intermittent, unpredictable shocks, and watch what happens. Initially, the rat scurries around the cage looking for relief. When none is found, the anxious rat begins climbing the walls, urinating, and eventually lies down, exhausted and powerless.

Health and management experts studying how much people control and participate in decisions surrounding their jobs and lives find that their health is affected by feelings of control and involvement, too. Lack of control quickly translates into an assortment of disorders, including alcoholism, cardiovascular disease, anxiety, and depression. Research confirms this:

- A six-year study of men with heavy work loads and limited control over their jobs found their risk for cardiovascular disease 1.4 times higher than normal.

- A study of men under age fifty-five performing hectic work and possessing little control over its tempo showed increased incidence of myocardial infarction.

- A study of Swedish workers who changed to positions that gave them more control found they had fewer coronary symptoms than workers who had less control.

- A study of American women with heavy work loads and little job control found them three times more likely to develop coronary heart disease than women with the same work load but more control. Women doing clerical work had a 420-percent greater chance of developing this disease.

and outright destruction. With no psychological ownership, the substance of one's work and its consequences become irrelevant; one becomes unconcerned whether a job is unfinished, a product is shoddy or defective, a customer walks out, or money is wasted.

But when the feeling of ownership is high, everything matters. An employee who owns his or her work is concerned about the entire environment, from the quality of communication, to the efficiency of the process, to all aspects of the product. Some executives describe this relationship as covenantal. "The best people working for organizations are like volunteers," says Max DePree, retired chairman of Herman Miller, Inc. "Volunteers do not need contracts, they need covenants . . . covenantal relationships induce freedom, not paralysis. A covenantal relationship rests on shared commitment to ideas, to issues, to values, to goals, and to management process."

What follows are suggestions for instituting ideas and programs to help managers and companies overcome the crises of commitment and leadership. I will begin with an examination of personal obstacles, then move on to ways to blend these suggestions into business relationships that forge a healthy-company environment.

INSIDE OUT

Are You a Controlling or an Empowering Leader?

One of the biggest destroyers of leadership is the misuse of power. What you think about power in general—where it comes from, how you get it, and what it can do—and how you wield your power determine your effectiveness. Regardless of your position, you have some power. Do you use it or abuse it? These questions will help you explore your thoughts about power. Score them:

1 Never	3 Sometimes	5 Always
2 Seldom	4 Often	

1. Do you closely watch employees so that they won't take advantage of you or the company?

2. Do you consider yourself the best problem-solver in your work group?

3. Do you ask employees to give you constant progress reports on their work?

4. Do you determine the hours for arrival, breaks, lunch, and leaving around your office?

5. When you hear criticism of your management style or work output, do you get defensive or vengeful?

6. Do you believe employees need to receive information on only a need-to-know basis, that is, if it directly affects their jobs?

7. Do you keep confidential information about company finances, competitors, market trends, company strategy, and future plans?

8. Are employees reluctant to share problems or warn you about risks or possible bad outcomes?

9. Do you believe your employees should not go around you to communicate with your boss?

10. Do you avoid holding meetings and assigning team projects because people seem to waste a lot of time when they work together?

11. Do you feel employees frequently avoid taking initiative or duck responsibility?

12. Do you sometimes see yourself as a kind of hero to your employees?

13. Are your meetings tightly structured, with people speaking only when asked or offering only prepared comments?

14. Do you find it hard to delegate responsibility and believe that for a good job, you must do it yourself?

15. Do you tend to discount or ignore employee suggestions or ideas?

16. Do you believe some people are born leaders and some are born followers?

What Your Answers Mean

Your answers indicate whether you regard power and control as a weapon to fend off threats and challenges or as a tool to empower coworkers and enhance their productivity. A score of 64 to 80 suggests that you are a controlling manager who keeps employees on a very short leash; a score between 35 and 64 indicates

Empowering is the opposite of control. Empowering managers create the climate for innovation in their organizations. They see their most important work as enabling the men and women working with them to succeed—to develop as individuals. Empowering only works in organizations that drive decision-making to the people closest to the problems, closest to the issues, and that encourage taking risks. And it only works if the empowering leaders then get out of the way —even if it hurts.

LARRY PERLMAN
CEO, Control Data
Corporation

ⒼⒹ CONTROL DATA

that in some instances you can share leadership and empower employees, but in others you do not let go; and a score below 35 indicates that you are a leader who empowers those around you.

Most of us possess more than a few controlling qualities—a touch of impatience, a fear of losing control, a little insecurity about status, or occasional outbursts at employees because they do not do their job *our* way. But in private conversations with managers, I can sense those who are excessively controlling, because they talk about fear of being taken advantage of, are preoccupied with appearances, promise to even scores, and believe employees are fundamentally lazy. In conversations with empowering managers, however, I find maturity and confidence. Secure within themselves, they are not afraid to allow coworkers to shine on their own; they know that the more power they share, the more they gain.

Warren Bennis, an expert on leadership and author of *On Becoming a Leader,* defines leaders thus: "Leaders are people who are able to express themselves fully. They know who they are, what their strengths and weaknesses are, and how to fully deploy their strengths and compensate for their weaknesses. They also know what they want, why they want it, and how to communicate what they want to others in order to gain their cooperation and support." Here are some truths I have learned about leadership and power from leaders—truths that are important to remember as you manage your working life.

INFLUENCE IS EARNED, NOT SEIZED. Many people believe you can buy influence, but leaders have proven you can buy only position or status. Influence must be earned with hard work and the respect of others.

LEADERS ARE DEFINED BY THEIR FOLLOWERS. Leadership does not occur in a vacuum. It is not some mysterious quality like charisma that people are born with. True leaders are elevated from the pack by their colleagues and achieve their leadership because it is granted to them.

LEADERSHIP SPRINGS FROM ACCEPTING IMPERFECTION. We are told from early childhood that presentation is everything—that we should hide mistakes and avoid looking vulnerable at all costs. However, people feel more secure around others who are imperfectly human. They identify with them and gladly follow their lead.

POWER INCREASES AS YOU GIVE IT AWAY. Often our immediate reaction is to hoard power so others do not steal it. But paradoxically, power builds on itself only when you share it with others.

SHARING POWER PREVENTS STUPID MISTAKES. Recently, an executive said to me, "I can't tell you the screw-ups I avoided by allowing people underneath me to set me straight when I didn't know what the hell I was talking about."

POWER BUILT ON FEAR IS AN EXPRESSION OF IMPOTENCE, NOT LEADERSHIP. People who try to lead by intimidation—bending the will of others—produce more fear than followers and expose their own feelings of powerlessness. In leadership, fear and ego cannot replace strength and character.

NO MATTER HOW BRIGHT YOUR REFLECTION, IT WILL ALWAYS FADE. As Andy Warhol once said, "We are all famous for fifteen minutes once in our lives." Unfortunately, many managers lose sight of the time and do not realize that others do not really care anymore.

What the Manager Can Do

As a manager, your role in the healthy company should be one of a liberator, allowing people the freedom to do their best. At times this means destroying the hierarchical barriers that impede innovation and taking risks, while at other times it means leading and inspiring, even pushing people to perform beyond their image of themselves. Occasionally, you must be vulnerable, open to influence, actively soliciting others' ideas, or seeking consensus. While often you are a leader, creating ideas, acting as a model, and liberating others, there will be situations when you are a follower, taking directions, listening, and assisting colleagues. The liberating leader is a master of both roles and knows that, frequently, terms like *manager* and *worker* are arbitrary, because responsibility is shared according to ability, not title.

No leader is omnipotent, so asking people to fill in where you are inexperienced or unskilled shows them that your ego does not dominate your thinking. It indicates that you value accomplishing something over appearing infallible.

In putting into action these qualities and truths, a liberating manager tries to implement the following seven directives:

I can speak from experience. It has been difficult for me to accept the fact that I don't have to be the smartest guy on the block—reading every memo and signing off on every decision. In reality, the more you establish parameters and encourage people to take initiatives within those boundaries, the more you multiply your own effectiveness by the effectiveness of other people.

ROBERT HAAS
Chairman and CEO,
Levi Strauss & Co.

If we let our people flourish and grow, unleash people to be self-confident and take on more responsibility, if we use the best ideas they come up with, then we will have a chance to win. The idea of liberation and empowerment for our work force is not enlightenment, it's a competitive necessity.

JOHN WELCH
CEO, General Electric

Tailor Your Leadership Skills

The first rule of empowering leadership is to tailor your style to accommodate everyone's individual talents and energy levels. You need to seek out gradations of participation, depending on a person's experience, the work situation, available time, and other relevant factors. Your role as leader greatly depends on your assessment of each situation. For employees who are short on skills and perception, you must wear your coach's cap, directing and advising along the way. For those employees with talent and initiative, delegating authority and providing support will accomplish the task. Ultimately, you want all your employees to develop and implement their own goals; your role here is to train them and then get out of their way.

One caveat to this issue is that you must remain flexible. Employees and jobs may change, yet your assessments of them often do not. Though the secretary who needed initial coaching may have grown and developed, you may still view her as the office neophyte. The executive who never seemed to need your attention may now be struggling with a tough assignment and wasting valuable time and resources. When we misread people's abilities, our expectations of them are often inconsistent with how they behave. We then perceive them as stepping on our turf, not pulling their weight, or challenging the mentor-protégé relationship. When this happens, both you and the employee are likely to feel resentful and misunderstood.

Open Yourself to Feedback

Nothing is more important to healthy companies than the constant flow of ideas between leaders and followers. Soliciting ideas from others takes time, often requiring that you give up some control and opening the door to personal criticism. Asking for suggestions from your employees can also be interpreted as not having all the answers. Frieda Caplan, founder and CEO of Frieda's Finest, a California-based distributor of fruits and vegetables, offers an alternative approach: "When I face a tough decision, I always ask my employees, 'What would you do if you were me?'"

We are usually not the best judge of ourselves, so soliciting evaluations of your management style is another way to avoid self-delusion. Your employees may well be better judges of your

Leaders Who Make a Difference

After years of studying leaders and followers, James Kouzes and Barry Posner report in their book *The Leadership Challenge* that leadership is an observable, learnable set of practices. These are the five fundamental practices and ten behaviors (shown in small caps) in exemplary leadership:

1. *Leaders challenge the process.* They SEARCH FOR OPPORTUNITIES to change the status quo. They look for innovative ways to improve the organization. They EXPERIMENT AND TAKE RISKS. And since risk taking involves mistakes and failure, leaders accept the inevitable disappointments as learning opportunities.

2. *Leaders inspire a shared vision.* They passionately believe that they can make a difference. They ENVISION THE FUTURE, creating an ideal and unique image of what the organization can become. Through their strong appeal and quiet persuasion, leaders ENLIST OTHERS in the dream. They breathe life into visions and get us to see the exciting future possibilities.

3. *Leaders enable others to act.* They FOSTER COLLABORATION and build spirited teams. They actively involve others. Mutual respect is what sustains extraordinary efforts, so leaders create an atmosphere of trust and human dignity. They STRENGTHEN OTHERS, making each person feel capable and powerful.

4. *Leaders model the way.* They establish values about how employees, colleagues, and customers ought to be treated. They create standards of excellence and then SET AN EXAMPLE for others to follow. Because complex change can overwhelm and stifle action, leaders PLAN SMALL WINS. They unravel bureaucracy, put up signposts, and create opportunities for victory.

5. *Leaders encourage the heart.* Getting extraordinary things done in organizations is hard work. To keep hope and determination alive, leaders RECOGNIZE CONTRIBUTIONS that individuals make to the climb to the top. And every winning team needs to share in the rewards of their efforts, so leaders CELEBRATE ACCOMPLISHMENTS. They make everyone feel like heroes.

All of us have had our share of bonehead ideas. Having someone tell you it's a bonehead idea before you do something about it is really a great blessing.

WALTER SCOTT
retired Chairman, Grand Metropolitan, USA

strengths and weaknesses. If you can listen to them without becoming defensive, aggressive, or dismissive, you may learn more about your leadership capabilities.

Retired GTE chairman Theodore Brophy discovered this late in his career when GTE instituted a program that let employees assess managers: "I was the first person to be evaluated. I was told that I did not praise people enough. I would tell them when I was dissatisfied, but I didn't tell them when they did a good job. This program was something I wished I'd gone through thirty years ago. It would have helped me be a better manager."

Symbolize Your Beliefs

Sweeping actions that symbolize your commitment to instilling leadership can serve as important markers to others. Using symbols helps communicate what you are thinking so that employees do not have to guess your thoughts. Sometimes these gestures may be simple or small and other times they are large, but whatever shape these gestures take, they must be sincere. If employees doubt the conviction behind them, your gestures will ring hollow.

Ren McPherson, former president of Dana Corporation, for example, demonstrated his disdain for bureaucracy by publicly dumping the company's foot-thick stack of rules and regulations into the trash, then presenting the board with company procedures outlined on a single sheet.

Mike Warren, CEO of Alabama Gas, signaled the end of the old era of company-union antagonism and the beginning of a new partnership with a twenty-foot paper-maché dinosaur. He stuck a stake through its heart, then dragged it from department to department. Two years later, the union reciprocated: it sent him a brontosaurus statuette inscribed, "Dinosaur Killer of the Year."

Consciously or not, words and actions like these convey powerful layers of meaning. They send signals to people about what you believe is important; they show that you believe leadership means sharing power; and they show that everyone can benefit from learning leadership.

Reject Showy Signs of Power

Being a liberated leader means being a role model that people respect. Flaunting one's status or achievements, however, sets the wrong example, because it suggests you value appearances more

You always have to maintain credibility. That requires a sixth sense, one that tells you when your credibility is in question. You know it. You can hear it out on the shop floor. You can feel it. To be a good manager, you have to have that sixth sense.

JACK STACK
CEO, Springfield
Remanufacturing Corp.

than content, public envy more than private respect. Pricey symbols also undercut your credibility. "If I buy a factory one day and show up in a Lamborghini the next, can I then go and talk about the company being at risk? Would anyone believe me?" asks CEO Jack Stack.

Especially avoid these flourishes:

- Layers of personal staff, secretaries, and gatekeepers that isolate you; dress and title do, too. Take off your tie sometimes and don't be afraid of your first name.

- Offices larger than human-scale, executive dining rooms, exclusive limos, private elevators, private bathrooms, and special parking places.

- Talk peppered with first-person pronouns, formal names, and specialized vocabulary known to just a few. These all send the wrong messages.

The liberating leader instead connects with others outside his or her circle, has lunch with employees, and stops by people's offices. Be approachable; invite employees to come to you with thoughts and suggestions. Keep meetings informal enough to allow people to speak their mind, be open to criticism, and let people address you by first name.

At Chaparral Steel in Midlothian, Texas, company president Gordon Forward demonstrates the epitome of informality. He holds most of his meetings in the wide flange mill or in a hallway, primarily because that is where he can see and hear the people who, by his reckoning, produce "more tons of steel per employee per year than any steel mill in the world."

W.L. Gore & Associates, a $700 million fabrics company, goes one step further. Each of its 5,300 employees is considered an associate. Perks such as executive parking spots and big offices are taboo, while leaders must share the power to hire, discipline, or fire associates with peer committees. They can't give orders, either; they can only seek commitments from associates.

Give People the Tools to Lead

Many of today's workers show up at work to find an empty toolbox. Either they lack the information or skills to get the job done or they know a given situation is bound to fail because of

What employees are looking for from me—the first word I think of is "coxswain"—they want to know that we're headed in the same direction, everyone is given a voice, and each person participates.

BILL O'BRIEN
CEO, Hanover Insurance Company

not enough time, inadequate instructions, not enough money, too little support, or a dozen other reasons. As a leader, you need to recognize these obstacles and put more and more accountability and authority into the hands of people who are closest to the products and customers. To ensure their success, people must have access to five essential tools:

The leader has to focus on the process, not just the end. He asks people what they need to be accountable. And he accepts the responsibility by giving them what they need to be successful.

MICHELE HUNT
Herman Miller, Inc.

- **Information.** Without knowledge, people operate in the dark. Information is like nourishment; spread it around. Teach employees everything about the business: operating plans, unit results, financials, competitors, pay schedules, and more.

- **Skills.** Being underskilled is like being asked to drive a car with a manual transmission but not knowing how to use a clutch. It is a setup for frustration and failure. People must be adequately skilled to feel empowered.

- **Responsibility.** When people are given responsibility, they typically act in a responsible fashion. There is a self-fulfilling prophecy here. But so often companies program employees to fall short by treating them like teenagers.

- **Control.** Lack of autonomy and control over one's work is the single loudest complaint among American workers and one of the greatest sources of stress. Eventually people get angry and give up trying.

- **Rewards.** B.F. Skinner once said, "Reinforcement is the fuel of human psychology." Without positive rewards directly linked to desired outcomes, people stop producing. They slow down on the treadmill and eventually shirk their duties or leave.

Your challenge is to make sure these tools are properly distributed, because if there are shortages, employees rebel in one way or another. This issue will be examined further in Chapter Four, but for now keep in mind that in the new service economy, the new tools are information, skills, responsibility, and control.

Let People Run with Good Ideas

Good, profitable ideas often get lost in companies not because they will not work but because of where or with whom they originate. But when everyone assumes responsibility for leading and following, ideas are evaluated on their inherent quality, not where they came from. When people feel comfortable taking risks and experimenting with ideas, excitement and innovation follow.

Occasionally, certain ideas are not worth pursuing—they are impractical, too costly, or politically unwise. When such ideas are proposed, do not mislead the employee with reassurances and encouragement; gently, honestly tell him or her why an idea will not fly, yet reinforce your openness to ideas and tell the person to keep thinking and keep suggesting.

The company 3M makes sure its motto, "Thou shalt not kill a new product idea, just deflect it," is fulfilled by an assortment of programs that encourage, nurture, and execute new ideas. For instance, its Genesis program provides scientists and technical personnel with support and funding to pursue research projects that may not hatch for years. Similarly, the Venture Career Path encourages employees to develop embryonic ideas into products that can be marketed. 3M's appreciation of new ideas has paid off—every year, it introduces more than 100 new products.

Encourage Acts of Civil Disobedience

Employees standing up for what they believe, alerting their bosses to bad news, and disagreeing with superiors are unusual occurrences in many companies. The best ideas and objections often get shoved aside because of insecurity, indifference, or fear of reprisal. But learning to fight for ideas and allowing others to do so is a trait well worth cultivating. By encouraging your employees to question the status quo, you will cultivate your own in-house entrepreneurs.

Syntex, a multinational health-care company in Palo Alto, California, believes no one has a monopoly on all the facts, so it teaches employees to speak up by offering these suggestions:

- Alert superiors to both opportunities and problems in a timely manner.

- Avoid surprises by providing frequent updates.

- Admit and take full responsibility for mistakes or disappointing results.

- Be obliged to offer your opinion with reasonable alternatives.

- Once a decision is made, support it.

People don't want to be worthless. But they don't get to be meaningful unless they're given some responsibility—and are held accountable for their decisions. When people are let into the system and get involved, they'll feel more accountable for what happens. Participation won't work unless people also feel a sense of ownership.

MAX DEPREE
retired CEO,
Herman Miller, Inc.

One in three employees is reluctant to go over his or her boss's head, belying the notion of open-door management in many companies, according to management consultants Towers Perrin.

A Harvard Business School survey reveals that 72 percent of managers view employee involvement to be good for their companies but only 31 percent view it as good for themselves. Managers resist employee involvement for three reasons: job security, confusing responsibilities, and additional work.

As these suggestions illustrate, leadership and commitment occur simultaneously when leaders and followers learn to develop adult partnerships. For their part, leaders should be challenging, inspiring, and encouraging, learning to empower and liberate all those around them; followers should be natural team players, participating, collaborating, and staying involved. Studies show that there is a clear relationship between what leaders say they do when at their personal best and what followers say they admire most in their leaders. As more and more partnerships develop, the differences between leaders and followers become less relevant and less visible. In fact, in a healthy company, they are generally the same person.

Corporate Policies and Strategies

Participative management is a familiar, accepted, and laudatory business principle, yet in many companies it has been more honored than implemented. Company efforts to institute participative management have generally resulted in a smattering of programs or activities that are launched, then forgotten, and lack any true sense of direction or larger purpose.

But imagine a company where people are accountable for their results, encouraged to take risks, and responsible for their actions; where every employee feels involved and committed to the success of the business; where employees share authority and decisions are made at the lowest possible level: where people work in teams and task forces, not pyramids and totem poles; and where communications are open and flowing, with rewards shared by all. This is the empowered workplace, an environment that goes beyond traditional ideas about participative management.

Examples of the new empowered workplace are unfolding around the country:

- Schreiber Foods, Inc., a Green Bay, Wisconsin-based cheese processor, has been organized around work teams for five years. Its rotating team coordinators oversee all administrative activities previously handled by management.

- In Palm Beach County, Florida, Palms West Hospital, a HealthTrust affiliate, established an employee-owner committee that meets monthly with the CEO. The open agenda addresses issues ranging from hospital income statements to rumor control.

- Aid Association for Lutherans (AAL), a fraternal benefit society headquartered in Appleton, Wisconsin, has nearly half its work force operating on teams. Since 1987, productivity has increased 24.2 percent.

- Sewing machine operators are now running the Blue Ridge, Georgia plant of Levi Strauss. They are making the rules and changing how jeans are made.

These are just a few of a vast stockpile of programs and activities. The suggestions that follow are mainstays of developing an empowered workplace. Some pause at interim stages while others reach for complete psychological and financial ownership, but what is important to remember is that separately and together they are pathways to total employee involvement.

If you really believe in quality, when you cut through everything, it's empowering your people, and it's empowering your people that leads to teams.

JAMIE HOUGHTON
CEO, Corning, Inc.

Flatten the Pyramid into Circles and Teams

The more layers in a company, the more impediments to communication and involvement. Pyramids get in the way because they create a we-versus-they mentality that blocks communication and undermines people and their participation. Pyramids can be transformed into circles by restructuring an organization, rethinking people's roles, and broadening everyone's responsibilities.

Aid Association for Lutherans

Clarke Home Nursing Service in Novato, California did all three. Since its founding and until recently, Clarke had been managed, top-down, by its founder, Kenneth Clarke, who described himself as a benevolent dictator. To break this managerial hierarchy and, more important, push employees to make decisions and be accountable, Clarke created a seven-person management team with complete responsibility to run the service. He describes the situation after the team made a few initial, tough decisions: "What happened next was that the people who perform the skilled care in the field or the administrative work in the office began to make decisions of their own. Thus by me, the benevolent dictator, deciding to try and let go, seven people found they could make good decisions and enjoyed doing so."

Leading a team is like playing volleyball: you probably consider yourself better in one position than another, yet the rules of the game require you to rotate through the line-up. You have to serve, set up, or play front line and spike. Roles and responsibilities are shared by all.

Successful work teams are similarly self-managing: members share control, influence, and consequences, passing around leadership depending on what needs to be accomplished. Authority and responsibility are constantly redistributed so that the people closest to the customer, the product, or the end result have the power to make decisions, as appropriate. Work teams have no ladders; they have circles with employees learning all tasks, crisscrossing jobs, and interacting with everyone else. When they are effective, teams take over many of the supervisor's responsibilities—scheduling, hiring, firing, and troubleshooting. The supervisory role of the manager thereby changes, from director and manager to advisor and coach.

Teams have to be given support from upper management and real responsibility, not superficial power that truly doesn't affect a company. Their freedom to cut through bureaucracy is essential to their success. Their strength is also increased when they have a sense of common purpose about why the team exists and the function it serves. Most important, teams must be self-aware, with members open and willing to learn, diverse viewpoints discussed and defended; and a deep, enduring respect for the process and the product. Warns John Sculley, CEO of Apple Computer and leader of some of the most famous teams in the business world: "One of the biggest mistakes a person can make is to put together a team that reflects only him. I find it's better to put teams together of people who have different skills and then make all those disparate skills function together."

Quad/Graphics, a Wisconsin printing company, has no employees but partners who operate in peer groups that virtually run the company. These peer groups make decisions at all levels, set disciplinary standards, and can even fire people. Each group is responsible for quality and production. The truckdrivers' group arranged for backhaul loads on empty returning trucks, a practice that has become a dependable source of profit for the company. The press crew group keeps its own records and has almost complete authority for cost containment, quality control, customer relations, and work schedules.

The struggle to rebuild business on post-bureaucratic lines is partly a struggle to de-colonize the organization—to liberate these suppressed groupings. In fact, one might say that the key problem facing all big companies today is how to unleash the explosive, innovative energies of these hidden colonies.

ALVIN TOFFLER
Powershift

Here is how other companies are putting teams into action:

- Federal Express has organized 1,000 clerical workers into teams of five to ten people who have the authority to make significant changes or corrections in the areas of their responsibility.
- Donnelly Corporation, a Holland, Michigan auto supplier, maintains a variety of equity committees, consisting of work-team members from around the company. Issues from wages to grievances are considered, and all decisions are reached by unanimous vote.
- General Mills has reorganized employees and managers at one of its cereal-production plants into teams that include machine operators, communication specialists, maintenance workers, and quality-control people.

Air Company Information

When executives share vital facts about a company, employees feel more ownership, involvement, and responsibility. In fact, the many positive effects of airing company information have been documented in a survey of forty high-performing companies, as measured in terms of productivity, customer service, competitiveness, profitability, and quality, by the American Productivity & Quality Center. The Center found that the highest performers regularly reveal to employees information about employee pay, unit operating results, advance notice on new technology, competitors' performances, and hiring practices.

Probably the most sensitive area of disclosure is salaries. Companies truly sincere about sharing information disclose data about salaries instead of waiting for employees to read about them in the "Executive Pay" issue of *Business Week*. The justification for disclosure is persuasive: salary facts allow employees to gauge their value and performance relative to those of other employees and to help them plan careers and future opportunities.

Semco S.A. not only believes in full disclosure but also goes out of its way to make sure everyone understands its financial information. The company conducts classes on how to read and interpret financial information, and every month it gives each employee a profit-and-loss analysis and a cash-flow statement with seventy-plus line items for his or her division.

I guarantee that if you come across someone who says teams didn't work at his company, it's because management didn't take interest in them.

JAMES WATSON
Vice-President,
Texas Instruments

The traditional, hierarchical structure based on power must be replaced by the network structure based on empowerment by trust and respect. Teams are built where members are chosen for their competence rather than their authority, to deal creatively with a specific task.

WORLD BUSINESS ACADEMY

Teach Employees How to Liberate Themselves

Empowerment skills do not come naturally for many employees, and people do not become believers overnight. They must see a participatory program in action and be taught how it

You have to ask, "How complex is the work?" The more complex, the more suited it is for teams.

EDWARD LAWLOR,
Director, Center for
Effective Organizations

Lessons from an Empowering Leader

Ralph Stayer, CEO of Johnsonville Foods, Inc. of Sheboygan, Wisconsin, learned to be an empowering leader from the inside out. Here are some of his thoughts as he discussed this issue in a *Harvard Business Review* article in 1990:

"[In the early 1980s] the very things that had brought me success—my centralized control, my aggressive behavior, my authoritarian business practices—were creating the environment that made me so unhappy. I had been Johnsonville Sausage, assisted by some hired hands who, to my annoyance, lacked commitment. But why should they make a commitment to Johnsonville? They had no stake in the company and no power to make decisions or control their own work. If I wanted to improve results, I had to increase their involvement in the business.

"The early 1980s taught me that I couldn't give responsibility. People had to expect it, want it, even demand it. The goal was not so much a state of shared responsibility as an environment where people insist on being responsible. I had come to realize that I didn't directly control the performance of the people at Johnsonville, that as a manager I didn't really manage people. They managed themselves. It surprised me how readily people accepted this ownership.

"Team[s] gathered data, identified problems, worked with suppliers, even visited retail stores to find out how retailers handled the product . . . [they] took complete responsibility for measuring quality and then used those measurements to improve production processes. . . . People in each section of the shop floor began to collect data about labor costs, efficiency, and yield. They posted the data and discussed it at the daily tasting meeting. . . . Teams [took on] responsibility for selecting, training, evaluating, and when necessary, terminating employees. Now they began to make all decisions about schedules, performance standards, assignments, budgets, quality measures and capital improvements.

"For the last five years, my own aspiration has been to eliminate *my* job by creating such a crowd of self-starting, problem-solving, responsibility-grabbing, independent thinkers that Johnsonville would run itself."

will affect their jobs and careers and where the payoff comes. At first, both manager and employee may feel awkward and unsure how to act and what to do next; this is true about most learning. Occasionally, you will find employees who are totally resistant to the idea of liberating—leading and following as the situation demands—and you may either have to transfer those persons away from the team or to suggest they find another employer.

At Corning, Inc., managers spend 15 to 20 percent of their time (the equivalent of one day a week) in training. Training begins by communicating the rationale for the change in management style, followed by learning the concepts of work teams and the skills necessary for team members: problem-solving, resolving conflicts, asking advice, and giving feedback. Even at this company, where employee involvement is a way of life, the transition to full participation took time and hard work, but it is already paying off.

At MBNA, the fourth-largest bank credit-card company in the country, supervisors and executives team up to interview every candidate for every job, regardless of its level. People feel part of the selection process; as a result, they are more likely to choose candidates whose values are consistent with their own.

Suggestions from employees saved companies $2.2 billion in 1988, a 10-percent increase from the year before. Their suggestions garnered rewards totaling $160 million, according to the National Association of Suggestion Systems.

Cultivate and Celebrate New Ideas

Participation is meaningless if people do not have a voice that is taken seriously. Companies that liberate people create elaborate systems to penetrate deep into the company to extract suggestions and generate ideas. Properly heeded, new ideas within a company become self-perpetuating: employees know a company listens to their suggestions because they see them implemented, which then inspires more ideas and more suggestions.

Eastman Kodak Company, which created its suggestion system in 1898, has a suggestion office staffed by four full-time personnel who forward ideas to relevant departments and people. Every suggestion is responded to and the company reports that it adopts one-third of all the suggestions it receives. Kodak is very clear about how much it values employee suggestions: it offers cash rewards of up to $50,000 for ideas it uses.

Equifax, Inc. draws out suggestions from employees by surveying them regularly and asking them what they would do differently if they were president of the company.

Twice a month, five employees at the 150-employee company

Resource Information Management Systems meet with the four principals over lunch. The purpose of the lunch is solely to solicit ideas and suggestions.

At Peavey Electronics Corporation, a guitar and amplifier manufacturer in Meridian, Mississippi, hourly workers receive 8 percent of the first year estimated savings on labor and materials that result from their suggestions.

Form Employee Task Forces and Committees

These groups go by a variety of names and their functions are as diverse as their members. The common denominator in all is fostering input and involvement by employees on a range of company-wide concerns.

The chief executive at Beaumont Enterprises, a Texas newspaper, created its first committee to solve a seemingly simple problem: employee discontent over a parking policy that gave preferred spots to advertising and sales staff. Led by an editor and composed of representatives from all departments, the committee abolished the preferred parking and inspired employees to address other aggravations. Production workers then jumped on the bandwagon, improving the paper's printing process by researching and installing a better lighting system. While the system cost $5,000, it saved the company $47,000 over five years by eliminating wasted newsprint.

Beth Israel Hospital in Boston has arranged its entire staff into committees. Each employee participates in a departmental work team. Some people serve on standing work teams dedicated to researching and planning hospital missions; others work on single-issue, ad hoc teams.

In Omaha, Nebraska, Central States Insurance Company uses company-wide task forces to solve its future human-resource challenges. Employee-led committees examine major concerns, including family support, health-care costs, communications, and employee recognition. For example, the title-and-level committee reassesses all roles and evaluation criteria for the company.

LESSONS FOR ALL COMPANIES

The crises that Ford Motor Company and countless other companies have faced are often easy to identify, and until now the preferred solution was some type of participatory management

---

In any organization, there are lots of people just waiting for you to give them some responsibility, some sense of ownership, something they can take personal pride in. And it's amazing how once you take those first steps, suddenly a thousand flowers bloom, and the organization takes off in ways that nobody could have predicted.

GENERAL BILL CREECH
retired Commander, Air
Force Tactical Air
Command

 Beth Israel Hospital

that transferred some control and responsibility down through the ranks. Yet participatory management often has not been taken to its logical end and inculcated into the fabric of an organization. What has been missing is a new concept of leadership that applies the principles of participation, teamwork, and ownership to every level and to every employee of the company.

This chapter has offered a model for that leadership and for the managers and employees who will be the leaders and followers of their companies. The next chapter illustrates how vital establishing this kind of leadership will be to a healthy company. Without it, the currents and tides that are now constantly buffeting companies will overwhelm them. Leadership at all levels is essential to not only manage and harness change, but also to turn it into a positive force that propels a company to better health and greater success.

A 1989 survey of 476 Fortune 1,000 companies shows the concept of employee involvement on the rise. Eighty percent of the companies report some employee involvement activity, but only 25 percent have made significant changes in how they manage employees.

CHAPTER THREE

If You Don't Manage Change, It Will Manage You

THE WASHINGTON, D.C. BOOKSTORE Politics and Prose did not change overnight, but it literally changed over a weekend. On a Friday afternoon, it was a small shop known for its cozy atmosphere, personalized service, and a book-smart staff who more or less shared responsibilities equally. The following Monday morning, it had moved and altered its identity by doubling its size, creating individually managed departments, and spinning off a new bookstore, Secondhand Prose. The store's twelve employees were largely responsible for this burst of growth, having pushed for the change and then successfully orchestrating a smooth move. As with many business decisions, the owners listened to their employees and, after much discussion, opted to move.

Helping employees make the transition was the owners' decision to turn moving day into a memorable event—an experience that would acknowledge and celebrate the store's identity as a highly personalized, customer-oriented kind of place. The event would also mark the beginning of a modern, larger bookstore

Change has considerable psychological impact on the human mind. To the fearful, it is threatening because it means that things may get worse. To the hopeful, it is encouraging because things may get better. To the confident it is inspiring because the challenge exists to make things better. Obviously, then, one's character and frame of mind determine how readily he brings about change and how he reacts to change that is imposed on him.

KING WHITNEY, JR.
Personnel Laboratory, Inc.

where employees would learn new ways of managing inventory but also have a chance to expand their offerings and service.

Moving day involved 400 customers on a Sunday morning carrying boxes of books across the street. Employees supervised not only the actual moving of the books, but also the organization in the new store. Coffee, bagels, and orange juice were handed out, along with T-shirts stenciled with the slogan "Why did the book store cross the road? . . . To get to the other side." Although the move was official and final by evening, it nevertheless took employees months to adjust.

Some employees resisted the change, preferring to stay in familiar surroundings and cling to the business's old-fashioned, quirky bookstore image. During the preparations for the move, one employee summed up a popular sentiment: "We had real character in the old store—skylights, old wood, ceiling fans. One of the things we're selling here is character. The architectural ambiance was perfect. Everyone was afraid of losing what is at the heart of our business."

"This has been a hard transition," said another employee. "People resisted being held accountable for their sections or functions."

Explains a third employee: "Some of the problems since we have moved here are interpersonal. There are a lot more people and I sometimes have the feeling that important things are happening when I'm not here. This can lead to blaming people for things that were done in your absence. This is a stress that I didn't have to deal with at the old store. I also don't trust people as much, yet. In the old store, people owned up to their mistakes. But now we're left to find mistakes."

While the passage of time has helped employees accept the new store, the owners have eased the process by not forcing them to make instant changes. The original plan to have all employees work at the Secondhand Prose shop was scrapped when people complained that they felt isolated there and uncertain of their job. Instead, one employee has been put in charge and regards her assignment as an opportunity to build a profitable new venture.

Politics and Prose is a small company with a big vision—one that saw clearly the obstacles and opportunities in managing the human side of change.

Paper shuffling has its correlates in people shuffling. All this rearranging of industrial assets and people has made it more difficult for American enterprise to undertake basic change. It has enforced short-term thinking, discouraged genuine innovation, and consumed the careers of some of our most talented citizens. It also has transformed many American companies into fearful and demoralized places by cynical indifference and opportunism.

ROBERT REICH
Professor,
Harvard University

A CORPORATE EARTHQUAKE

The experiences of Politics and Prose are being repeated in retail stores, offices, and factories around the country: shock waves of change are pummeling American business, and these waves are coming from all directions. The nature of these changes varies depending on their content, pace, and desirability. Nevertheless, to the people and companies going through them, their impact is momentous and unstoppable.

The changes that are altering the content and composition of business can be categorized as structural, technological, and managerial, or human. The structural changes span not only entire companies but also entire industries and include such transformations as up-sizing, down-sizing, reorganizing, expanding, spinning off assets, streamlining, merging, acquiring, and contracting. These changes are happening across the land: we can see them in airline companies consolidating, factory closings among auto makers, food companies developing new products, retailers joining forces to broaden offerings, entrepreneurs launching new service businesses, and advertising agencies streamlining operations.

Then there are the ever-present technological changes, inundating all layers and aspects of our working lives: PC networks, fax machines, laptop computers, cellular telephones, and so on. These have flooded the workplace like a tidal wave, dramatically rearranging how people do their jobs and relate to one another. Not all these changes are in the realm of high tech; some are high-touch advancements, such as the revival of recycling and the demand for comfortable, ergonomically sound office furnishings.

Finally, changes in the way people manage and are managed are also sweeping through businesses. Brought about for a host of reasons, alterations in management practices are changing roles, responsibilities, and chains of command. At times, outsiders force internal, managerial changes, such as those instituted when state or federal regulators issue new safety rules that managers must implement. The changes caused by factors within are usually more amorphous but no less dramatic. Many can be attributed to broad demographic trends, such as the growth in the

It used to be, "You have something I need and I have something you need." Now both employers and employees have become more protective, distant and skeptical. And to validate these feelings, both sides have come to believe that "people are taking advantage of me." Individuals these days are more likely to walk out for something better, while companies are more inclined to fire people.

TERRY ELLEDGE
Management consultant

number of employees whose native language is not English, working mothers, and experienced employees demanding sabbaticals.

Some changes—such as the move at Politics and Prose, an industrial accident, or product sabotage—happen quickly while others are incremental, taking months or, occasionally, years to affect everyone in a company. One such incremental change has been the steady revision of company policies on mandatory retirement. While some changes are clearly for the better and desirable and others are clearly damaging and undesirable, there exists a huge middle ground of uncertainty and ambivalence about most changes. We do not always know how a change is going to affect people and business and whether we want to encourage or curb it.

In short, change has many forms: some familiar, some strange, some attractive, some not; some large, some small. Regardless of the exact shape it takes, constant change in the workplace has become inevitable and, in truth, the norm. Companies and people must change if they are to grow healthier and more productive. So for the manager—and really for all working people—the critical issue becomes not just identifying the nature of change but, more importantly, learning how to manage its impact.

Many companies and managers have not harnessed the human side of the corporate earthquake. Typically, companies in the throes of change pay more attention to such matters as debt structure, telecommunications networks, or asset redeployment than they do to employees struggling to adjust. Consequently, businesses that mismanage change suffer both financial and personnel losses. Companies lose money because their employees are not able to adapt to corporate advancements: even the best-laid improvements are undermined by people who do not know how to implement them. And people lose jobs, self-esteem, hopes, and dreams.

This chapter is about managing the human side of a changing workplace. As a manager, you need to understand the change process and the pressures it puts on people and how to adapt your reactions so that ultimately you benefit and emerge better off than when you started. You need to help your employees grapple with the tides and undertows of the changes that are inexora-

An Industry Week *poll of 800 managers on the effects of buyouts and takeovers reveals that 66 percent said they hurt employee morale; 85 percent said shareholders and top managers were the main beneficiaries, while only 15 percent said employees benefited; and only 20 percent said that efficiency has improved, with almost 50 percent saying it had suffered.*

The Gamut of Change

- In the past five years, more than 12,000 U.S. companies and corporate divisions have changed ownership.

- The 100 largest mergers in the United States in a recent year affected 4.5 million workers.

- In 1988, 450,000 American workers were laid off. Since 1983, almost five million workers who held their jobs for at least three years were terminated.

- Of the nearly 81,000 positions eliminated in 1,219 U.S. corporations in 1990, 44.6 percent were managerial or professional—up from 34 percent a year before, according to the American Management Association.

- By 1995, five million employees will work by telecommuting—not going into an office every day but working by telephone, fax, and other electronic machines.

- A 1991 survey of 1,005 corporations conducted jointly by *Fortune* and the Wyatt Company consulting firm has found that 86 percent of the companies have reduced their management ranks in the past five years, 52 percent of them in 1990.

bly altering their working lives. Finally, you need to create an environment that first and foremost recognizes and supports the human dimension of change.

INSIDE OUT

How Do You Cope with Change?

What happens to you when your organization changes is as powerful and deep as any corporate upheaval. Listen to this employee's reaction to such an overhaul: "You see the guys to the right and left of you get it, and after that, you're not the same man. Suddenly you realize you might as well be a coolie digging a trench. You know there's a bullet out there with your name on it. It just hasn't been fired yet."

As this manager found out, change can have a profound personal impact, altering one's identity and personal relationships.

And over time, the reverberations can sap a person's strength and good health. The crucial first step for managers is to understand how they personally react to change so that they can temper and guide its impact.

Whatever the change—from employees reporting to a different boss to their learning a new product line to being transferred to an unknown city—it brings out our best and worst emotions: exhilaration and excitement, but also greed, fear, a sense of loss, and resentment. Few of us have been taught how to cope and manage through the spectrum of feelings.

Think about a recent change at your workplace, such as being assigned a new project or client, being placed on a departmental task force, having to learn a new work procedure or phone system, or possibly facing a layoff or reorganization. How did you react to these changes? The following questions highlight the emotions and attitudes that comprise your arsenal for dealing with change. They reveal whether you are a resilient person who is always open to a new challenge or are firm and rigid in your ways and so avoid change. Perhaps you fall between these extremes, eager for some changes and afraid to contemplate others. If you are in the middle, as most people are, the next question becomes "Why do you embrace some changes and fight others?" Use this scale to score your answers:

Most managers are scared to death of emotion. It's a lot easier to put on a macho act and come across as a heartless cost cutter. But if you can't do the "soft" stuff, as well as the tough stuff, you'll never get people's total support.

NOEL TICHY
Professor,
University of Michigan

1 Never	3 Sometimes	5 Always
2 Seldom	4 Often	

1. Do you look forward to meeting people and being put in new situations?

2. Do you prefer an unstructured workday?

3. When your daily schedule is unexpectedly disrupted, do you adapt and make adjustments easily?

4. Does routine quickly bore you?

5. When you leave a job or get a promotion, is it easy for you to say good-bye?

6. At a party, are you comfortable talking to people you don't know?

7. Do you seek out new adventures and experiences in your life?

8. Do you make new friends easily?

9. When confronted with a new problem, do you feel challenged and excited?

10. Are you quick to accept new ideas in the office?

11. Do you listen and try to comply when someone close to you asks you to change something he or she doesn't like?

12. Do you feel you can handle any change that comes your way?

13. When change occurs at your office, are you quick to accept it and move on?

14. Do you feel you have control over changes at work?

15. When change occurs in your life, do you get excited about all the new possibilities?

16. Do friends and family describe you as being able to roll with the punches?

What Your Answers Mean

If you scored between 64 and 80, you are probably a resilient person who enjoys and can handle change; if you scored between 32 and 63, you are somewhat flexible and can adapt to some changes much better than others; and if you scored below 32, you are fairly rigid in your habits and preferences and tend to avoid change if at all possible.

Some people thrive on change. They gravitate toward the unpredictable, quickly lose interest in routine or regular schedules, and like to try new ways of doing things. Their lives and psyches are always in motion, ready to embrace the next challenge. If you received a score above 64, you may be this kind of person.

Liking change is not harmful to your health, yet it can create problems if you are constantly pursuing new jobs, new situations, and new people in a kind of thrill-seeking to avoid commitment. People who job hop, grab on to new ideas yet discard them just as quickly, refuse to plan ahead, and reject any kind of routine or discipline are allowing themselves to be whipsawed by change. The kind of life such people lead may be unpredictable and exciting, but it also borders on chaos, and the person who does not have control over the events and situations in his or her life loses purpose and direction.

At the other end of the scale (scoring 32 points or fewer) are those who deny change, who are cemented into a routine surrounded by ideas set in concrete and bordered by unscalable fences. Should any of their usual activities be changed, such people feel threatened and fearful of losing something. The unknown terrifies them, so they cling to familiar patterns. Sometimes they appear impassive, another sign of rigidity. By and large, these people deny change, but when it is forced upon them, they resist it by trying to alter its course toward something more familiar. Since change often defies such maneuvering, they are left frustrated and dissatisfied.

Ideally, a person should regard change as a challenge, not as a source of either thrills or fear. Any obstacles it may present should not be insurmountable. The person who copes best adapts to change and recognizes that it offers potential profits and pleasure, although the process may take patience and persistence. To assimilate this mentality into your managerial arsenal, you need to develop these four qualities:

Understanding. The healthy manager understands the ramifications of every change in the workplace, large or small. He or she knows that change is rarely a one-time event that is absorbed and then forgotten; it has aftershocks and undercurrents that must be watched and tracked. Too often, people underestimate the impact of a seemingly simple change and then become self-critical when they have trouble moving forward. Bringing in a new computer software program, for instance, may look like a simple upgrade, but to the people who must use it and continue to produce quickly and efficiently, such a change can have major personal ramifications.

Flexibility. When it comes to change, the healthy manager possesses the ability to adjust, make compromises, learn new skills, and adapt to new surroundings. This manager knows that being fixated on one way of doing things clouds creative thinking and impedes progress. Even though someone may be trained as a marketing expert, he or she should be flexible enough, for instance, to learn budgeting or inventory control, should the job demand

Some people really get scared [when change occurs]. Maybe they shouldn't but they do. You have to be able to relate to that and to say to yourself, "I have to be tolerant of that and I have to assuage it, and channel it constructively."

MICHAEL BLUMENTHAL
former CEO, Unisys

change. Flexibility means being open to new ways of working, knowing what adaptations you can accept and endorse, while maintaining your personal and professional standards.

Resilience. This is the ability to survive and thrive, while wrestling with changes you may be able to control as well as those over which you have no control. The resilient manager is self-confident, capable of weathering stressful situations, and willing to take risks, all with the knowledge that he or she will learn from experience and bounce back from setbacks. Hearing that a friend or mentor has been made redundant by a merger and is leaving can be devastating, but the resilient, healthy manager says goodbye and, after briefly mourning, learns to work with the new people coming in.

Momentum. Change is growth, forward motion, and eagerly seeking out new experiences. Managed properly, the entire company and individual employees should benefit from changes, as long as they maintain personal and professional momentum. To keep the momentum, healthy managers must have a sense of direction and goal.

 ### What the Manager Can Do

When change occurs in your department, managing it may be one of the most troublesome tasks before you. Few people are comfortable handling uncertainty and ambiguity, especially your employees. So your role must be one of a guide—leading people through the wilderness, clearing the trail for each employee behind you, and keeping in mind that some will be more bewildered and disoriented than others and that you must regularly check their progress. This guiding involves vision, planning, involvement, and motivating so employees emerge more informed and enthusiastic than before. What follows are three general guidelines for managing through the wilderness.

1. TAILOR YOUR ACTIONS TO THE CHANGE. The terrain of your journey will vary depending on the nature of the change confronting you. Some changes—such as a spurt of growth, a departmental

The first thing that happens when people become aware of an upcoming change is, they stop working. The rumor mill starts to heat up and employees begin to experience fear for their continued employment. You see an increase in the amount of anger, hostility, and feelings that while they have been loyal to the organization, the organization is no longer loyal to them. The employee who does not have the personal resources to deal with the emotional pressure may experience problems at home or with work relationships.

DAN EVANS
Personnel Manager,
Xerox Corporation

restructuring, or launching a new service—are first apparent at the organizational level and demand that managers react immediately and strategically. Changes that affect the entire structure of a company, such as a merger, require managers to exercise their full panoply of communications skills to keep employees informed. When changes are sudden or dramatic, such as the resignation of the CEO or a very public lawsuit against a company, a manager's initial response should be decisive and unequivocal, dispelling fears and articulating for employees their role in the changed environment. Slow, incremental changes, like a steadily declining market, compel a manager to undertake methodical, step-by-step planning with employees.

2. OVERCOME YOUR PERSONAL OBSTACLES. One of the greatest barriers to change is our own reactions. One common response is to accept a change but ignore or not see floundering employees. One reason you may not recognize struggling employees is the assumption that talented, valuable employees do not need help adjusting. During a down-sizing, for instance, managers mistakenly believe that some people can fend for themselves and that regardless of how much their jobs and companies change, they will continue to excel. However, grappling with and adapting to change is an emotional event, and even the most able employees need reassurance and guidance.

Another misdirected approach is concentrating on the wrong elements of a change. When a change is in motion—such as accelerated product cycles, relocation, reconfiguring offices, closing plants, or opening branches—a misfocused manager only dwells on the tangible, physical changes and overlooks the more crucial human side. For example, he or she may become preoccupied by furniture and finances and ignore the tension between two merging departments.

Managers also have trouble when they misjudge how to pace an employee's adjustments to change; they may race through a change and be far ahead of lagging employees who need more time to adjust. When this happens, a manager often feels annoyed and frustrated because employees seem to be dragging their feet and not coming to grips with the change. Conversely, a manager may move too slowly and be reluctant to accommodate a change while employees are eager for the new order. In this instance, a manager reacts defensively and may well sabotage a change.

There's nothing wrong with getting lean and mean. But after all the bloodletting, after the carcasses of dismissed employees have been hauled away, what exactly do you do with your business? That's where the tough decisions are, or aren't, made.

IAN MITROFF
Co-director, Center for
Crisis Management,
University of Southern
California

Mismanaged Change May Be Hazardous to Your Health

Mismanaged change is often the silent killer inside organizations. When combined with unpredictable working conditions, little control over work, and excessive stress, too much change can be the straw that breaks the camel's back.

- After years of studying blue-collar workers and managers, Michael Matteson and John Ivancevich, University of Houston business professors, have found that change may trigger illness. Harmful change, the researchers say, generates instability, ambiguity, surprise, and discord. These feelings make some people self-interested, manipulative, and insensitive to others. Other employees develop heart disease, anxiety, and other physical and emotional symptoms.

- A ten-year study in Belgium found that employees in banks under increased competition and organizational changes experienced a 50-percent higher incidence of heart disease.

- Data from Johns Hopkins University indicates that every 1-percent increase in national unemployment is associated with an additional 36,876 deaths and a 2-percent rise in mortality from heart disease and cirrhosis.

- A study of 1,900 office workers in Sweden whose companies had been reorganized, had been relocated, or had changed work procedures found a connection between a person's health and the kind of change he or she experiences. Workers whose job changes included more decision making and more influence on others showed much lower levels of cardiovascular risk and fewer psychological problems.

You have to help people appreciate the need to deal constructively with the changing environment. If we're doing our job, we need to understand the rapidity and magnitude of the changes taking place and provide people with all the tools we can to cope with change.

ROBERT HAAS
Chairman and CEO,
Levi Strauss & Co.

Different managers react different ways, but unless a manager champions the change and has assimilated the four qualities of understanding, flexibility, resilience, and momentum, the consequences for employees will be unpleasant, at the very least. Employees are left stranded, their talents and enthusiasm wasted or misdirected and the full benefits of the change lost.

3. USE VALUES AS YOUR GUIDE. Managers deep in the wilderness of change, groping to find a safe path out for their employees, will discover that above all else, strong company values are the best

We believe that we have to manage for the long term, protect our people from cyclical, changing markets, and if they know we're going to do that, they will help us solve the problem. When external realities create changes in the market . . . your obligation is to find a way to retrain and redeploy those employees, rather than saying, "Oops, the markets changed. Too bad, gang, you're fired."

IRVINE O. HOCKADAY, JR.
Chairman and CEO,
Hallmark Cards

guide. A few years back, the Miami-based Ryder Truck Company and its chief executive, Tony Burns, were caught in a forest of change: deregulation of the transportation industry had altered the entire economics of the business, including routes, fare structures, and taxes, and in response, the company was expanding beyond trucking leasing into other forms of transportation. Throughout this tumultuous time, Burns took every opportunity to reaffirm for employees the company's core values of respect, trust, support, and striving. He posted plaques and posters and distributed plastic, wallet-sized cards carrying the message; he reiterated it in video interviews for distant offices; and he spread it throughout the company magazine. The company is now firmly, and successfully, ensconced as a leader in the transportation business.

As Tony Burns discovered, firm values that define what is most important to a company can help it weather even the most turbulent times. Values provide stability in a sea of change, assuring employees that no matter what happens to a company, it will always honor respect, teamwork, and openness and treat them fairly and honestly.

LEADING EMPLOYEES THROUGH THE STAGES OF CHANGE

A manager has a choice between being shoved around by changes within a company, hoping for the best, or seizing the reins to help navigate the direction and outcome. To take control of change, you need to find out how your employees are reacting.

Organization experts Drs. Dennis Jaffe and Cynthia Scott have taught me a lot about how people experience change. Everyone goes through four stages: denial, resistance, exploration, and commitment. People experience them in that order, but not at the same pace and not to the same end. Some people never find their way to commitment; they become stuck in one stage, always denying or resisting a particular change.

To assess where your employees are vis-à-vis these stages, you need to look at how a particular change is affecting them. For example, a department in the middle of down-sizing may seem to hit everyone the same way: people struggle to adjust to the loss of coworkers, assume expanded responsibilities, and search for expenses to cut or eliminate. While this may be how you view the change, employees may be experiencing something else. They may be battling survivor's guilt, the uncomfortable feeling that comes from *not* being cut while friends are made jobless, or with a profound but unconscious sense of mourning over the death of the company as they knew it.

The best way to appraise employees' reactions is to talk with them—individually or in small groups—about the tangible and intangible changes they are going through, such as moving offices, meeting new people, saying good-bye to friends, or adjusting to smaller budgets. This conversation may become an emotional, personal exchange. Don't be afraid of this expression of feelings; they are a natural and necessary element of any kind of change.

In asking employees to describe these changes, you will see signs of which stages they are experiencing. Watch and listen to your employees, keeping attuned for signs, behavior, and statements that indicate how they are handling the change. After these discussions, ask yourself the following questions:

A poll of senior managers at down-sized companies by Right Associates found that 74 percent believed employees had lower morale, feared future cutbacks, and distrusted management.

- Is the department rife with rumors?
- Are employees holding secret meetings in offices, bathrooms, and hallways?
- Is there more tension and chaos in the office?
- Are there more accidents, absences, and health claims?
- Are your employees asking for more advice and assistance?

Overcoming Denial

Everyone, including people who enjoy change, starts out with some degree of denial. When a change appears at work, you may not recognize an employee's initial reaction as being denial. Reasonable caution, particularly if it persists, is actually disguised denial, as I discovered a few years ago. I was consultant to a young, fast-growing computer software manufacturer that had just brought in new operations managers to help it bridge the gap from dynamic start-up to established business. In its early days, the company was casual, unstructured, and collegial: employees wore blue jeans, worked flexible hours that included evenings and weekends, kept few records, and devised their own systems and solutions.

This was all to change. The new managers wanted to institute formal policies and practices, and most of the employees were agreeable. The design engineers were being asked to keep better records of project progress, log hours on time sheets, work regular hours, and use standard design methodology. However, one design engineer flatly refused to use the new design methods, insisting that they were too rigid and stifled his creativity. When I talked to him about the changes, his attitude was, "What's the big deal? It's never going to last. Anyway, these guys will go away; just give them time." However, the company's commitment to the new order indicated the new procedures would be permanent, and his cavalier attitude was obviously an attempt to deny the changes.

Employees may have a good reason for denying change, for it can be personally and professionally threatening. Underneath their denial may well be a fear, such as fear of:

Our culture has a lot of denial concerning the human pain associated with significant loss. If a parent dies, for example, you are expected to be back to work in a few days, and back to "normal" in a few months. Being laid off after many years of steady employment can be like an unexpected death or divorce.

EARL HIPP
HealthAction

- losing security—their job future is uncertain.
- losing the feeling of competence—they are asked to do new, unfamiliar tasks and no longer know whether their skills are adequate.
- losing a sense of belonging—established, comfortable groups, teams, and cadres of coworkers may be broken up.
- losing a sense of direction—change may mean new priorities and goals.
- losing control over psychological and physical space—work space and assignments may be altered.

Denial, this fear of loss, is expressed as numbness, apathy, and a wishful assumption that the changes will soon pass. It also appears in other attitudes and expressions, such as refusing to believe ("They'll never go through with it") or minimizing the impact ("This is really just a minor adjustment").

When an employee denies a change is taking place, he or she halts all progress, learning, and forward motion. Denial is akin to being stopped in the middle of a dash across quicksand—a person freezes and refuses to recognize the unstable ground, then sinks. In a business, employees as well as managers who refuse to accept the new order drag down people around them. Two ways to cope with denial and get beyond it are to honor the past and keep employees informed.

HONOR THE PAST. Moving beyond denial is easier if employees acknowledge the value of the past, giving it its rightful place in the growth and development of a company. Employees will reach out to grab hold of changes and the future if they know that what has gone before has not been wasted or discarded. Their sense of loss will be lessened. Some companies even throw parties in tribute to the past. At Honeywell, employees held a mock wake to mark the closing of a plant and to say good-bye to other employees. "It was done in a positive manner, where everyone talked about the good times, told stories, said good-byes, cried a bit and generally honored the ending in an upbeat way," explains Ken Kostial, Honeywell director of employee relations.

So tell employees what you know is going to happen, even if the news is unpleasant, and allow time for that news to sink in. Weeks—even months, for long-term employees—may pass before balance is restored. Suggest ways they can prepare for the upcoming changes, such as by reading about a former competitor the company is joining forces with or about a new piece of technology just purchased.

INFORM REGULARLY. People whose immediate reaction is one of denial have an insatiable thirst for information. Although they do not want to admit a change is happening, a small part of them is very curious. The perceptive manager will feed this curiosity with constant, accurate information through meetings, notices, videos, and memos. You should explain why a change is taking place, the sequence of the transition events, how and who will implement the changes, who will be affected, and how company operations and services will differ. You have to be a better and more reliable source of information than the employee grapevine, which works overtime during an upheaval. Even if your information or facts are spotty, share them. When you know little, explain this to employees rather than filling in the blanks with silence or letting them assume something you know is not true.

If there is anything I really picked up on, it was making sure that gobs of written communication went out and that good people were in charge of that. But I also personally did a lot of traveling in that period. One must not underrate the importance of a personal appearance of someone who has become a symbol of the change.

MICHAEL BLUMENTHAL
former CEO, Unisys

However, recognize from the start that your employees have different informational needs. Some want a full-scale, panoramic description of the future, others a step-by-step plan, and still others only a snapshot of the immediate future. Whether the clamor for information is great or small, do not close down lines of communication and hide out in a comfortable office.

Moving Through Resistance

The symptoms of resistance—anger, complaining, foot-dragging, frustration, and depression—are painfully clear. As a manager, you will find resistance unpleasant, but remember that it is natural and will pass. Under no circumstances can you ignore it, for if you do, it can fester into sabotage, accidents, sickness, absenteeism, and turnover. When employees are resisting, a manager needs to listen to and acknowledge the validity of their emotions rather than try to talk them out of their feelings, telling them to hide their emotions or to pull themselves together. If you do not encourage them to express themselves, you cannot guide them through this difficult time. If you overreact and return anger with anger, emotions will escalate and become destructive. By sharing fears and frustrations, employees begin to allay them.

The resistance I witnessed among employees at a major museum faced with new leadership, changing responsibilities, and financial instability was as obvious as bright flags fluttering across the front door. At this organization, the top-down hierarchy was being dismantled for a more participatory, team-oriented approach. One group, former project directors, felt especially betrayed as a result of the reorganization, certain that it meant being demoted into the pack with fewer perks, less travel and status, and fewer creative opportunities.

Brenda, a director of special exhibits who had been with the museum for seven years, was especially resentful of being forced into being a team player instead of an undisputed leader. She refused to attend meetings about future exhibits and was unwilling to share her years of experience with junior staff. For more than a year, she expressed her resistance by declaring: "This is a stupid idea" and "I can't see the point of this. It's inefficient and you can't make me. What's the difference, this organization doesn't care about me anymore." Brenda was stuck in the abyss of resistance.

If there is one silver lining for out-of-work managers, it is that merger mania has partly removed the stigma of being laid off. Five years ago, if we saw a résumé come in of somebody who was laid off, probably we would have been a lot more skeptical. Before, you might have said, "I don't want to pick up somebody else's bad news." But that's not true today.

Human Resources
Director, John Hancock
Financial Services

When employees resist changing, their productivity dips drastically, because they are often upset, complaining, and threatening to quit. Or perhaps they engage in pointless arguments, become sullen and withdrawn, have accidents on the job, or claim a number of mental-health sick days.

Underneath an employee's anger is insecurity and trepidation about the future, based on such concerns as:

- I don't know what this means to me.
- I don't see a clear direction.
- I'm afraid I'm going to lose power, prestige, and money.
- I've been burned before by other changes.
- I may not be able to learn enough and adapt to the new ways.
- I'm being forced to change my dreams and goals, which is unfair.
- Things were better before the changes.

Employee resistance, however, may be a good sign, because it can represent progress from denial toward acceptance and be a healthy expression of emotion. In a sense, an employee is acting out the grief he or she feels from losing something familiar. By vocalizing anger and discontent, or by raising the subject of quitting, an employee is beginning to alter his or her attitudes. The person is subtly saying good-bye to the old and contemplating the new, and the sooner this process is begun, the quicker the advance to more positive emotions.

Denial and resistance are the initial reactions to change. During both of these stages, a person tends to be self-absorbed and self-interested and to dwell on the past and what has been lost. Yet these stages are unavoidable, like a deep valley an employee must descend into before climbing out on the other side.

Some people may try to cut these two painful stages short and immediately go through the motions of accepting and embracing the changes. Hoping to avoid the pain of change, they force themselves to appear as if they have instantly integrated the changes. Managers trying to help employees circumvent denial and resistance may even hire outside motivational speakers to give pep talks to employees about the can-do spirit. Alas, this rarely works.

There was no warning or explanation for the cutbacks, but each time they assured us that this was the last time around. I learned more from the gossip going around than from anything the company told us. My feelings about the company have changed: I don't feel the company is being up-front with us. Everyone in my department is ready to jump to another company.

Employee of a Fortune 500 company

These stages cannot be leapt over by positive thinking or pretending as though there are no great expanses to traverse. Ignoring them does not make the feelings go away; it only makes them fester. You can help employees cross the valley of resistance by sharing your vision of what is beyond and being honest with the promises you make.

SHARE YOUR VISION. Imagine yourself on a satellite hovering far above your department, your view becoming clearer and clearer as you ascend. This big-picture perspective should help you formulate a new vision of the shape and future of your organization.

People who can visualize the future often turn it into reality, and so envisioning the future should be an activity you share with employees. Invite them to see the larger perspective and postulate what tomorrow should look like. A shared vision helps to focus people's energies and fosters a feeling of ownership and commitment. It helps them to be part of the change by choice, to be enrolled for their own benefit. If their vision is to have any link with reality, they must see the whole picture, warts and all. So explain your point of view and any limitations that a change may bring. A shared perspective also helps people look beyond their personal concerns to a more panoramic view and so be less self-absorbed.

Creating a new tomorrow takes time and patience. Your employees will need opportunities to rethink the problem together and to draw a road map they are all comfortable with. Allow them time to discuss their conflicts, disagreements, and contradictions as they prepare for the next business challenge. By listening and learning, your own vision will be broadened and clarified. Through this process, you will build consensus and allow your employees to buy into the change.

DON'T MAKE PROMISES YOU CAN'T KEEP. You will be tempted to reassure employees or make commitments that you may not be able to fulfill. Be careful about what you promise, because employees will take you at your word. For instance, do not tell people their jobs are safe or budgets are fixed unless you are certain of these facts. (And sometimes even certainties are reversed by higher-ups.) Promise only what you personally can deliver, and remember that if you renege, you will damage people's faith in you and in the value of the changes. "You can't give people mush," declares Bob Beck, an executive with Bank of America.

False promises hurt people, because they create the impression that change is easily handled and needs only an assurance from a person in power to render it smooth and trouble-free. A rose-tinted view of a change distorts it and creates additional obstacles for the employee advancing through the stages. People can accept and handle bad news, even half news; intolerable to them are lies, deceptions, cover-ups, and unpredictability.

Future shock is the shattering stress and disorientation that we induce in individuals by subjecting them to too much change in too short a time.

ALVIN TOFFLER
Future Shock

Advancing to Exploration

People in the exploration stage of change are ready to move ahead. Although still uncertain, they are beginning to feel a little better about a change. A manager seeing employees at this stage must help them establish priorities and short-term goals and determine what skills or training they now need.

Exploration is an exciting, exhilarating stage—a time when employees test new ideas, forge new bonds, try out different approaches, reshape expectations, and conceive goals to fit the new reality. Be aware, however, that even at this point, the path is not completely clear. During exploration, employees may feel tangled up by too many ideas and too much to do. They may launch into frenzied hyperactivity that can lead to frustration and an inability to focus or concentrate; they may overanalyze, overwork, get bogged down in details, or grasp at quick fixes.

At this stage, you may hear an employee say things like "Let's give it another try" and "We should meet every day to iron out these problems."

Although these statements sound upbeat, the exploration stage may feel like chaos and result in poor management of time, endless training or preparation, excessive risks, or snap judgments. Someone in the middle of an exploration high sees no boundaries or limits. At this stage, a manager needs to channel this fresh energy and help employees stay more focused and merge their high-energy fantasies with practicality. This is best accomplished by involving employees in the mechanics of a change and paying attention to the messages you send them.

INVOLVE EMPLOYEES IN THE MECHANICS. Employees need to talk about the change process, offering opinions and speaking out. Arrange formal and informal meetings to solicit suggestions and opinions, even to brainstorm. Not everyone will jump at the chance to get involved; some need time to complain about those responsible for the change.

When Trans-Matic Manufacturing Company was planning a 25,000-square-foot addition to its plant, it posted the blueprints for all employees to see and comment on, and they proposed some very useful alterations. One employee noted that the door openings were not large enough to accommodate all the new machines on order; another suggested that the tool rooms be equipped with wash basins.

At Cummins Engine Company, which has undergone severe retrenching and layoffs largely because of foreign competition, employees are encouraged to send their ideas via electronic mail directly to the president. Every day, his computer mailbox is filled with signed statements from workers. When one employee complained about receiving overtime pay while a coworker was being laid off, the president tapped out an explanation: he could not bring back people just to fill orders that might take longer than expected. However, the opportunity to communicate directly with the president about the mechanics of a change was reassuring to the employee.

Assign and recruit employees to help put the change in effect by letting them make some decisions and carry out critical assignments. Create transition teams with specific functions to give people a vested interest in the success of the change, but ensure there are enough low-risk or sure-win tasks to help them succeed. For example, when Burroughs was merging with Sperry to become Unisys, executives formed task forces co-chaired by representatives from each company and assigned in-depth analyses—fact-finding and problem-solving—to every company operation.

At Levi Strauss & Company, managers formed Crisis & Loss groups to address the emotional impact of announced layoffs. In these groups, employees could air and share their grief as well as the confusing emotions that beset them.

You may need to cultivate new leaders in your office. These people are usually natural leaders who have moved through their stages of change and have a firm vision of what is coming. By giving them leadership roles, you utilize their momentum and energy to help move others ahead. You can reward these new leaders by offering one-time bonuses. If you cannot afford money, offer words of encouragement and thanks or simply an afternoon off.

PAY ATTENTION TO SYMBOLS. Symbols take on special significance when people are forced to change. These symbols, which may be logos, slogans, rearranged offices, gestures by managers, altered uniforms, or even a new paint color on company buildings, help people recognize the seriousness of the change and are a visible sign of the change itself. When Burroughs and Sperry were meshing, employees were given baseball caps with the new company logo; these were dubbed thinking caps so that people would cease thinking with a we-versus-they mentality.

Sometimes surprise gestures grab the attention of your work group and help concentrate its attention on a change at hand. An extreme example of this involves Chiyoshgi Masawa, Japan's largest home builder, who sends out a memo whenever there has been a momentous shift in the industry (for instance, after the last energy crisis) announcing that he has died. Thus, when employees resist changing because they are accustomed to the old way, he tells them, "That was the way things were done under Mr. Masawa. He is now dead. Now, how shall we proceed?"

Symbols do not always have to be large; small, seemingly trivial activities can take on heavy significance for employees, especially if they are in the dark about what is happening. During the merger of USAir and Piedmont Airlines, employees grew very concerned about an apparently small detail—a proposal that the new airline discontinue the Piedmont tradition of giving passengers full cans of soft drinks and instead hand out more economic, single glasses. The so-called Coke-can dispute symbolized employees' concerns about whether the new company would value service and thoughtfulness. Management, perhaps not realizing the significance of the proposal to stop handing out soft-drink cans, eventually decided to continue the custom.

Little changes can either boost or undercut morale. When management ignores details and employees notice that they are being ignored, as when they see litter in parking lots, messy bathrooms, tattered office furnishings, or a forgotten event such as annual performance evaluations or a company party, the message seems clear: the company no longer cares about small things and, quite possibly, no longer cares as much about employees.

Arriving at Commitment

A person's last stage in the journey through change is one of cooperation, excellence in performance, and eagerness to enrich the future. At this point, an employee not only accepts and understands the change, but also uses it as a catalyst for a new sense of mission and goals, heightened productivity, and seeking even more challenges. When employees have arrived at commitment, they often declare that they can do things even better. They seek out teamwork, have a clear focus and plan, and even look forward to and expect more changes. Once achieved, this energy and vision last until the next change cycle begins.

However, even at this stage, you need to continuously monitor the level of commitment in your office. One company I worked with brought in an outside consultant to help facilitate a reorganization. After a few workshops, people were able to vent their feelings and move forward. Yet, a few months later, the department had a relapse; people fell into their old routines because there was no regular follow-up and review. Once your employees have entered commitment, the next change will appear on the horizon, telling you it is time to start the process again.

Corporate Policies and Strategies

At the corporate level, companies are finding that they must give employees both psychic and professional support in their struggles to adjust to the changes besetting them. The psychic support comes in the form of a corporate attitude and company atmosphere that signals to employees that all managers understand the turmoil they are experiencing, want to help them ride it out, and believe the process can benefit both the individual and the company. The professional support is more tangible; it consists of programs and policies that reinforce the psychic message and provide concrete backing during a change cycle.

In a four-year study of companies undergoing change, Harvard Business School professors Michael Beer and Russell Eisenstat found that the most effective way to change behavior is to put people into a new organizational context, which imposes new rules, responsibilities, and relationships on them.

This support depends on a company devoting much of its attention during a change to its human assets. By paying attention to the people, a company can keep a change on course, avoid costly personnel losses, and steer it toward its desired end. If managers and employees are flexible and a company creates an environment that recognizes and supports people during change, everyone will prosper.

To create a resilient organization that not only survives change but thrives on it, a company must institute programs that anticipate change, further its implementation, and smooth the process. Such programs include educating people, retraining, seeking out alternatives to layoffs, and crisis management.

Educate Your People

Like the blind man and the proverbial elephant, people often recognize only fragments of an event; and when a change is sweeping through a company, employees typically see only what is affecting their individual jobs and not the totality of the change. Managers also need information and support so their employees don't think their boss is acting alone. So the first task of a company is to educate employees about the scope and consequences of a change as well as about the change process and its effect on individuals.

Seminars, classes, and group meetings dedicated to talking about a coming change or the mechanics of a current change are essential to employees who must adapt to a new order. Change-management seminars can be generic or specific; they can address the psychology and nature of change or the specifics of what is happening inside your company. These programs must be tailored to your needs and considered alongside other change strategies.

For example, to cope with turmoil in the airline industry, the Association of Flight Attendants holds continual seminars on the trauma of surprise unemployment or being assigned to a new employer. An association director, Barbara Feuer, explains the underlying philosophy of these seminars: "We're letting them [flight attendants] know that this is very stressful, like losing a member of your family. Having gone through strikes, I saw that there was nothing out there to deal with the psychological stress."

The Eighties were just the tip of the iceberg, and we're going to see dramatic reductions in the Nineties. Corporate America is still as much as 25% overstaffed.

DANIEL VALENTINO
President,
United Research

A survey of 1,468 restructured companies by the Society for Human Resource Management reports that employee productivity either stayed the same or worsened after layoffs.

Almost one-third of Americans working abroad return early from their assignments because of culture shock, lack of human services, depression, isolation, and dislike of the host country.

ADVANCED
MICRO
DEVICES

After it merged with Monolithic Memories Inc., Advanced Micro Devices saw that the employees were dissatisfied and unsettled, and so it developed a program called Managing Merger Transitions. Aimed at managers, the program included regular sessions on accepting the challenge, communicating the change, negotiating personal commitment, building connections, and taking responsibility.

Minnesota-based Honeywell pays attention to remaining employees, as well as those leaving, by conducting special training programs entitled How to Thrive in the Midst of Corporate Change to deal with aftershocks of reorganization. A manager from another midwestern manufacturing company explains the importance of helping all employees: "If you're nasty to the people who are leaving, morale takes a terrible dive because those who stay conclude that they're working for a bunch of sadistic idiots."

Incorporate Retraining

To manage change rather than allow it to decimate a work force, a company has to make retraining a centerpiece of its operations. Depending on the nature of a change, employees may need to learn new skills, assume new responsibilities, train for unfamiliar equipment, work in a different office or different city, or adjust to different coworkers and supervisors.

The expert in guiding employees out of the maelstrom of change is IBM. Big Blue doesn't guarantee jobs, but it does promise employment security. In the past five years, the computer giant has cut costs not by widespread layoffs, but by moving around 21,500 employees. IBM presented this redeployment and relocating in such a way that most employees who moved did so voluntarily and often regarded the change as a promotion from blue-collar status to white-collar positions. Managers met regularly with employees to tell them what was happening and who was moving, and the company distributed information packets so that everyone was informed at the same time with the same facts. Employees were directed away from manufacturing, research and development, and administration into sales, marketing, and programming, but their new assignments were not random. Each employee had to take aptitude tests and pass interviews, after which the company matched a suitable employee with a new position, then solidified the assignment through months of rigorous classroom and on-the-job training. During this time, IBM spent almost $700 million on education and training.

In a similar way, Hallmark Cards thoughtfully shifts work loads among its various plants and retrains workers for new assignments. Pacific Northwest Bell uses a computerized skills bank to match people and jobs. Pitney Bowes provides displaced employees 100-percent tuition reimbursement to learn new skills. Even companies without multiple factories or extensive computer systems can help their employees retool by bringing in experienced teachers from the community or other firms who can share their knowledge.

Small companies lacking big-company resources need not neglect retraining; they simply must tailor their efforts so that the resource expenditure is appropriate for the employees affected and the magnitude of the change. One twenty-person consulting company in Alexandria, Virginia manages change by hiring only generalists who are flexible and open to retraining. The company worked out a deal with a nearby supplier who allows employees to participate in their in-house training programs.

Look for Alternatives to Layoffs

Healthy companies are constantly expanding and contracting to meet the demands of the marketplace. The most painful and difficult of these changes is the trimming of its operations and work force. While this change may be inescapable, its exact course and timing can be guided and anticipated, and there are ways to shrink a company that are more humane and more profitable than others. Here are alternative ways to modify a work force and lower wage costs without massive dismissals and the damage that comes from employees who are frightened and uncertain about their jobs. They illustrate that when management is determined to keep people and applies a little imagination, ways can be found to keep a valuable work force intact.

Temporary salary cuts. When the computer-chip manufacturer Intel was forced to reduce personnel costs, it chose progressive salary cuts according to employees' individual paychecks. Pay cuts ran from none to 10 percent, with the lowest-paid workers losing nothing from their checks.

Over the years the relentless pressure of cost cutting had created with Heinz a mounting feeling of bile. There was an ever-increasing feeling of hostility among the employees. Layoffs create a degree of insecurity because workers wonder if 50 people were cut last year and 100 cut this year, how many will go next year?

ANTHONY J. F. O'REILLY
Chairman and CEO,
Heinz Inc.

We don't want people to come to us as a marriage. We want them to think of it as dating. Don't come here for security, come here for excitement.

Human Resources Manager, American Federal Savings Bank

Do's and Don'ts of Down-Sizing

Do's

- 💼 Do establish teams of employees to identify how to distribute the new work load and avoid duplicate responsibilities, needless activities, and outmoded methods.

- 💼 Do solicit opinions, reactions, and suggestions from employees on how to handle change. If you decide not to act on them, explain why.

- 💼 Do establish short-term and long-term responsibilities, rewards, and goals.

- 💼 Do be careful about timing. Watch out for clustering events too close together as though they are connected when they really are not. Watch out for making announcements at bad times—for instance, around anniversaries of earlier cutbacks.

- 💼 Do keep top management visible and talking, even though they may be very busy orchestrating the change.

Don'ts

- 💼 Don't shrink the company with general edicts about fixed, across-the-board reductions, such as 10 percent from every departmental budget. With such edicts, people are cut and suffer first; eliminating employees may not be the best way to cut costs.

- 💼 Don't eliminate jobs while maintaining bureaucracy. Assess each department and division to find extraneous expenses and identify where cuts can be made.

- 💼 Don't eliminate employees while maintaining the same work level. The remaining employees will become overburdened, resentful, and exhausted.

- 💼 Don't make impulsive, poorly conceived changes; they only add to the atmosphere of unpredictability. Think through the consequences of both small and large changes. Says Bob Tomasko, author of *Downsizing*, "Use a scalpel, not a meat cleaver."

- 💼 Don't keep people in the dark. Employees want answers to these questions: How stable are we as a company? Who is in control? Who is in charge of operations? Is my job in danger? What am I supposed to do?

- 💼 Don't stress only the short term. Discuss what will happen after new people arrive, procedures or policies are rewritten, and employees move or change offices.

Layoff rotations. Climax Molybdenum, a mining company in Colorado, chose layoff rotation when falling demand for steel necessitated work-force reductions. It transferred more than half its miners to the mine maintenance crew and rotated jobs every two months. Under this system, employees could choose their rotation, deciding which weeks to work and which not.

Shortened work week. Nucor Corporation, a specialty steel company, keeps its ranks intact by putting all employees—from the CEO to production workers—on a bonus system. Everyone knows that if production slows too much, jobs will be lost. During slack periods, employees go on a four-day work week and get smaller bonuses.

Flexible employment. At Worthington Industries, production workers were asked to paint walls, sweep floors, or repair equipment. While workers were willing to learn new skills, management was flexible enough to rearrange jobs.

Early retirement. Northwest Airlines offered lump-sum payments of $20,000 plus fringe benefits and lifetime free or reduced-rate travel privileges for senior flight attendants.

Delaying projects. The St. Louis brewing company Anheuser Busch discovered from its records that it had numerous employees nearing retirement and that if it delayed completion of a project for two years, it could avoid layoffs.

Tin parachutes for hourly workers. Kodak created a tin-parachute plan to anticipate change and protect employees in case of a hostile takeover. The program promises severance pay, health and life-insurance benefits, and outplacement help to all 80,000 employees, should new management cut people.

Invite employees back. At Super Value Stores, management believes that downturns are everyone's responsibility, so it makes extra effort to hire back former employees when business picks up again.

Fortune Magazine *offers this advice to laid-off employees: Negotiate for a better severance; stay calm; save your network of contacts and friends until you're ready to act; be flexible; don't limit your search; try to avoid emotional highs and lows; don't pretend you weren't fired; maintain a daily routine; stay involved in other activities like volunteer work or hobbies; and consider all aspects of a new job.*

OUTPLACEMENT THE RIGHT WAY

Ten years ago there really was a stigma—people assumed there must be something wrong with you if you were fired. When it's happening to everybody, it's easier to accept that it's not your fault.

JAMES CABRERA
President,
Drake Beam Morin

Personnel cuts and layoffs are no longer unusual in American business, and when a company is shrinking, some people inevitably do not fit into the newer, smaller organization. Nevertheless, there are right and wrong ways of dismissing people. For instance, public firings are devastating, demoralizing, and dehumanizing for both employees and the people who carry them out. Although it is more painful, you should lay off employees in private, individually. If conditions warrant, you should make clear that the position is being eliminated, not the person, and so allow an employee's sense of his or her accomplishments and skills to remain undiminished. The benefits of dismissing people the right way are improved morale among employees staying with a company, fewer separation costs from disgruntled employees, and less resentment from the community.

In 1985, Stroh's Brewery decided it had too much beer capacity and so had to shut down its Detroit brewery, which had been operating for seventy-one years. When chairman Peter Stroh announced the layoffs, he made special plans. Rather than outplace the traditional way, he opened Employee Transition Centers that would deal with all the needs that employees might experience, not just that of finding a job. The center, located in a renovated private school, was equipped with vending machines, personal computers, phone service, and resource materials. All employees were given a source of income after termination, extended insurance coverage for catastrophic illness, and a variety of early-retirement benefits.

Employees completed individual development plans covering biographical information, work histories, aptitudes, and career aspirations so that center staff could address specific needs. Seminars and ongoing counseling assisted laid-off workers with such issues as job loss, interviewing skills, résumé writing, and networking. Basic remedial education was also offered.

Special job developers made inquiries and referrals to nearby employers to identify job openings for employees, and a biweekly newsletter kept people informed about the center's job opportunities. The transition center closed a year later. The overall placement rate was 98.3 percent—most with salaries comparable to or above those at Stroh's.

MANAGING CHANGE WHEN IT TURNS TO CRISIS

Whether they are environmental catastrophes such as Union Carbide's Bhopal disaster or industrial accidents such as NASA's space-shuttle explosion, an alarming increase in business disasters is being faced by companies around the world. Since 1900 there have been twenty-eight major industrial accidents in the world, and half of these have occurred in the past eight years. Many of these crises are the result of mismanaged change. Here is a sampling of crises that can alter a company:

- Product defects
- Environmental accidents
- Plant or equipment defects
- Computer breakdowns
- Lawsuits
- Product recalls
- Accidents
- Sabotage
- Boycotts
- Terrorist activities including kidnappings
- Bribery charges

Not all changes are crises, but all crises generate change, and companies should plan for them in advance. Ian Mitroff, crisis-management expert, says the following four qualities are essential to controlling a problem so that it doesn't blow up into a disaster:

ENLARGE YOUR PERSPECTIVE. When a crisis hits, companies must look beyond the damage done to their individual business and understand the impact on the community, employees, other businesses, customers, and stockholders. Otherwise, management's response is narrow and limiting, and the crisis quickly spreads beyond its domain.

MAINTAIN CLEAR VISION. A crisis must immediately be recognized for what it is. Attempts to diminish its import through wishful thinking, rose-tinted glasses, or selective vision only exacerbate the damage and prevent quick responses.

ACCEPT FALLIBILITY. No company or executive is perfect; a company must immediately recognize and accept its shortcomings, misdeeds, failures, and accidents so that corrective measures can be launched.

ESCHEW QUICK FIXES. Crisis responses that address only the immediate, most visible damage and do not consider long-term psychological, emotional, environmental, and health hazards are only half-remedies. With a Band-Aid approach, the crisis never goes away but simply is hidden from sight for a short while before resurfacing.

Johnson & Johnson's handling of the Tylenol poisoning has become a classic in crisis management. Within days of the news about the poisoning, the company, although obviously a victim itself, accepted responsibility for protecting its customers and recalled all Tylenol capsules. The company estimates that the recall cost $300 million, yet money was far down on its list of priorities. Concerns about public health and safety, internal manufacturing controls, and the effects on the company's reputation among shareholders and its own employees preceded financial implications.

One of the most frequent things I hear is: "When the next downturn in the business happens, is top management going to remain committed to Aspirations?" The only answer to that one is, "Test us."

ROBERT HAAS
Chairman and CEO,
Levi Strauss & Co.

HOW A HEALTHY COMPANY CHANGES

All change involves some kind of painful, arduous stretching for both individuals and institutions. Whether a change entails introducing new technology, moving to new office space, or closing down a plant, employees and managers need to learn how to function in their new configuration. Thus, everyone in the resilient, healthy company is learning all the time, and the company itself becomes a learning institution. The next chapter is about how employees, managers, and companies can foster the ability to learn and grow continuously.

Lifetime Learning Pays Lifelong Dividends

EVERY COMPANY HITS A potentially fatal snag in its early years—a time when sales begin to slow, when spending exceeds earnings, and when employees and managers pull in different directions. To break free of this snag, all workers must learn new ways to optimize their skills and find new ways to improve operations. Failing to learn and adjust through an awkward corporate adolescence can stunt a business's growth, or worse.

Consider Moving Comfort, Inc., an Alexandria, Virginia company launched from an apartment bedroom by Ellen Wessel sewing running shorts tailored specially for women. The company started quickly; by its second year it posted sales of $400,000, almost doubling that in its third year of operation. But by year seven, expenses were exceeding revenues, the company was overstaffed, and Wessel and her two partners were at odds with each other in their individual management styles. Moving Comfort was on the verge of bankruptcy, and something had to change. When the partners called me to help out, I discovered a company that had stopped learning and was not preparing for the future.

Stinging interest rates, a cash crunch, and mounting payroll

The 1980s was the decade of improving the quality of our product. The 1990s will be the decade of improving the quality of our people.

A. WILLIAM WIGGENHORN
Vice-President, Motorola

In contemporary speech, the meaning of learning has been dragged down to "taking in information." We should think of learning as the expansion of one's capacity— to create, to produce results.

PETER SENGE
The Fifth Discipline

expenses forced Wessel and her partners, Andy Novins and Elizabeth Goeke, to reexamine their assumptions about their own skills and those of their employees. The company was quickly outgrowing their limited knowledge about management and finance. While they had been hiring other people's expertise and ignoring their own education, company survival now demanded that they look within themselves in order to learn better management skills and improve their people skills.

Their immediate financial crisis demanded that the company cut staff from twenty-one people to twelve, so their first lesson, a hard one, consisted of learning how to better utilize fewer employees. Their best source for learning how to do this was each other, while my role was that of a facilitator, pushing them to ask tough questions of themselves and one another.

Wessel, Novins, and Goeke began to meet regularly to talk about their strengths and weaknesses as a management team. While Wessel was the visionary manufacturing partner, Novins's area of expertise was computers and finance, and Goeke was skilled in design and marketing. Each had to acknowledge what he or she did not understand and learn to be comfortable being instructed by a peer.

Ellen Wessel's education consisted of the slow process of accepting that even though she was the founder, she didn't have to know everything and had to be more tolerant of her own and others' shortcomings. To run her budding company, she had adopted the demeanor of a hard-driving business person, blind to her own ignorance and intolerant of mistakes by employees. Her aggressive, self-deprecating style made her a critical, impatient boss.

"During the early days of the company, I felt I had to assume the persona of a businessman, not show the soft side or a lack of knowledge. Be more strident, less flexible," she admitted to me. "I used to be very impatient with myself and others when we made mistakes. I found out that I was not always treating people with respect. Before, each person was trying to assert his own sovereignty. Now we are better sharers of power."

The education of Andy Novins, vice-president for finance and operations, surrounded the substance of the business— women's apparel—and its manufacturing and marketing. Andy had to learn that Moving Comfort was much more than a collection of numbers, be they its credit line, cash flow, tax rates, or earnings. Thus an essential element in his education was learning to defer to employees who knew more about the company's retail operations. "The hardest thing was to see someone doing something in a way that might have been different from how I would have done it," he said. "Letting someone do it their way, biting my lip and letting them learn in the process. In most cases, it came out just fine."

Elizabeth Goeke, executive vice-president, sales and marketing, had several lessons to learn: she needed schooling in the financial side of the business, in communication skills, and in teamwork. "Our financial difficulties helped me develop a sense of discipline," she said. "I used to operate as a maverick, but now I am more of a team player. I learned how to communicate better, admitting when I didn't know something and when I needed help from my partners—such as with calculating cost factors, respecting margins, and understanding certain marketing budgets."

With the success of their own retraining, the Moving Comfort partners knew their education could not stop with themselves: their employees also had to develop broader areas of expertise. Rather than constantly hiring the right person from outside, they opted to school and train existing employees. Each partner set out to share his or her newfound managerial talents with an assistant in a kind of mentor program.

Wessel tutored a young woman to help as a production assistant. "When I started supervising her, I realized I didn't have the skills myself," Wessel remembered. "I had to do a lot of learning. I had to convey to her a sense of exactness with the work—the extreme need for quality and accuracy, and to be more precise, more thorough."

Novins, who needed to teach someone computer skills and inventory tracking responsibilities, chose a man whose job had been simple data processing. "In the warehouse, we implemented a new bar coding system that computerized the inventory," he related. "I bought the equipment, gave it to Mark, and told him to do it. He found ways to integrate with the existing system that I would not have dreamed of doing. In fact, now I need to learn what he did so I can back him up."

Everything else being equal between two businesses in the same industry, the one with people who can learn faster, who maintain flexibility and exploit information for value-added products and services will win in any economic competition.

SHOSHANA ZUBOFF
In the Age of the Smart Machine

Goeke took under her wing a customer-service representative with the goal of cultivating her into a new sales manager. "I needed to shift my personal responsibilities and get Deana to learn the sales management job," she said. "I tried to teach her everything I could about sales reps, major accounts, liaison between sales reps and Moving Comfort . . . it was an evolving mentor role. I took a lot of pride in the relationship."

When they were on the brink of bankruptcy, the Moving Comfort partners were a group of bright, eager individuals who lacked the skills and insights to go to the next stage of their business. Today, they have learned how to function as an experienced, knowledgeable management team with each person's skills complementing the others'. They have become savvy business people who can analyze a problem, work collaboratively, and lead employees to get results. Their numbers confirm the success of their education: Moving Comfort's twelve employees have doubled the sales they posted with twenty-one and increased pre-tax income from a $150,000 loss to a $500,000 gain. Better yet, the company is growing again, eyeing plans for expansion and new markets.

WHY LEARNING IS IMPORTANT

For Moving Comfort, the education of its principals and employees was essential to survival. If they had not acquired new management skills, the company would have withered and died. But Moving Comfort's dilemma is repeated across the country in all kinds of companies, not just young ones and not just manufacturers. Today's constantly changing business environment demands continual self-evaluation by managers, employees, and entire companies to assess their knowledge, skills, and capacities. In short, they must become lifelong learners.

We are all potential learners, capable of growing and recreating ourselves through new knowledge and experience. Learning provides the skills, insights, and competence to perform well at work. Even more important, learning enables people to adapt and grow in their jobs, becoming better problem-solvers, more creative thinkers, more confident people, and more proficient workers. As an individual becomes more knowledgeable, he or she becomes a better, more valuable employee. Learning is also a significant factor of self-esteem, a way to achieve personal mastery, and an opportunity to thrive in the face of change. By learning to solve our own problems, we create reality out of dreams.

Just as individuals must commit themselves to learning, companies, too, must dedicate themselves to becoming learning institutions. Within the business setting, a learning institution is a company that constantly encourages and nurtures education. Through its policies and programs, such a company demonstrates each day that employee development is fundamental to its operations. A company's competitive edge is determined by the continued advances in the performance of its employees, and if an organization expects to grow 10 to 15 percent year after year, each employee must stretch in similar proportions. Organizational learning enables companies to solve their own problems, to expand their capacity to create new ideas, and to build their own future.

THE CORE COMPETENCIES

The task of learning, whether by an individual or by an institution, entails the acquisition of six basic competencies. These are the raw material that employees, managers, and companies must develop and refine in order to be a healthy organization.

Ability to learn. First and foremost, the ability to learn—to continuously acquire new information, different insights and perspectives, and basic skills—is fundamental to every employee inside a healthy company. The process of learning requires the ability to analyze problems, understand cause-and-effect relationships, and utilize sound logic. Other components of the process are a facility to recognize patterns, to learn from experience, to test mental hypotheses, and to use trial-and-error methods of problem-solving.

Technoknowledge. The lean office of the 1990s insists that everyone cover a number of functions and be competent in one or more disciplines. Marketing people have to know accounting; accountants have to know about production; and salespeople have to know how to use a computer. Employees are breaking out of functional boxes and more and more are becoming generalists. Technical skills and knowledge enable people to handle all the

Here's a report card on the American worker:

- *20–40% of the job applicants at Motorola flunk an exam requiring junior high level English and math.*

- *In a survey of Fortune 500 companies, 58 percent reported difficulties finding employees who possessed basic arithmetic and reading skills.*

- *Southwestern Bell had to process more than 15,000 job applications to find 3,700 people able to take its entry examination. Of the 3,700, just 800 passed.*

- *Every fifth worker hired by American business is illiterate and innumerate, according to a professor at Columbia University Teacher's College.*

The *Wall Street Journal*

Knowledge itself, therefore, turns out to be not only the source of the highest-quality power, but also the most important ingredient of force and wealth. Put differently, knowledge has gone from being an adjunct of money power and muscle power, to being their very essence. It is, in fact, the ultimate amplifier. This is the key to the powershift *that lies ahead, and it explains why the battle for control of knowledge and the means of communication is heating up all over the world.*

ALVIN TOFFLER
Powershift

information and technology that are effectively integral to any job: written literacy, computer literacy, and basic mathematical skills.

People skills. The diverse workplace demands that people be able to communicate with individuals who think and work in noticeably different ways. People skills enable a person to relate effectively with peers, bosses, and subordinates; to be a persuasive public speaker; to be perceptive about the strengths and weaknesses of others; to collaborate successfully; to be responsive to various stakeholders; to negotiate without turning the exchange into a competition; to participate in a mentor relationship; and to know how to listen.

Emotional literacy. This competency requires insight into one's own emotional make-up and how it affects work relationships, as well a perspicacity regarding other people's emotional tides. Not only are emotionally intelligent people committed to personal growth, they read the feelings and intentions of others as clearly as they read the morning paper; they have a second sense, an instinctive insight. Although it is difficult to acquire, people can develop this skill by learning to express their feelings, question their intentions, and nurture character development in themselves and others.

Intuitive abilities. This competency is essentially a confidence in the unseen, the unknown, the unprovable. The manager who demands evidence and facts before making any decision is uncomfortable with intuition. Yet intuition often provides people with creative solutions and preferable alternatives to the usual way of doing things. With this competency, a person can rely on hunches, dispense with normal linear thinking, and have visionary insights about the future. Exhibiting stronger judgment, appreciating strategic issues, and adapting well through uncertainty are by-products of intuition.

Personal management. This competency is the ability to control one's life, from setting specific, challenging goals to combating the pressures, stresses, and strains that sometimes threaten to disrupt it. The personally competent manager anticipates needs and takes charge of them. He or she also has a sense of balance and well-ordered personal priorities. This individual knows the importance of sound physical as well as emotional health and the importance of avoiding extremes, whether they be workaholism or a destructive relationship at home.

THE GAPING KNOWLEDGE GAP

Unfortunately, most employees, managers, and companies lack the full complement of these competencies. Huge gaps exist between their previous education and what is needed to stay competitive in a job. Until this gap is closed, individuals will underperform at work, while companies stagnate and atrophy.

There is plenty of evidence that this learning gap is widening everywhere. Employees are not keeping up with the technological demands of their jobs, such as advances in computer sciences and automation. They are not cultivating their emotional intelligence and personal management skills, misjudging the people they work with and letting themselves become incapacitated by stress. And they are losing jobs, because they cannot read instructions, take initiative, or assume responsibility. As the former president of Wilson Learning Corporation, Matthew Juchtner, explains, "When people are underskilled or undertrained, they become infantile. They close down and exhibit clinging behavior, they hold onto old procedures and old relationships, continue to make products that have lower and lower profit margins. Employees give up and become dependent on the system."

Companies, too, are sinking in this learning gap. They are struggling to find entry-level employees who are literate and can handle basic math. They are misreading what employees need from work and so are facing hordes of frustrated careerists. They are communicating poorly, causing employees to be fearful and dependent rather than innovative and energetic. They are refusing to consider alternative business strategies and so are missing new markets. And they are grappling with declining product quality, because their employees are ill-trained. A shortage of skilled, knowledgeable workers is hurting most businesses; they are hard to find and even more difficult to keep. Warns Kay Whitmore, president of Kodak: "If you're not careful, you will retain the lower half of your population. The best half move on if you don't give these people a sense that they're fully engaged and that they have a future."

We must develop our human resources into a smarter, more productive labor force that can sustain our economic growth. We must close the troubling gap between the higher skill levels required in the new job market and the actual skills possessed by today's workers and labor force entrants. Closing this gap will require that we establish a life cycle learning process transcending age boundaries, and that we empower workers to adjust to changing circumstances.

Committee for Economic Development Report on Demographics & Jobs, 1990

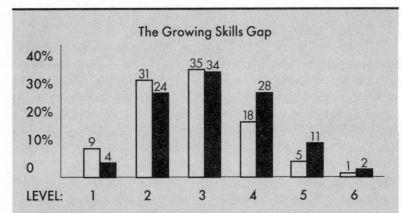

The Growing Skills Gap

☐ Percent of existing jobs requiring this skill level.

■ Percent of new jobs to be created between 1984 and 2000 requiring this skill level.

Level 1: Recognizes 2,500 words, reads 95 to 120 words a minute, writes and speaks in simple sentences. Can add and subtract two-digit numbers and do simple calculations. Example: laundry worker.

Level 2: Recognizes 5,000 words, reads 190 to 215 words a minute, reads comic books, writes compound sentences with proper punctuation. Can add, subtract, and multiply units of measure and compare ratios and percents. Example: assembly line worker.

Level 3: Reads variety of novels and magazines, writes and reports essays with proper usage, and speaks well. Understands basic geometry and algebra. Can do business calculations. Example: travel agent.

Level 4: Reads novels, poems, and newspapers. Writes business letters and reports. Speaks on panels on a variety of subjects. Does fairly complex algebra and geometry. Example: management trainee.

Level 5: Same reading, writing, and speaking skills as Level 6 but less advanced. Knows calculus, statistics, and econometrics. Example: accountant, personnel manager, corporate president.

Level 6: Reads literature, book and play reviews, and scientific journals. Writes novels, plays, and speeches. Knows advanced calculus, modern algebra, and statistics. Example: biochemist, computer applications engineer. *(Source: Hudson Institute.)*

WHY HAVE WE FAILED?

In identifying the causes for this country's crisis in learning, there is no shortage of culprits. The responsibility is shared equally by schools, businesses, and individuals. The American school system is the most obvious target, for many people believe that it has not only failed to educate its graduates but has also failed to instill an appreciation of learning. However, the damage done by schools is much more insidious than not passing along adequate skills and knowledge. The damage is in the attitude it has engendered: that learning is simply a phase of one's youth, not a lifetime pursuit, and that learning and working are mutually exclusive activities. As a result, schools graduate legions of students who have diplomas, perhaps even advanced degrees, and a smattering of book knowledge but who are totally bereft of long-term learning skills and the capability to fill this gap continuously. Their education has ended, and they will learn no more—they do not know how to learn outside a classroom. They are not comfortable asking questions or experimenting with ideas; they do not know how to solve problems analytically or to think creatively; and their teamwork and communication skills are woefully inadequate.

Learning requires stepping back from day-to-day operations. In a lot of organizations, that's not considered a legitimate use of time.

MARK PAICH
Professor of Management, Colorado College

Yet, just as schools have failed, so too have our business institutions. Business has perpetuated the above myth about learning by ignoring the importance of continuous employee training and education. Most companies are not learning institutions; instead they relegate learning to an activity akin to a support function, on a par with building maintenance. As a result, business rarely makes a sincere effort to educate its workers, and when it does, the programs are often ill-conceived, underfunded, or quickly abandoned.

Outdated short-term attitudes are also preventing companies from taking on the role of a learning center. Business pressures that force a company to show instant improvements and immediate results usually overshadow efforts to promote learning. In this atmosphere, there is scant time for employees to accumulate knowledge methodically and gradually, a pace that is essential for proper learning. There is also little tolerance of trial-and-error approaches that are an integral part of learning. In many companies, mistakes and wrong decisions are not viewed as learning opportunities and must be avoided at all costs. Thus, companies calculating costs and benefits quickly conclude learning is not worth the expense. This belief is further reinforced by employees who do acquire education and training, then leave for another company. As American business finds more of its skilled workers overseas, it has become less—not more—concerned about whether it has a skilled work force at home.

Individual employees are not blameless in this predicament. Psychological barriers against personal growth and development are major impediments to most people taking responsibility for their own education. Should they make the effort, people typically lack the necessary persistence and the tolerance for ambiguity that are part of being a learner. To learn, an individual cannot be afraid of asking questions, making mistakes, or appearing ignorant. Yet many people are, and thus they limit their capacity for growth and mastery.

Learning also demands patience and a willingness to temporarily relinquish the thrill of competition and winning, qualities that reign supreme in many companies. Competition produces stark conclusions—a final score, a winner and a loser. In competition, the process, the activity itself, counts for little; only the outcome matters. Competition usually emphasizes all the wrong aims and attitudes, and competitors learn little about themselves or from their colleagues.

None of these barriers is insurmountable and each is perhaps already changing. The education system is trying to heal itself; many leading companies are making major investments in employee retraining; and some people are shedding ancient notions about self-development in order to acquire the discipline and drive to learn. Whether you are an employee, an entrepreneur, or a manager, success depends on your ability to develop a lifelong learning program.

The remainder of this chapter offers ideas and activities for how managers can turn themselves and their employees into lifelong learners and how companies can turn themselves into learning institutions. It will begin with an examination of your personal learning style—what it is, how effective it is, and how it can be improved. The next section asks you to apply this understanding to your employees so that they, too, can learn how to develop in their jobs. Lastly, the chapter identifies company activities that stimulate employee education by creating an atmosphere in which personal and professional learning has an important place.

INSIDE OUT

Are You a Lifelong Learner?

To a degree, everyone knows how to learn; we all possess an intellect, learned skills, innate talents, and acquired experiences. These form the bedrock of any education. But learning is a lifelong process of self-discovery, study, and mastery—a never-ending adventure in which you are constantly exploring yourself and the world around you. Not everyone grows the same way, at the same pace, or in the same direction. These questions will help you discover your personal resources and attitudes about lifelong learning. Score them:

1 Never   3 Sometimes   5 Always
2 Seldom   4 Often

1. Can you admit to yourself when you've made a bad business decision?

2. Are you curious and always wanting to know more?

3. Can you admit your areas of ignorance?

4. Can you accept your professional shortcomings without feeling inadequate?

5. Are you comfortable being a beginner when learning something new?

6. When you start a new project, do you get excited about it?

7. Do you prefer long-term projects to ones that promise immediate results?

8. Are you an adventurous person who seeks out new experiences?

9. When you fail, can you extract lessons from your mistakes?

10. Do you seek out people who know more or have more expertise than you?

I look for people to hire who have the strength that life experience gives you when you've had your wins and losses. You can learn how to capitalize on the lessons you've had so you can come back and do a better job the next time.

ROBERT MAYNARD
Publisher,
Oakland Tribune

11. Do you bounce back quickly from personal rejection or setbacks?

12. When people around you make mistakes, are you able to help them without feeling the mistakes are a reflection on you?

13. How often do you ask for help, advice, instructions, or directions?

14. Are you comfortable changing your mind about an event, fact, or person?

15. Did your parents stress learning for themselves and you?

16. Do you compete more to improve yourself than to be better than someone else?

17. Do you often think about what you want from life or form distant goals?

18. Are you interested in other people's hobbies and interests?

19. How often do you attend concerts, movies, plays, or cultural events?

20. Are you involved in projects or activities aimed at personal self-improvement?

What Your Answers Mean

If you scored between 80 and 100, you are probably a natural lifelong learner; growing and developing is part of your personal life philosophy, and the unfamiliar, the untested, and the unknown are enticing to you, not frightening. If you scored between 40 and 80, you are a selective learner, eagerly pursuing some kinds of knowledge and timid in pursuing other types of learning. If you scored between 20 and 40, you are a reluctant learner and possibly grew up in an environment where new ideas and taking chances with the unknown were discouraged, and where opportunities for personal, intellectual growth were limited.

Without learning, people stagnate and never reach their full capacities. A good learner is first and foremost open, inquisitive, and undeterred by self-conscious fears of appearing ignorant or unschooled. Such learners are more aware of what they do not know than what they do know. Excited by knowledge and experience, they consciously seek out people and perspectives to broaden their horizons. They search for what they want out of life and work, cultivating a personal vision, then setting challenging, realistic goals. Developing the qualities of a lifelong learner takes time as you adopt learning styles that can be applied to all situations and integrate key philosophical tenets into your work life. The following suggestions will sharpen your personal learning skills.

Cultivate a Flexible Mind

Researchers have found that each of us possesses multiple intelligences, or what Harvard professor Howard Gardner calls *seven kinds of minds.* Each type of intelligence has its own thinking pattern and course of development, and most people are strong in a couple of areas and underdeveloped in others. While the focus of Gardner's research was children, psychologists believe that his classification applies to people of all ages. The seven kinds of minds are:

- *musical:* indicating a strong sense of rhythm and melody
- *interpersonal:* by which one relates well and easily co-operates with others
- *logical-mathematical:* involving thinking in concepts and looking for abstract patterns
- *intrapersonal:* by which one learns best alone and is good at self-teaching
- *linguistic:* indicating a knack for language and an ease with words
- *spatial:* by which one learns visually through images, colors, and metaphors
- *bodily-kinesthetic:* by which one learns by movement and repetition of the body and hands

Everyone has at least a germ of each of these intelligences. The goal of the lifelong learner is to identify first which intelligences predominate. The most direct way is to catalog your

Nobody makes mistakes on purpose. When you do make a mistake, I urge that you shouldn't let it gnaw at you, but should get it out into the open quickly so it can be dealt with. And you'll sleep better, too.

LEO BURNETT
founder of advertising agency Leo Burnett, Inc.

educational strengths and weaknesses by making a list of what you excel at, then linking each entry with the appropriate intelligence. For instance, I work with a woman who is an exceptional tennis player, is very adroit at computer operations, and prefers to figure out problems alone rather than ask for help. Clearly, her bodily-kinesthetic and intrapersonal intelligences are her strong suits; she is less developed in mathematical and interpersonal skills.

Be honest about what tasks you excel at and those you avoid for fear of failure. Arrange your weak areas by degree, pairing them with the appropriate intelligence. Perhaps you are a division manager who has an abundance of energy and a penchant for rhetoric but clashes with colleagues in the office; a restaurant owner who hates to keep the books but is talented at interior design and a terrific motivator; or an airline supervisor with a love of foreign languages but very little talent in learning them. After identifying your strengths and weaknesses, the next step is to build up your underdeveloped areas. You can do this by reading books, taking courses, or finding a mentor.

Another way to expand your perspective is to broaden your repertoire of learning styles. Creativity consultant William C. Miller has identified four specific learning styles that individuals use to solve problems. No one has a single style, and most people use a blend of approaches. Miller suggests that learners first identify which style they favor, then work on enhancing the others. They are:

> *Experimenting style.* You use a systematic process of fact-finding to combine different elements and test the viability of each solution.
>
> *Exploring style.* You question basic assumptions, break down paradigms, and use insights to discover new connections. Insights are used to perceive new combinations.
>
> *Visioning style.* You develop a clear long-term purpose or goal to guide your actions. Insights are used to guide innovation.
>
> *Modifying style.* You build and improve on what is already learned and accomplished. Facts are used to create new combinations.

Lifelong learners develop and actively apply all four styles. So, for example, when faced with declining product sales and disgruntled customers, you might reexamine your long-term goals, question your assumptions about the market, target the most receptive clients, and initiate a customer survey.

Direct Your Personal Development

You are your own best teacher. Ultimately, you are responsible for your own personal and professional development. This means you need to begin with a personal lesson plan consisting of instructions to yourself. This plan must go beyond declarations about becoming a lifelong learner; it must also include a commitment to these six promises:

Discover your personal vision. When people are asked what they do for a living, a sad majority describe their job tasks, not the purpose of their work. Lifelong learners are more concerned with clarifying what is important to them personally and expressing their talents. They ask themselves what is satisfying to them, why they are working, and for what purpose. They learn best when their job has personal significance.

Carve out some quiet, personal thinking time and ask yourself what you want to accomplish from your work. Conjure up a personal vision of who you want to be and where you want to go. Examine the big picture of life and how you fit in. You should focus on your passions and dreams as well as your talents and accomplishments.

Establish professional goals. Buttressed by a firm personal vision, you are now in a position to establish concrete professional goals. Whereas your personal vision is the dream, your professional goals are the road maps that will turn that dream into reality. By establishing goals—in essence, acknowledging the knowledge gap—you will make these dreams come alive. Peter Senge, director of Systems Thinking and Organizational Learning at MIT's Sloan School of Management, regards this process, which he calls creative tension, as essential to learning.

Professional goals are of two types: short-term and long-term. Neither should be so easy to attain that you lose motivation

Many people can innovate in processes and projects to make something work more efficiently, more smoothly or more profitably. We encourage them to do so. . . . one must have room for such wonderful activities as fooling around, making mistakes, being inspired, and failing.

CHRISTOPHER WHELLER
Executive Vice-President,
Human Resources,
3M Corporation

or so distant and hard to achieve that you give up. Both short- and long-term goals, with their measurable and tangible outcomes, are the building blocks to learning. They may consist of a certain salary, a title, specific job responsibilities, an award, or a sales figure, and you may have many goals, some more essential than others.

Although tangible goals are most common, those that are more experiential and process-oriented can be the most conducive to learning; for instance, goals that teach you about your strengths and shortcomings. Managing difficult clients, handling rapid-turnaround assignments, and seizing new responsibilities force us to learn about our true capacities and vulnerabilities.

A secret to effective goal setting is knowing when and how to set the right goals. These critical moments happen either when you reach and exceed your aspirations or as you strive and fail to reach them. Sociologist Gilbert Brim, chairman of the American Institutes for Research, who has studied ambition, explains: "We are constantly resetting our goals throughout our lives in response to what we see as our wins and losses. When we succeed in meeting some goals, we replace them with other, more challenging ones; when we fail, we lower our sights somewhat. . . . People tend to tinker first with their methods for achieving their goals. Then they begin to work on extending their timetables. Later they resort to changing their levels of aspiration, and finally, if necessary, they forgo certain goals." Lifelong learners can use these wins and losses to catapult them to the next phase of their life.

Identify your knowledge gaps. The essence of this promise is honesty with yourself about what you know and do not know, because dishonesty will undermine learning. While few people think of themselves as a know-it-all, many act like one, clinging stubbornly to a collection of ironclad opinions or assuming an air of unassailable authority. Admit your areas of ignorance and aggressively try to eradicate them. If you conclude you are too critical with employees, take a course on how to build collaborative teams. If you discover your computer skills are becoming obsolete, seek out more training and spend time every day on the computer with a personal project to learn new functions or software.

As people get older, they are forced more often to lower their aspirations and change or abandon their goals and to restructure and reorganize their lives. Among white-collar workers this process is usually launched around ages 45 to 50; among blue-collar workers it can start almost 10 to 15 years earlier as their work life tops out.

GILBERT BRIM
Director, MacArthur Foundation Program on Successful Midlife Development

Seek out mentors. Learning by watching or imitating others is one of the most powerful methods of lifelong learning. Whether you form a relationship with a mentor or simply identify someone whose knowledge you admire, watching how that person handles professional success and failure, personal difficulties and triumphs, ethical dilemmas, interpersonal conflicts, and his or her own continuing education offers an invaluable model. What cannot be gleaned from observation can be learned by asking questions; by seeking out suggestions, feedback, and even criticism; and by simply talking with a mentor about experiences, ideas, and useful lessons in life.

Pursue new interests outside of work. Developing new hobbies and interests outside of work can be the source of much learning in professional life. While most people tend to segregate personal and work interests, what you learn and know in one sphere often affects the other. Proficiency in skin diving or hiking, for instance, can make you a healthier, more energetic, more confident employee. Discovering racquetball, taking up photography, or learning to garden helps you cultivate a new skill. That new ability will show up unpredictably at work and open up new opportunities. For instance, I know a lawyer who has always been successful at researching and writing briefs but who is shy and gets tongue-tied in court. Recently, she became active in the animal-rights movement, talking to community groups. In the course of her volunteer activities, she discovered her voice and now enjoys the courtroom.

Turn mistakes into opportunities. Learning is a trial-and-error process, and inevitably, the process produces mistakes, whether they be wrong decisions, misjudgment, or simple carelessness. But mistakes are as natural a part of learning as sore muscles are of athletic training. Mistakes, like sprains and pulls, indicate that a person is working hard, and can be merely an indication of someone's knowledge gap.

While mistakes themselves are not harmful, people's attitudes about them are when those mistakes become the basis of conclusions about their character or worth, leading them to feel powerless or helpless. When people impose standards of

We have an environment here that says it's OK to make mistakes as long as you're doing your best. If someone screws up out of laziness or carelessness, that's not going to be looked on very favorably. But if you mess up because you had a great idea and it didn't work, that's another thing altogether.

MICHAEL BLEDSOE
Founder and President,
Telecalc

perfection on their performance, they set themselves up to feel rejected and depressed. Mistakes usually have a short life span, with little meaning or few consequences beyond the immediate situation. Only when people exaggerate them or persist in reliving them rather than forgetting them do mistakes grow into something to be feared.

Mistakes should be considered as signposts pointing in right and wrong directions, highlighting strengths and weaknesses. For instance, giving an assignment to an undependable employee does not mean you are an incapable manager; instead, this mistake reflects on your people skills and indicates that your powers of personal assessment need improving. People who play it safe and never make mistakes learn and grow little, spending their working lives wandering in circles, recycling the same stale information over and over.

Lifelong learners develop a mental process for dealing with mishaps: quick assessment of the situation and its possible consequences, weighing and valuing the perceptions and judgments of others and making corrections immediately without blaming others. Instead of avoiding mistakes, they use their newfound knowledge and skills as a foundation for further learning.

Executives should have a line in their budget for failure. A former associate of mine calls this investment spending.

WALTER WRISTON
former CEO, Citicorp

 ### What the Manager Can Do

As a manager, your success depends on your ability to inspire the best in your employees, to expand their competence and capacity, and to create the right conditions so that they can learn. Just as you can shape yourself into a lifelong learner, your job is to prepare and stretch your people, to help them discover their personal visions and professional goals and to expand their careers. Their learning, like yours, is a series of stages that begins with an assessment of knowledge and ignorance and proceeds to a plan of action to acquire the competencies that fill their gaps and shortcomings.

As you lead employees through the learning process, remember that employee development is a shared responsibility. No one can cram knowledge, facts, or skills into a mind—they must be sought out and firmly grasped. But while you cannot do employees' learning for them, you can act as teacher, guide, and resource by following these guidelines.

Conduct a Personal Career Audit

Your first task is to develop an ongoing process for employee appraisal and development. In many companies, these responsibilities are kept separate; in the healthy company, they are conducted as two complementary activities in the learning process.

You begin by assessing the unique skills and aspirations of each employee, writing a three-part assessment of the person's personal and professional education, job performance, and career potential. This document is not long, but it does require thought in order to be useful. It is a guide for future career discussions and makes performance reviews more meaningful, exploring in depth an employee's abilities and future goals. The audit covers these areas:

Education and experience. In this first part, you and the employee examine his or her formal education as well as informal learning and valuable experiences he or she brings to the job. What new training or education has the employee acquired recently? Included here are any seminars, weekend courses, night classes, or lecture series attended, as well as learning from hobbies, special interests, reading, or unique experiences such as traveling or athletic achievement.

Knowledge and performance. The second part relates to work: it describes what skills and knowledge are required for day-to-day job performance and how well an employee's abilities meet those requirements. Remember the core lifelong learning competencies (technoknowledge, people skills, ability to learn, emotional literacy, intuitive abilities, and personal management) and assess the employee in light of these, indicating where he or she is weak and strong.

Filling in the blanks in this area may seem simple, but you will need to dig below the surface with probing and persistent questions. You want to learn about an employee's true strengths and weaknesses, as well as the substance of his or her knowledge gaps. Then ask yourself whether that person's skills and resources match the demands of the job. How well did he or she perform on special assignments or fast-turnaround projects? Was he or she able to learn from you or constantly trying to prove him- or herself? When the employee made mistakes, was he or she

Helping human beings fulfill their potential is of course a moral responsibility, but it's also good business. Life is aspiration. Learning, striving people are happy people and good workers. They have initiative and imagination, and the companies they work for are rarely caught napping.

RALPH STAYER
CEO, Johnsonville
Foods, Inc.

sullen and preoccupied or did he or she rebound quickly? Could the person work independently, or was he or she always at your door? Did he or she surprise you with spurts of talent or mediocrity?

Potential and possibilities. Lastly you must consider potential and try to match competencies, interests, and abilities with opportunities at work. Together, you and the employee should ask what this person could be doing in one or two years' time. What does he or she enjoy and excel at? What activities or responsibilities are constantly unsatisfying or unlikely to bring success? This is the time for you to ask questions and for the employee to discover what he or she truly enjoys doing and where he or she finds satisfaction and success. These questions will help an employee discover his or her heart at work:

- What do you find most frustrating or rewarding about your work?
- Describe your ideal job. What types of work bring out the best in you?
- Do you recall your most recent success? Your most recent failure?
- What would you like to be doing in five years?
- If you could learn anything (given enough time and resources), what would it be?
- What practical skills do you wish you could pick up?

When you finish this process, you will possess a wealth of information about your employees' talents and potential. Now your job is to figure out whether their interests and abilities are consistent with your assessment and whether there are opportunities for the future. Regard this information as a deep talent pool that will guide you for future planning and staffing.

A personal career audit, like a financial audit, takes time, patience, and questioning. The audit is rarely painless, because it delves into employees' personal beliefs, dreams, and disappointments, as well as their fantasies for the future. This is sensitive material, and a manager must proceed slowly and thoughtfully. Some employees may resist the process because they are uneasy with introspection; others may be more comfortable with the status quo and disinclined to exert themselves. When this happens, you shouldn't hold this against the employee but perhaps counsel him or her to explore alternative career interests. Nevertheless, your patience and persistence will go a long way to completing the career audit. Here is how some companies assist employees in this assessment process.

At Tandem Computers, with the help of employee handbooks and self-paced career-planning guides, employees work directly with their managers to determine their learning goals and responsibilities.

Mattel Toy Company holds career-planning seminars for executive secretaries to help them assess their transferable skills, identify career goals, and take action to begin working toward them.

At Dow Chemical, engineers are given personality and personal skills tests that highlight strengths and weaknesses, including personality traits suited or unsuited to their work. The engineers then discuss test results with their supervisors and design a plan of action for future learning.

Digital Equipment Corporation employees explore career possibilities through their company-wide career awareness network, DECscan. Given the large size of the company and its fast-changing technology, Digital is eager to match employees' individual career growth goals with its requirements. Employees complete self-assessment profiles (information on current job, work experience, skills, education, performance reviews, career objectives, and personnel facts) that are compared with DEC's employment database on vacant positions. The system also assembles a talent pool for managers to tap for unusual abilities, such as a talent for learning foreign languages.

Formulate an Individual Learning Plan

The next step, formulating an individual learning plan, uses the information you gathered about strengths and shortcomings to devise a plan for the future. Not every employee's plan looks the same—each is tailored to the individual and to the available resources, both human and corporate. Discuss this plan with your employee at least once a year. Coca-Cola USA calls their discussion times People Days, held each year for all employees, from secretaries to executives. Establish that this meeting is devoted solely to performance review and career development, and do not

---

Conducting a Healthy Performance Review

Consider the performance review as a periodic side trip on a long journey of employee development. It is a time when the employee learns about expectations, current performance, and future directions. The review should emphasize analysis over appraisal; process over paperwork; and problem-solving over blame-placing. Make sure you evaluate performance on all the core competencies. Here are some suggestions:

- *Be prepared.* Study the facts prior to the interview. Tailor your approach to suit the specific employee.

- *Participate as equals.* Make sure that the employee feels at ease before you plunge into the actual appraisal.

- *Talk in specifics, not generalities.* Tell the employee what you think honestly and clearly, using concrete examples.

- *Be a good listener.* Resist the temptation to take center stage. Ask for the employee's assessment of his or her performance. Generally this self-assessment will be more critical than yours.

- *Share your assessment with the employee.* Highlight the strong and weak points. Look for similarities and differences between your assessment and the employee's, and allow plenty of time for discussion or disagreement.

- *Repeat what each of you heard to prevent misunderstandings.* When the employee leaves the review, each of you should be clear about strengths, weaknesses, and next steps.

---

mix it with a salary review. You will maintain your focus if you remember to concentrate on the future, not on past events. Each plan should include the following:

Education. What types of training and skill development will close the employee's knowledge gaps?

Experience. What jobs and work assignments will add to his or her repertoire of talents and perspectives?

Responsibilities. What new roles and responsibilities will offer a heightened level of maturity and mastery?

Opportunities. What resources and opportunities for learning are available inside the organization?

During the follow-up interview, be candid about your assessment, the opportunities available, and any concerns you may have. Ultimately, your job is to help employees see future possibilities. Listen carefully to what they are saying—perhaps they are implying doubt about their future, unrealistic expectations about timing or opportunities, or a reluctance to take charge of their own careers. If you hear such messages, raise them with the employees and talk about them. Air any anxieties you may have about their abilities or ambitions. Finally, try to come to agreement on a direction for the next year, with both of you responsible for ensuring that the plan is implemented. Consider these corporate learning plans:

At IBM, managers and employees participate in the Performance Planning Process by sitting down together to plan employee goals, including responsibilities and career directions. They plot a series of objectives, and reevaluate these regularly. The company has identified eighty-five separate job categories with specific knowledge and skills required to perform each job.

Xerox employees take part in a three-phase career-evaluation system. The program is implemented by line managers, who volunteer to help employees plot their careers. Step one is self-evaluation of needs, wants, strengths, experience, and training. Step two consists of information about career choices, job requirements, business outlook, and realistic options. Step three produces a development action plan that can encompass formal education, company training, job moves, or educational materials. Employees go through these steps with the aid of a workbook the company has entitled "Failure to Plan Is Planning to Fail."

If you ask people who have been putting on car fenders for 20 years to learn computers, then you're taking their dignity and skills away from them. They are no longer experts. If you want to retrain people, you must do it in a way that doesn't threaten their lives.

WALTER WRISTON
former CEO, Citicorp

Teach People How to Learn

Many employees are accustomed to compartmentalizing their lives, isolating job activities from learning activities. This separation is habitual and destructive; employees are never free to grow and develop at work. The greatest learning opportunities occur on the job in day-to-day working relationships. Your challenge is to transform these daily tasks into long-term learning opportunities. Whether as mundane as sweeping floors or as complex as purchasing new equipment in Argentina, every business activity is an opportunity for teaching the core competencies. Peter Senge, author of *The Fifth Discipline,* has addressed the dilemma of teaching employees to be learners while they are on the job and offers these questions to help you get started:

- Do employees see the consequences of their actions?
- Do they think about systems—cause-and-effect relationships, and patterns in behavior and problems?
- Are employees asked to analyze and separate problems from solutions and to examine the forces underlying business events?
- Are employees pushed to find quick fixes that focus only on symptoms, not the causes? Or are they given enough time for reflective thinking, time to think about long-term actions and consequences?
- Are employees taught how to brainstorm, to vision, and to focus on desired results?
- Are they allowed to question assumptions, hypotheses, paradigms, sources of data, generalizations, and theories?
- Do employees know how to advocate a position or persuade, and how to probe someone else's position?
- Do they feel comfortable expressing and defending their ideas in a group?

Crotonville [General Electric's training headquarters] is a giant workshop, not just a training center. It's a total experience . . . a physical, mental, challenging, mind-bending, stretching, exciting experience that, in the most constructive sense, blows people's minds into the next round of competitiveness and excellence and innovation and leadership.

Director of
Crotonville Facility,
General Electric Co.

Bill O'Brien, president of Hanover Insurance Company, has taken these questions to heart. "The greatest unexplored territory in the world is the space between our ears," says O'Brien. "If you believe, as we did, that there's an enormous reservoir of untapped potential in people that can be channeled more productively than it is, you try to build a value-based, vision-driven environment . . . in [this] type of organization, the fullest development of people is on the equal plane with financial success."

This Massachusetts-based insurer offers managers a three-day seminar dedicated exclusively to thinking and learning. The Merit, Openness and Localness seminar examines various thinking models and encourages participants to explore beyond most people's usual linear, mechanistic thinking habits. Another seminar, which lasts five days, is called Thinking about Thinking and explores various philosophical systems, from the Occidental to the Oriental, and evaluates the merits of each. The company's most innovative learning program is Learning Labs, a computer program that simulates for managers business situations, decision options, and possible outcomes. A manager using this program can experiment with short-term and long-term consequences of a decision, plot causes and effects, and learn how to improve his or her decision-making abilities.

As Hanover Insurance learned, employees need time to learn. This means providing sufficient time for training, ample opportunities for teamwork and brainstorming, and support for thinking about long-term business decisions. Employees also need space for learning. For large companies, this might be a learning center staffed with training specialists and sophisticated equipment. Smaller companies may simply invest in a special study or reading room for learning only (no meetings) that is equipped with computers, audio and videotapes and recorders, or perhaps a library well stocked with books and periodicals employees need and want.

Master the Mentoring Process

The mentoring relationship is often misunderstood, because people tend to think of a mentor as a largely political connection to help them maneuver upward through corporate layers. Yet it actually can be very different, if used properly. Mentoring is more than a flesh-and-bone ladder for professional advancement; it is a learning process that teaches employees how to grow, personally and professionally. While it is typically a safe relationship in which one can learn technical skills, it can also be a rich environment for teaching the principles of learning.

The Center for Creative Leadership in Greensboro, North Carolina has studied organizations, specifically looking at what happens when people clash during their rise up the corporate ladder. In assessing why managers fail, the center found the most commonly cited causes of career setbacks to be the inability to get along; failure to adapt; preoccupation with oneself; fear of action; and the inability to rebound. These hardships are due to poorly developed people and psychological skills.

The mentor relationship is ideal for preventing these problems. By teaching principles, sharing personal experiences,

The expense isn't what it costs to train employees. It's what it costs not to train them. You realize that as you grow.

GARY WILBER
CEO, Drug Emporium, Inc.

demonstrating good judgment, and pointing out acceptable and unacceptable behavior, a mentor can teach employees how to function and communicate inside a healthy company. Ideally, a mentor teaches these insights:

- humility and patience
- acceptance of one's strengths and weaknesses
- respect for other perspectives
- adaptability to changing business realities
- ability to cope with events beyond individual control
- balance in one's personal and work life
- a more humane approach toward people

Authors Morgan McCall, Jr., and Michael Lombardo (Off the Track: Why and How Successful Executives Get Derailed) *studied dismissed managers and found that 75 percent had poor people skills: they are poor listeners, avoid conflict or see it as negative, and do not equally give and take criticism.*

Once a mentoring relationship has been established, it needs to be nurtured and also to be monitored for disagreement or disintegration. People outgrow each other, hidden areas of conflict may emerge, and even jealousy and competition can arise and spoil the relationship. Sometimes people idealize mentors and harbor unrealistic notions. Cautions Jim Perkins, senior vice-president for personnel at Federal Express, "I still think it's important, even though you may be a role model, that your public behavior actually reflects what your normal behavior is. . . . I have some flaws, I'm not perfect, and I don't think anyone should consider a role model as absolutely perfect. Part of a role model's job is allowing people to see that you don't have to be superhuman in order to accomplish certain goals and tasks."

Be watchful for when it is time to sever a mentor relationship. This may be a natural outgrowth for you and your employee.

Here are some examples of mentoring programs formed by companies:

- At Jewel Companies in Salt Lake City, each new MBA is assigned a senior manager as mentor.
- General Alum and Chemical Corporation has hired on a per-diem basis retired managers from other successful companies to act as advisors to its promising employees.
- At Sequent Computer Systems, every new employee is assigned a sponsor for the first couple of weeks who is

responsible for showing him or her the official and unofficial ropes. The sponsor gets the employee plugged
into the electronic mail system, rounds up supplies, and
shares insights about the company culture.

- New recruits at the J. Walter Thompson advertising
  agency in Chicago may be assigned two mentors. The
  senior mentor, who usually has at least seven years' experience, gives advice; while the junior mentor, a relatively new entrant, offers encouragement and informal
  social connections.

Corporate Policies and Strategies

As a learning institution, the healthy company has a commitment to instituting programs and policies that support a true
learning environment. The company first invests in teaching a
wide range of competencies, from basic technical and literacy
skills to communication and teamwork skills. But even more important, the healthy company creates an arena where employees
can use and improve upon their talents. In this atmosphere, employees feel safe and comfortable making mistakes, taking
chances, testing new skills, and pursuing their personal visions.
Inside these healthy companies, learning is not just an accepted
practice, it is part of the organizational fabric. Each lifelong
learner is a microcosm of the whole company, and as personal
education expands, so too does a company's capacities.

Being a learning institution is more than simply providing
once-a-year job training to your sales-and-marketing staff. It
means more than teaching secretaries the latest word-processing
program, more than paying tuition costs for engineers, and more
than sending your most contentious manager to a communications workshop. Being a learning institution means that your
company fosters personal and professional development at every
level, making learning available to every employee.

While being a learning institution clearly makes a company
healthier and more prosperous, few American firms have instituted a comprehensive learning strategy. My observations are
borne out by statistics reported in the *Wall Street Journal,* indicating that while Japanese and European firms spend 4 to 6 percent

If 80 percent of the products a company turned out were defective, would the chief executive solve his problem by asking employees to work 20 minutes longer each day? If you wanted to turn your business around, you would be asking, "How can we fundamentally restructure what we are doing?"

ALBERT SHANKER
President, American
Federation of Teachers

Does Your Organization Sabotage Learning?

These signs indicate that your company does not offer enough learning opportunities:

- There is a shortage of promotable, high-potential employees, forcing you to always hire from outside.
- Employees feel stuck and lack career mobility or have unclear career paths.
- You offer little information on career opportunities.
- Managers feel inadequate in advising employees on their careers.
- There is little planning for job succession.
- Many employees stay in the same job for years.
- The company consistently makes the same mistakes.
- New employees leave soon after starting.

Source: © Career Systems, 1982.

---

of operating budgets on employee education, U.S. firms spend only 1.5 percent. It should be no surprise that the quality, competence, and productivity of the U.S. work force have fallen behind those of their Japanese and European competitors. Companies aware of this shortcoming are beginning to institute programs that address these concerns:

- What are the strategic goals of the organization? How can employee education help meet those goals?
- What are the current strengths and weaknesses of the work force? What kinds of programs can the company implement to eliminate these weaknesses?
- What is the organization's projected growth for one year, five years, and ten years? What employee skills and qualifications will be needed to accomplish this growth?

Following are the types of programs companies need to implement.

Get Serious About Training

American business spends about $210 billion a year on formal and informal training. Although the expense is large, it is minuscule compared with our real education needs. According to the American Society of Training and Development, the need for training at all levels is glaring; only 10 percent of American workers who need training actually get any. This half-hearted attitude will come back to haunt companies, because, experts believe, by the year 2000, 75 percent of today's employees will need retraining.

The problem would not be so dire if companies were making the best use of their current investment, but that is not the case. Typically, training is tangential to daily operations and future plans. It is an afterthought, a modest perk or reward often for those who need it least. Much of this training is directed toward one specialized group or focuses on only a few competencies, and even those lessons are rarely reinforced on the job. Yet without proper training, few employees will be able to perform jobs of the future, which will require constant relearning and skill upgrades. Tomorrow's jobs will overwhelm today's untrained employees.

Companies that are starting to fill this gap are devising an array of innovative programs. For them, being a learning institution means that they must see to it that everyone becomes proficient in the six basic competencies: ability to learn, technoknowledge, people skills, emotional literacy, intuitive abilities, and personal management. Above these, some people in certain positions will need to constantly upgrade their technical and professional skills. The benefits of this investment are increased output, improved quality, enhanced flexibility, and reduced replacement costs. These are common features among these leading-edge companies:

- They invest from 3 to 5 percent of payroll into employee education.

- They establish visible, measurable links between business strategy and training goals.

- They tailor training to the organization's problems and skill gaps.

- They teach a broad range of competencies (knowledge, attitudes, and skills) and apply them directly to job performance.

Data Bank

- *According to* Business Week, *13 percent of American seventeen-year-olds are illiterate, compared to only 1 percent in Japan and Germany in the same age groups.*

- *Another study shows that only 12 percent of managers receive any job training from their employers when they start work and only 17 percent receive formal training for job advancement.*

- *The Hudson Institute estimates that more than half the 18 million jobs expected to materialize by the end of the century will require advanced skills— at least some technical training after high school.*

- They utilize whatever works: formal courses, satellite broadcasts, conferences and seminars, internal trainers, outside consultants, personal learning guides, and computer-assisted instruction.

- They rely on their operating managers to determine what programs have failed and what new programs are needed, and they ask their employees to diagnose their own training needs.

- They evaluate what knowledge was gained, how it translates to performance, and what impact it has on organizational effectiveness.

- They follow up regularly.

A person entering the work force today can expect to be retrained five times in his work life.

JOHN YOUNG
CEO, Hewlett-Packard
Company

A study by the Rand Corporation found that recipients of on-the-job training earn 16.9 percent more on average than the untrained; people who seek outside vocational training earn 11.9 percent more when they return to work; and people armed with vocational training are less vulnerable to layoffs.

Though the kind of training your company needs or how much you should be spending is an individual matter, here are some examples of the best company education programs.

Few companies educate better than Motorola, which has made training an essential part of its operations. In January 1987 the company increased its investment in the retraining and education of all 100,000 employees in order to redirect the company focus toward five key initiatives: six sigma quality, total cycle time reduction, product and manufacturing leadership, profit improvement, and participative management.

Says William Wiggenhorn, president of Motorola University and corporate vice-president for training and education, "We learned that line workers had to actually understand their work and their equipment, that senior management had to exemplify and reinforce new methods and skills if they were going to stick, that change had to be continuous and participative, and that education—not just instruction—was the only way to make it happen."

The curriculum at Motorola University includes periodic classes that last half a day to two weeks and covers such topics as quality, risk taking, managing change, basic skills courses in reading and math, and teamwork. Each of the functional classes —engineering, manufacturing, sales, and marketing—is divided into three parts: relational skills (customer satisfaction, effective supervision, negotiation, and persuasive presentations), technical skills, and business skills. Often training mingles company departments, with employees from marketing, production, and engineering learning together. At any one time, 1,200 people are involved in training and education, including 110 full-time teachers and 300 part-timers, with an annual budget of $70 million. Motorola's total investment in training and education is approximately 22 percent of the company's after-tax profits. The company saved no less than $1.5 billion over the past three years through work force improvements.

Aetna Life & Casualty offers its entry-level employees from inner-city Hartford two months of training when they begin work. The training recognizes that employees may lack many job skills, so it covers reading and writing, using computers, and guidance on communicating and interacting with other employees. Aetna estimates the training costs $7,000 to $10,000 per employee, including salary, but finds the training essential because of a dramatically shrinking pool of qualified job applicants.

American Communications Group, Inc., put a classroom at the back of one of its buildings and gave experienced telephone wiring technicians time-and-a-half for training new employees.

Captive-Aire Systems, Inc., a ventilation company in Raleigh, North Carolina, offered people skills and problem-solving training to employees through lunch-time classes. Every Monday, the CEO bought lunch for all twenty-five administrative employees so they could eat while he talked to them about customer relations as well as technical ventilating problems.

The Travelers, a Connecticut-based insurance company, identified management competencies by using employee surveys and analyzing the traits of their high-performing workers. These competencies shaped the company's training efforts.

Polaroid doubled their training budget even though the company was going through a 30-percent reduction in force. They saw training as a vital economic force as they reorganized for the future.

Corning, Inc. devotes 5 percent of all hours worked in 1991 to classroom training, up from 4 percent in 1990 and far more than the 1 to 2 percent at most U.S. companies. The result: Corning's return on equity jumped from 9.3 percent in 1984, when it began emphasizing training, to 15.9 percent in 1989.

The Body Shop, an international company founded in Britain with stores in thirty-eight countries from New York to Tokyo,

You can't train anybody to do anything that he or she doesn't fundamentally believe in. That's why we've designed leadership week to give people an opportunity to reflect on their own values and to allow them to say what they want to get from work.

ROBERT HAAS
Chairman and CEO,
Levi Strauss & Co.

offers unique training to every employee and franchise holder. The training has less to do with running a shop—with management skills and financial controls—than with educating every employee and franchisee about the origins, ingredients, and characteristics of its products: skin- and hair-care products inspired by nature and traditional practices. Employees are trained in such areas as herbal hair care and aromatherapy. Explains company founder and president Anita Roddick: "[Other cosmetic companies] train for a sale. We train for knowledge."

Lincoln Electric, a Cleveland manufacturer, puts managerial trainees to work in its welding school so that they know the company from the bottom up.

A Menu for Training

Training comes in all shapes and sizes, depending on your business needs and the people involved. Consider these ideas for training programs:

Leadership. Mission and strategy development; public policy; communication and motivation; global thinking.

Management. Teamwork; performance feedback; project management; financial management; employee development; diversity management; empowerment skills; safety; administrative skills.

Literacy. Reading; report writing; computer literacy; company mission, vision, and goal setting; emotional literacy; foreign languages.

Communication. Public speaking and presentation skills; interpersonal skills; organizational behavior; mentoring; conflict resolution.

Customer service. Quality service; negotiation; selling; customer skills; telephone skills; product knowledge.

Technical. Software development; engineering; automated manufacturing; quality control; computers; personnel management; labor relations; information management; data processing; professional skills; federal, state, and local law compliance.

Creativity. Brainstorming; intuition; problem-solving; idea development.

Personal management. Time management; stress management; career development; self-development; wellness; assertiveness.

Open A Skills Bank

Many companies are stuck in a merry-go-round of continuous turnover. One way to break their plunge is by improving the match between employee and job through a company skills bank. Healthy companies accept the reality of constant change and adjust to it, not by always looking for new workers, but by educating existing employees and promoting from within. They are keenly aware of their internal talent and their future needs.

Skills banks centralize information and announcements about openings and new jobs in a company. They are primarily a repository of information about what skills employees currently possess and the company's present and future needs. Of course, skills banks are useful to management for filling slots, but they also give employees, through job postings, a clear description of the kinds of skills they need to learn in order to advance. Here is how some companies organize skills banks.

Pacific Northwest Bell has computerized its job bank, which it updates weekly with listings of openings and their required skills. The company then matches these positions with employees' professional-development profiles. The computer, in effect, goes headhunting and matches jobs and people. When it finds a match, the personnel department notifies the employee and the department with a vacancy. Employees praise the system, because the computer eliminates personal bias, making matches based on actual skills.

Lawrence Livermore National Laboratories in California operates a career center that offers postings for educational opportunities, career planning, personal counseling, computerized job information banks, skill- and job-related periodicals, study materials, and community resources for job training.

Healthy companies believe their success depends on their ability to prepare for the future. Knowing and tapping the special strengths of their work force through skills banks gives them that added competitive edge.

Reward Learners

While employees are responsible for their own education, the good employers have found that incentives quicken people's motivation. Rewarding people for learning reinforces their behavior and helps ensure its long-term impact. Here are examples of company reward programs:

- Nissan Motor Manufacturing Company, USA, has instituted a Pay for Versatility incentive. Under this program, employees receive a bonus—twenty-five cents an hour for production workers and thirty cents an hour for maintenance workers—for learning how to do more than one assembly-line job.

- Burger King Corp., anxious to reduce turnover, sets aside as much as $2,000 per employee in an education-and-training fund if an employee stays with the company for a certain length of time. Some Burger King owners encourage employees to use this money for advanced education.

- At 3M, researchers are allowed to spend up to 15 percent of their time (almost one day a week) on personal projects with only distant payoffs, not immediate results.

- Texas Instruments has a program called IDEA to finance new business ideas from employees. Executive approval is not required for these ideas, and funds are funneled through sponsors who watch over an idea's development.

- The Military Avionics Division of Honeywell asks employees to rate their managers' mentoring skills. The Chance to Grow program helps supervisors create an environment that encourages employees to grow both personally and professionally. Supervisors who score above a certain level receive $200.

- Student employees at the Sonic Drive-In in Tucson receive bonuses based on their grade-point averages, with a 2.5 to 3.0 average earning an extra fifteen cents an hour and a 3.0-plus GPA earning an additional twenty-five cents per hour.

- Houghton Mifflin reimburses 80 percent of tuition for job-related courses, and so do many other companies. All told, they have found that rewarding learning pays off.

Institutionalize Learning Stretches

Employee learning is a gradual process that takes many shapes and directions. Sometimes learning is vertical, such as when an employee receives a promotion; other times it is horizontal, such as when there is an expansion of an employee's existing abilities through a new assignment. Learning can be unexpected and forced, as happens when a crisis strikes, or carefully planned and modulated, as when someone enrolls in a training seminar. Regardless of what kind of learning seems to dominate a company, employee development must be a critical component of organizational life.

Just as companies routinely announce that they intend to grow 10 to 15 percent a year, so, too, should employees. The best time to introduce such a learning stretch is when an employee has mastered 80 percent of his or her job. Learning stretches are activities and projects that allow employees to expand, learn, and discover personal and professional rewards within the boundaries of their work responsibilities. At their heart, they are solutions to company and career stagnation, a recurring problem for many.

Remember that learning is not an issue for everyone all the time. Sometimes people are comfortable having mastered their current job and want to wait before the next stretch occurs. Your challenge is to find the right stretch for the right person at the right time. You must allow time for learning to soak in, during which employees can absorb their experiences and reflect on what they want to learn next.

Here are samples of learning stretches to rekindle organizational learning. The first is a vertical advance that adds responsibility and status, whereas the rest are lateral moves that place an employee the same distance from the top as before but enrich his or her job by developing more skills, control, and intrinsic rewards.

Fast-track advances. Keep an eye out for employees with high potential. Offer them special learning experiences and opportunities, and evaluate how well they meet your expectations. Be careful not to penalize those who turn down promotions. At NCR, a Dayton, Ohio computer maker, an early identification program identifies high-potential employees with fewer than five years' experience. Employees are given early cross-discipline experiences that typically last two years.

Turnaround projects. Give employees the freedom, resources, access, or control to remedy a difficult situation. For example, a line foreman who has ideas for improving plant efficiency might be put in charge of upgrading a production area; an operating head might be asked to turn around a dying product line; or a

The world accepts more career diversity than it used to. You can zigzag your way up and down and still hold up your head at the neighborhood store.

ANDREW S. GROVE
CEO, Intel Corp.

marketing manager could be given responsibility for a region that has lost part of its market share. In these kinds of situations, it may be necessary to strengthen the mentoring relationship and give more time for training and development, but the learning will pay off.

Special assignments. Accepting a special work assignment sometimes feels like turning down an untraveled path on a weekend hike. Although not sure what is behind the next bend, explorers may encounter a beautiful view or an adventure. Participation on company task forces, switches from line to staff jobs, transfers to other functions, and exposure to nearby departments bring an employee in contact with new people and ideas. Sending employees to management training or giving them a special overseas assignment are other ways to provide lateral movement. Offer employees more to do, more people to supervise, or more areas of influence. However, whenever you add responsibilities, make sure employees view the shift as adding meaning to their work. DuPont sends promising executives on academic sabbaticals. One molecular biologist took a three-month executive development program at Massachusetts Institute of Technology's Sloan School of Management. At PepsiCo Inc., where a lateral move used to be the equivalent of a death warrant, it is now standard for six of every ten management-track employees.

Alternative assignments. These assignments can entail rotating a person around different departments or jobs and ensuring they get trained in all of them. Workers learn a variety of jobs and move around the company as needed. Observes Ian Browde, a learning expert at Apple Computer Company: "No one here stays at a job for longer than nine months; my dad worked at the same job for thirty years."

Opportunities to handle different customers, coworkers, bosses, and subordinates all enhance employees' skills. Each position should include a new challenge, some novelty, and enough authority to get the job done. Make it clear that sideways moves aren't a dead end by offering them to everyone. Nissan Motor Manufacturing Company, USA, teaches assembly-line workers numerous jobs—all the operations within a supervisor's zone—and every couple of hours each worker shifts to something new.

We are starting to have broader bands for people. Instead of getting a $10,000 raise and moving on, they can earn much more within a job as they grow in and grow their business.

HAROLD BURLINGAME
Senior Vice-President,
Human Resources, AT&T

Plateauing Can Make You Sick

Consider the consequences when employees are stuck and frustrated with their careers:

- A study of middle managers at Lockheed Corporation found that a poor fit between an employee and his or her work was related to increasing stress and a higher risk of heart attack due to higher blood pressure, cholesterol level, and adrenalin secretion.

- A study of twenty-eight-year-old Swedish men found that restricted learning opportunities at work were associated with increased adrenaline and, in turn, high blood pressure.

- A study of two thousand telephone operators, some of whom were chronically sick and others relatively free of illness, found that the sicker group was better educated but much less content in their jobs. Employees in the sick group had a professional background with some higher education and described their jobs as boring or confining, were frustrated, and felt stuck in the wrong positions. The healthy group was more content with their jobs and their lives.

Research on managers' careers at AT&T from 1955 to 1985 found the following changes: from lifetime to short-term career perspective; from sole concerns about advancement to dual concerns of advancement and accomplishment; from supervisory-managed careers to employee-managed careers; from one career to several careers; and from one family income to dual career and wage earners.

Alternative career paths. In today's workplace, only a handful of employees will reach the top spots, although literally legions of managers are aimed in that direction. However, while many managers find their careers blocked and promotions deferred, their education and advancement need not halt. Companies cognizant of the log-jam in upper-management ranks are opening other avenues for managers to achieve, grow, and succeed by institutionalizing attractive lateral moves. Alternative career paths are a bifurcated corporate ladder that enables employees to reap the benefits of promotion and advancement without entering upper-management ranks. The best programs ensure that both ladders are comparable in status, prestige, and responsibility.

Monsanto has created for its scientists and researchers not headed for top management the new positions of associate fellow, senior fellow, and distinguished fellow, and it pays them executive-level salaries. It has done the same thing for computer employees in its information services department, with the

Monsanto

positions of technologist, senior technologist, and distinguished technologist.

At Eli Lilly & Co., upwardly mobile technical personnel can aspire to senior or principal research fellow status. A principal fellow has the equivalent in pay and perks of a vice-president. Nontechnical employees can reach for consultant status. (However, the company has found that dual paths among managerial, nontechnical personnel are less workable, because they result in too many people on management tracks.)

Atlantic Richfield Company has created nonmanagement career ladders with these positions: advisor, senior advisor, distinguished advisor, and executive advisor.

Counsel the Working Wounded

A twenty-five-year study of 5,000 business careers found that the decade of the forties is the most dangerous and turbulent on the job. People find themselves increasingly isolated, fearing obsolescence, and worrying about long-term job security.

As you talk with employees about their career stretches, you will likely hear frustration from people whose careers are not working. Notes psychologist and career consultant Judith Bardwick: "The youngest baby-boomers are 26. They're going to plateau at 40 or so, 10 years younger than their fathers did. They're not psychologically prepared for it." Such feelings are almost a demographic certainty, given the bulge of aging, aspiring baby-boomers competing for a shrinking number of career plums. Says Douglas LaBier, psychotherapist and author, "The drive for success—and its criteria of money, power and prestige —exists alongside a parallel, but less visible, drive for increased fulfillment and meaning from work . . . the tension between these two drives has unleashed a serious problem in our society." Career plateaus are growing more numerous as the working wounded struggle to find meaning in their work.

One of the most disturbing groups is the so-called troubled winners—people who find success and achievement at work but go home to a bewildering sense of emptiness, depression, and despair. They drain all their energies and emotions into their jobs, then burn out. So the corporate ladder loses its allure, and they step off and seek other outlets. However, they remain resentful and embittered for the time and loyalty they once dedicated to their employer.

Another upset group is known as the frustrated careerists. Driven by ambition, this breed of highly educated workers wants it all—advancement, participation, rewards, and responsibilities.

It is only a matter of time before their impatience runs up against the corporate realities of lateral transfers and limited opportunities. Discontent surfaces, because these employees possess all the skills that are needed and more, yet find themselves stuck on a plateau.

When either situation happens, talk frankly with these employees about their feelings and frustrations. The most effective remedy is to restructure their jobs to provide more flexibility, creativity, and participation. These are the people who are candidates for special assignments or alternative career tracks. Others, however, may enjoy a relaxation from the corporate climb with proper counseling. You can suggest they integrate their work skills with a pursuit outside of work and help them carve out a better schedule, one that allows more time for family and leisure. Perhaps they should even be encouraged to consider a sabbatical —possibly a few days, weeks, or months. It is inevitable that some of these employees will leave the company, but others will appreciate your sensitivity and return healthier and more motivated than ever.

Rohm & Haas, an industrial chemicals company in Philadelphia, is addressing the problem of stagnated careers and dissatisfied workers, having discovered that the typical professional employee spends twenty-five or more years on a career plateau. With few managerial promotions available, the company is eager to find a way to keep employees learning at work. It has hired outside consultants to work directly with employees in a midcareer renewal program, analyze their accomplishments, and provide realistic, honest, and useful counseling.

Create Educational Partnerships

Learning must not stop at the corporate gate. The best organizations highlight their foresight and commitment through alliances with local schools. Partnerships between business and educational institutions improve the practical education of future employees, bring students into the company to freshen up the learning atmosphere and show them what future skills they will need, and stimulate learning among employees by asking them to be teachers. They also help the transition from student-learner to employee-learner and emphasize the common qualities of school and work.

The best way for business to invest in educating the disadvantaged is to reach them early. By age five, they're already so deprived they can't benefit from schooling. It took us years to develop Tartar-Control Crest, years to make a profit on our investment. So we understand the economics of early childhood programs.

OWEN B. BUTLER
retired CEO, Procter & Gamble

United States students attend class 180 days a year; French and German children, 220 days; and Japanese children, 240 days.

the *Wall Street Journal*

Successful Career Moves: Yesterday and Today

Yesterday

- ■ Career moves were always upward.
- ■ Promotions came regularly, usually every two years.
- ■ Fitting into the company was more important than individual ambitions and dreams.
- ■ Job security was more important than job content.
- ■ Success was measured by a paycheck that was $1,000 times your age.

Today

- ■ Lateral moves are common, even desirable.
- ■ There is no set schedule for advancement—you may stay in the same jobs for many years, although your responsibilities may change.
- ■ Individual opinions and aspirations are as important as the corporate personality.
- ■ Job satisfaction and challenge are more important than security.
- ■ Success means having a job you enjoy and grow in, regardless of the title or paycheck.

Source: *Fortune* magazine, July 2, 1990.

Such partnerships can have many configurations: employees volunteering to be mentors to students; managers being given time off to teach in schools; grants made to local schools; a summer intern program being established at the company for students; and awards being made to students for achievement in studies related to your business.

Business cannot afford to work in its own ivory tower, separate from the community, schools, and young students, because its future hangs on the education and values of the youth outside its walls. Ill-equipped, poorly educated students can cripple a company's livelihood, draining it of critical talent and energy.

Here is how some companies are forging strong links with schools and guaranteeing that future employees are competent and qualified.

The Federal National Mortgage Association (Fannie Mae), in Washington, D.C., created the Futures 500 Club, a mentor program for selected students at nearby Woodson High School, including classes in writing, goal setting, and career development. Managers from Fannie Mae are assigned to students who get all As and Bs, and these students receive help landing summer jobs at Fannie Mae. The company also gives each student $500 a semester to be saved for college tuition.

In education as in business, trying to fix things is more expensive than getting them right in the first place.

JACK McALLISTER
CEO, U.S. West

Time Inc.'s employee volunteer program called Time to Read involved more than 700 employee volunteers who tutored students and prison inmates in reading.

Apple Computer donates computers to schools, thus helping students become computer literate. So far, the company has given more than $60 million worth of equipment and training.

Merck & Co. underwrites teacher education by sending New Jersey teachers to local universities for refresher courses and donates lab equipment to schools. Some of its scientists have volunteered to be pen pals with students, giving them ideas for experiments.

Central Fidelity Bank runs a minibank to teach finance at a local elementary school in Richmond, Virginia. Here students can open an account with $25 and make monthly transactions. Their savings are applied toward class field trips.

Secretaries and top executives from the oil company ARCO donate time to a nearby elementary school by helping out in classrooms and tutoring immigrants and minorities in English, math, geography, and computer science.

HEALTHY COMPANIES NEED HEALTHY LEARNERS

Regardless of how committed a company is to learning, it cannot cultivate lifelong learners unless employees are both physically and mentally healthy. People whose lifestyles and work styles make them sick or susceptible to illness are too distracted by health concerns to focus on learning. The next chapter addresses the issue of the healthy employee, with ideas and suggestions for helping employees become healthy and hardy.

CHAPTER FIVE

Healthy People Are Appreciating Assets

A FEW YEARS AGO, the bakery division of Safeway Stores in Clackamas, Oregon faced a major crisis. The accident rate among its 130 largely blue-collar workers was rising fast, absenteeism and turnover were high, and employee productivity was diminishing. In a single year, accidents cost the company 1,740 work days at $100 a day. Absenteeism, especially waves of Saturday and Sunday night "fever," knocked out eight people for every 100-worker shift. And in some jobs, turnover was reaching 100 percent.

Traditional corporate thinkers might have pointed the finger at poor training or inefficient equipment as the cause of the troubles. While it was obvious to the bakery manager that the problem stemmed from management, months of trial-and-error theories about the causes and gradual remedies would pass before he found the real cause of the problem. One of his last, and perhaps most startling, insights was that his moods had an immediate and marked effect on employees. When he would get upset at an employee for carelessness, he noticed that that employee frequently called in sick the next day. Conversely, employees singled out for praise generally did not miss a day's work for weeks.

In 1990, health-care costs were rising so rapidly that if unchecked, they would eliminate in ten years all profits for the average Fortune 500 company.

Washington Business Group on Health

Slowly, painfully, the bakery manager realized that his personal style of managing was the source of unhappiness, illness, and lost productivity in the company. The problem, he concluded with difficulty, was the employees' opinions and feelings about him, their jobs, and themselves. Employees were afraid of him, and were timid about making decisions and taking on responsibility for fear of his criticisms and displeasure. His aggressive management style—controlling everything, insisting that his point of view prevail, making all decisions—intimidated employees. They felt powerless, discouraged, and unimportant.

After months of watching employees, detailing their work habits, and studying his own performance, the manager decided to institute a number of programs aimed at restoring employees' confidence and loosening his iron-fisted management. To share control, he formed problem-solving groups for plant-wide concerns, such as sanitation, safety, and ergonomics. He announced a new openness to employee suggestions, and his positive reception of their ideas began to relax the atmosphere to the point where more and more workers started making suggestions, confident they would be heeded. Successful programs inspired more success, and momentum gathered: in a single year, the company implemented more than a thousand employee ideas, including a number of safety improvements.

Employee suggestions spilled over to virtually all areas of the business, such as the absentee rate and the work environment. Taking over a storeroom, employees built a small fitness center. Though crowded into just 144 square feet, the area contained a couple of rowing machines, a treadmill, and some weights. It also contained the seeds of a complete turnaround for the bakery division.

The fitness center became the focal point for a wellness program that reinforced the company's commitment to the total well-being of employees. Its popularity eventually prompted the division to construct a new 5,000 square-foot facility for not just employees but also their families. The fitness-center offerings expanded beyond exercise equipment and sports facilities to educational programs about health and lifestyle evaluations. The company began sponsoring special fitness events for employees, such as the Buns on the Run program which handed out T-shirts and psychological encouragement to regular exercisers. At the fitness center, employees learned everything from their percentage of body fat to how to eat more nutritiously to how to play pickle ball. One of the center's more imaginative programs was its Laugh Clinics, regular classes on how to worry less and have fun at work.

The fitness-center philosophy of tending to the whole employee spread to other areas of the company. The division decided to beautify itself so that employees would enjoy their surroundings more. Employees were encouraged to decorate their work spaces to reduce the monotony of their jobs and instill a sense of belonging.

The dramatic changes at this Safeway Bakery division brought even more dramatic benefits. The company reversed the troubles that first plagued the plant manager:

- Absenteeism dropped from 8 percent to 0.2 percent.
- Accidents slipped from 1,740 to two work days lost in a year.
- Turnover plummeted from the high in some jobs of 100 percent to less than 10 percent.
- Grievances and discrimination cases faded from seventy-five to eighty a year to one grievance, and no discrimination cases, in five years.

In real dollars, the company estimated that for every dollar invested in these programs, it has pocketed a return of $15. Put another way, the company estimates it has saved between $700,000 and $800,000 a year.

How employees feel about themselves and their jobs, as the Safeway Bakery manager discovered, can produce daily problems and annual budget drains. Unhealthy employees, whether physically ill or mentally stressed, are marginal workers, show up late for work, and call in sick frequently. For a manager, supervising overstressed employees means worrying about work getting done, more customer complaints, expensive and time-consuming medical appointments, and costly accidents.

Such managerial worries are then magnified into serious corporate concerns when companies realize how much unhealthy employees cost them in rising health-care premiums, disability

We know from our own experience that if we feel well, we do a better job than if we feel poorly. And if employees are sick, they will cost you a lot of money.

THEODORE BROPHY
retired Chairman and
CEO, GTE

costs, and worker compensation claims. Eventually, these costs eat away at operating budgets, and companies, regardless of their size or resources, lose profits and ther competitive edge.

In the past twenty years, corporate health-care expenditures have climbed 700 percent, and today we all recognize that they are out of control. In 1990 alone, health-care costs for American businesses rose 20 to 30 percent. The average cost per employee was $3,161, an amount equal to one-fourth of their net earnings. And the price of future poor health may become even more painful: the national standard-setting organization for financial accounting (FASB) has proposed that health costs for company retirees be expensed against earnings in company financial statements. This move could reduce corporate incomes by 10 to 20 percent.

The message for companies is clear: improve employee health in order to control these costs. But to accomplish this, managers must rethink their assumptions about what makes employees healthy and unhealthy and what companies can do to address the problem.

AN OUNCE OF PREVENTION

For decades, managers did not feel that employee health was their business. Illness was regarded as a single and personal event separate from work; it was something a person caught or an accident that kept him or her away from work. An employee was responsible for finding a competent doctor, getting necessary and appropriate treatment, and returning to work as soon as possible. A company's role was limited to paying health premiums, typically through a third-party insurance company. Managers had little responsibility for managing employee health; the expense was the domain of the personnel department and considered fixed and minor compared with other company expenditures.

With health costs out of control today, these assumptions simply do not hold true anymore. Business needs to make a major shift in its thinking and move away from treating costly illness to preventing problems before they happen—from prescriptive to preventative medicine.

Theories abound on why health costs are out of control, beginning with the rising cost of medical technology to bureaucratic insurance procedures. Although these factors certainly contribute, I am convinced the overriding reason is the changing nature of illness—from acute, infectious diseases to chronic, degenerative ailments, such as heart disease, cancer, strokes, accidents, and mental-health problems. These chronic, degenerative ailments constitute the majority of illnesses today, and their treatments—often long-term regimes of drugs, monitoring, and medical devices—enable people to live longer and better, but they carry hefty price tags.

The health of Americans is far more dependent upon personal behavior than it is upon medical care.

WILLIS GOLDBECK
Founder, Washington Business Group on Health

More than 60 percent of all disease is caused by the way we live—lifestyle risks that we impose on ourselves—according to the National Centers for Disease Control. The most powerful are smoking, diet, exercise, back problems, substance abuse, mental health, use of safety belts, and excessive stress. Fifteen years of epidemiological research has shown that these lifestyle habits pose major risks to our health. Consider these findings:

- A National Cancer Institute study of Alameda County, California followed 6,928 residents for nine years. It found the following personal habits to be directly related to a person's health: smoking, exercise, drinking, eight hours of sleep a night, weight, breakfast, and snacking patterns. Life spans for the healthier men were eleven years longer and for the healthier women, seven years longer.

- A Framingham, Massachussetts study has followed residents for more than two decades to discover links between personal habits and heart disease. They found risk of heart disease climbed among people who smoked, had hypertension, and were overweight.

- Harvard University has studied 17,000 of its male alumni over a number of years and found that exercise —even a moderate amount—dramatically increases life expectancy. Death rates for exercisers (people who burn 2,000 calories a week being active) were 25 to 33 percent lower than for the less active. Had all the men been physically active, 23 percent of first heart attacks would have been prevented.

■ The Multiple Risk Factor Intervention Trial, conducted by the National Heart, Lung and Blood Institute, has shown that programs to lower blood pressure, reduce cholesterol, and eliminate smoking can reduce the mortality associated with coronary artery disease.

■ The Lipid Research Coronary Primary Prevention Trial demonstrated that risk of coronary heart disease can be reduced by lowering blood cholesterol levels. The lower the cholesterol, the lower the risk of a heart attack.

A 1990 panel of advisors to the Environmental Protection Agency concluded that involuntary exposure to tobacco smoke causes lung cancer in nonsmokers and increases the risk of respiratory illness in children.

High-Risk Employees

Everyone's life includes some degree of health risk. Risk is like body temperature: it is always present but is only a danger when it exceeds a certain level. Lifestyle health risks push a person into the danger zone when they include certain unhealthy activities, a danger that lurks not only for the individual but for an employer, who must share the burden of an unhealthy employee.

High-risk employees cost more than low-risk individuals because they are less productive, are absent more, submit more and larger health claims, and spend more time in the hospital. Age is not necessarily a determining factor; no matter how old an employee, a high-risk lifestyle adds to the health-care tab. For instance, Control Data Corporation has found that unhealthy employees cost the company $509 a year more in absenteeism and health-care costs than do healthy employees.

While lifestyle risks are well known, many people are not aware of exactly how much damage they do. Here is a rundown on the major hazards.

Smoking. Experts and statistics alike confirm what many people already know: smoking harms personal health more than any other habit. Smoking weakens the immune system, causes serious illness such as cancer and bronchitis, and shortens lives. According to the Department of Health and Human Services, about 29 percent of workers smoke. The lifetime cost of smoking for the average forty-five-year-old, two-packs-a-day smoker is $46,334 in medical expenses, premature disability, and death. Absenteeism among smokers is 50 percent higher than among nonsmokers, and smokers have twice as many job-related acci-

High- versus Low-Risk Employees		
Risk Factor	Low Risk	High Risk
smoking	nonsmoker	40 cigs./day
exercise	4×/week, 20 min.	sedentary
weight	normal	over 30%
systolic BP	120	over 160
diastolic BP	80	95
cholesterol	160	300
seat belt usage	100%	0%

Source: William Jose, Control Data Corporation.

Your employees' eating practices can have an effect on your business' bottom line.

U.S. Office of Disease Prevention and Health Promotion

dents. Even a person who doesn't smoke at work is affected by the harmful effects of smoke in the air; many experts believe that working in an environment with secondhand smoke is as detrimental to a person as light smoking.

Diet. Most people do not eat healthfully, and it shows. The American Dietetic Association reports that nearly 70 percent of U.S. workers have poor eating habits: they consume too much saturated fat, salt, and sugar and too few vegetables and fruits, many of which have preventative powers. A poor diet is associated with five of the leading causes of death: heart disease, cancer, stroke, arteriosclerosis, and diabetes. Researchers at the National Cancer Institute believe that more than one-third of all cancers are directly linked to diet.

Obesity is another major problem, and Americans especially appear to be growing fatter. Studies in Minnesota and Rhode Island by epidemiologist Michael Sprafka show that, in general, women's weights over the past decade have risen six to seven pounds, and men's weights have risen three to four pounds. Major weight gain is also on the rise, with an estimated 16.7 million workers weighing 20 percent more than their desired weight. Overweight employees have 30 percent more hospital days and 48 percent more health-care claims than people of normal weight.

Mental performance after exercise is better in people who are physically fit. Swedish researchers have found that fit workers make 60 percent fewer errors on jobs involving concentration and short-term memory.

Substance-abuse-related workers'-compensation losses have increased fourfold since 1970. Substance-abuse costs for a typical large company (one thousand employees, average pay of $23,000) now reach almost $500,000 a year.

National Council of Compensation Insurance

Exercise. Most employees do not exercise enough, according to expert Dr. Steve Blair of the Institute of Aerobics Research, who concludes, "Only 10 percent of the adult population is following the Surgeon General's recommendation for twenty minutes of vigorous exercise three times a week." Exercise invigorates people and helps them control their weight and fend off illness. Those in good physical shape are healthier, happier people, less often absent from their jobs and more apt to work a longer, harder day. Studies of office workers by the space agency NASA have found that regular exercisers work a full day, while those who do not exercise lose energy and productivity in the last two hours of the day. Statistics also show that people who do not exercise regularly and vigorously have 30 percent more hospital days than those who do.

Exercise also can add years to a person's life. A fifteen-year study of more than 13,000 people who attended Kenneth Cooper's Aerobics Center found that those at the bottom 20 percent in fitness ranking were twice as likely to die early as the fitter people. Most remarkable about this finding was that exercise seemed to ward off not only heart attacks but chronic diseases such as cancer. A fifty-five-year-old man who exercises regularly has approximately the same level of physical fitness as a thirty-five-year-old man who does not exercise.

Back care. Experts estimate that about 30 percent of employees have back trouble, making it the second most prevalent disorder (after cardiovascular disease) and the number-one cause of absenteeism. The average work loss for a back problem is twenty-six days, and one-third of all workers'-compensation claims are related to low-back pain. Low-back injuries cost business $1 billion a year in lost output. DuPont Corporation reports that back problems, whether from on-the-job injuries or home accidents, cost it $40 million in 1987 at its U.S. operations alone.

The secret to preventing back troubles is exercise and staying fit, as discovered by Los Angeles County, which found that harder-working, stronger, more flexible fire fighters had one-tenth the back injuries of lesser-fit fire fighters. And, over ten years, their health-care costs dropped 45 percent.

Substance abuse. Alcoholism and drug abuse are the most menacing business problems, affecting up to 15 percent of the work force. Says Diana Chapman Walsh, professor at the Harvard School of Public Health, alcohol is a major contributor in all ten of the most frequent causes of death and disability; it creates a poisonous trail of adverse effects through the body to the brain, digestive system, liver, muscle system (including the heart), circulatory system, lungs, endocrine system, and sexual and reproductive systems.

Drug use among working people is rampant, too: in 1986, one in four working twenty-to-forty-year-olds said they had used an illicit drug, and one in five had used one in the past month. Prescription drugs are another abused substance: the National Institute on Drug Abuse estimates that prescription-drug abuse causes 60 percent of hospital emergency-room admissions for drug overdoses and 70 percent of all drug-related deaths.

The cost of all this abuse is enormous. Firestone Tire and Rubber Company reported that employees who abuse drugs are four times more likely to be involved in an accident at work, five times more likely to file workers'-compensation claims, and two-and-one-half times more likely to be off work for at least a week.

Substance-abuse problems are often hidden from view. One Massachussetts employer who believed substance abuse accounted for 8 percent of his company's health budget found a much different story when he looked more closely at his health claims: more than 28 percent of the claims were paid for alcohol and drug treatment.

Mental health. Personal and family problems weigh heavily on our health. According to the National Institute on Mental Health, 17 to 23 percent of the general population suffer from a major psychological disorder, such as depression or anxiety, at any point in time. Mental-health problems affect how people work and can set off a series of mishaps and illnesses, from job burnout to industrial accidents.

Unfortunately, mental health is a topic loaded with prejudices and sensitivities, and many companies underestimate the costs and numbers of employees with personal problems. Treating the diseases of the mind, they imply, is not as important as fixing physical infirmities. Consequently, one study estimates that only 27 percent of companies have mental-health inpatient coverage and only 3 percent have outpatient coverage that is

Data Bank

- *One in five workers suffer from emotional disorders.*

- *Over a twenty-year period, the Kaiser-Permanente Health Plan found that 60 percent of all physician visits were by patients who had nothing physically wrong with them. Another 20 to 30 percent were by patients who had physical illnesses (such as peptic ulcer or hypertension) with a stress-related component.*

- *In a New York Business Group on Health survey, two hundred managers reported that 13 percent of their employees experienced depression in the past year. Among the depressed, 36 percent had difficulty concentrating, 35 percent had sleeping problems, 27 percent had decreased energy, and 18 percent experienced loss of interest in work.*

comparable to coverage for physical illnesses. But employers should beware: mental-health costs are the fastest rising of all health-care costs. In 1989, mental-health and substance-abuse costs rose an average 18 percent nationwide, following a 27 percent increase the year before, according to Foster Higgins, a benefits consulting firm.

According to a 1991 Northwestern Mutual Life Survey, one in three Americans thought about quitting work because of stress.

A survey by Blue Cross/Blue Shield found that 80 percent of workers at all levels complained that job stress contributed to anxiety, depression, poor self-image, colds, asthma, and chest pains.

Stress. Invisible yet dominating, affecting nearly one-third of all employees, excessive stress is often the straw that breaks the camel's back. It compels people to smoke, drink, take drugs, and overeat, and it can induce a host of physical ailments—back problems, skin disorders, respiratory infections, and circulation problems. Stress is known to lower resistance to illness and weaken the immune system. Recent studies show that mental stress raises blood pressure, squeezing the coronary arteries and making them spasm and raise the level of dangerous chemicals in the blood. Over time, chronic stress weakens both coronary arteries and the heart muscle.

Stress is as individual as our fingerprints. For some, it is a result of constant minor hassles—days that begin with spilled coffee, march through traffic jams and arguments with coworkers, and fizzle to an end with evenings of paying bills. Other people can ignore the little things but are incapacitated by the major traumas like the breakup of a relationship or a chronic, recurring injury.

Stress is hard to recognize, yet many of us have a special symptom—headaches, stomach cramps, or simple anxiety—that tries to tell us that we had better slow down. Some people disguise stress with hard work and productivity. However, if you scratch the surface of these people, you see clearly that their productivity may be more frantic than efficient, their drive more toward a heart attack or depression than a promotion.

Some doctors believe that stress can trigger undetected or silent mini-heart attacks—spasms in the arteries that reduce the oxygen to the heart and thus weaken it. Studies have shown that people who ignore the toll of stress, such as heart-attack victims who continue to lead stressful lives, are two or three times more likely to suffer repeat attacks than survivors who learn to lower their stress.

On their own, each of these risk factors can trigger a serious illness, accelerate the course of a disease, or even cause disease. But lump these activities together in one employee and you are looking at a major health problem. Despite the obvious danger of poor health, many companies do not discourage dangerous lifestyle risks, continuing to invest only in costly after-the-fact treatments. Over 90 percent of most companies' health budgets are aimed at treatment, leaving minuscule amounts for prevention and wellness programs. Until companies reverse this spending pattern and begin applying resources to employees' total health to head off risks rather than applying a tourniquet to their illnesses, the cost of keeping employees healthy will continue to surge.

The remainder of this chapter is about building a healthy work force. The ideal healthy worker is an employer's dream: never late, never sick, and always positive and productive. While the model person may never exist, managers can take decisive steps toward approaching this ideal. Building a healthier work force requires three levels of activity:

- striving for health and well-being
- building a hardy work force
- creating a wellness culture

To be worthy of management responsibility today, a man must have an insight into the human heart. Unless he has an awareness of human problems, a sensitivity toward the hopes and aspirations of those whom he supervises, and a capacity for analysis of the emotional forces that motivate their conduct, the projects entrusted to him will not get ahead, no matter how often wages are raised.

CLARENCE RANDALL
former Chairman,
Inland Steel

INSIDE OUT

How Healthy Are You?

To be a healthy manager—one who inspires others to stay healthy —you have to first examine your own attitudes and lifestyle. This self-examination entails describing what you believe about your own health by exploring your mind and body, your strengths and weaknesses, your health history, and your future health.

Oscar Wilde once claimed, "Only the shallow know themselves." As much as we think we know ourselves, that knowledge is probably superficial, because we tend to bury or ignore sensitive information about our mental history and physical health. These questions will help you uncover your hidden attitudes and find your strengths and weaknesses. Use this scale to answer them:

| 1 Never | 3 Sometimes | 5 Always |
| 2 Seldom | 4 Often | |

1. Do you often wake up feeling tired and listless?

2. Do you often feel depressed, sad, and disinterested at work?

3. Do you get angry or lose your temper easily?

4. Do you suffer from chronic minor physical ailments such as headaches, backaches, muscle fatigue, colds, or stomachaches?

5. Have your friends or family expressed concern or warned you about drinking too much?

6. Do you set rules for yourself about smoking, drinking, or drug habits?

7. Are you concerned about being overweight?

8. Do you avoid vigorous exercise, such as jogging, swimming, or aerobic dancing, on a regular basis (at least three times each week, at least twenty minutes per day)?

9. Do you find it difficult to laugh at your own mistakes?

10. Do you tend to ignore your blood pressure?

11. Do you find you don't have time to take regular vacations or time off?

12. When upset, do you keep your feelings hidden?

13. Do you usually drive over the speed limit?

14. Is your diet lacking in high-fiber foods, such as whole-grain bread, cereal, fresh fruits, or vegetables?

15. Do you usually prefer food high in cholesterol or fat, such as marbled meat, cheese, fried foods, or eggs?

16. Do you take medications or drugs to change your mood?

17. When things go wrong, do you look to others as the cause?

18. Do you forget to wear seat belts when driving?

19. Are your close relationships a regular source of dissatisfaction, frustration, or anger?

20. Are you uncomfortable asking friends for help when you have personal problems?

What Your Answers Mean

If you score between 80 and 100, you are headed for a major health crisis, if you are not there already. Your life is filled with stress, and your daily habits are seriously undermining your health. If you score between 40 and 80, you fall into the medium-risk category, suggesting that you have certain habits that are hazardous but also possess a degree of control and moderation in your habits and are capable of reducing your health risks. A score between 20 and 40 indicates you are in the low-risk category—your good health and sound habits ward off illness and make you energetic and productive.

Two obstacles stand between you and a full awareness of your health: ignorance and denial. Step one is to educate yourself about your personal health risks by asking yourself questions about your family history, lifestyle, relationships, and general attitudes. While you probably know relatives' physical health—such as who has cancer, who has high blood pressure, and which side of the family is known for strokes—the age when these illnesses appeared is also important. Has anyone in your family had a heart attack or stroke before age fifty? If so, you are at risk. Also, explore family members' mental health. Often, their mental capacities and emotional difficulties trickle down to you. Is there a history of depression or alcoholism on your side of the family?

Step two is to be painfully honest about your own health and lifestyle and your willingness to change. Keep track of what you *do,* not what you *say* you are going to do, and explore your attitudes about yourself and others. How do you handle personal and external pressures? Are you aware of your personal symptoms of stress? Do you often sabotage close relationships? Are you sacrificing your health for your career? Here are some ideas to help you retool your attitudes and lifestyle.

Strive for Health and Well-Being

Modern researchers are expanding our definition of fitness, creating new models for what is considered a healthy, successful adult in the 1990s. The seemingly simplistic idea that physical and mental health are inextricably interwoven has taken on a new and deeper meaning as we learn more about human development. This new model focuses on continual growth and challenge, not stagnation and security; on hardiness and mental

"The more I look, the more I'm convinced that emotions are running the show," declares a National Institute of Mental Health neuro-pharmacologist investigating connections between emotions, brain chemistry, the immune system, and people's susceptibility to cancer, infection, and immunological disease.

well-being, not illness and disease; on values and character, not simply intellectual achievement; on mutually beneficial relationships, not just winners and losers; and on balancing and integrating personal and professional success.

Successful adults take active responsibility for all aspects of their well-being, establish balance between their work and home life, and constantly seek to improve and grow. Steve Covey, author of the best-selling *Seven Habits of Highly Effective People*, defines the healthy person as someone who applies a principle-centered, character-based approach to personal and interpersonal effectiveness. Put another way, healthy people focus on what they want to be (their character); on what they want to do (their contributions and achievements); and on what they believe (the values and principles that are the foundation of their being and actions).

Striving for health and well-being requires focusing on four areas of your life—a hardy lifestyle, an inner sense of control, healthy connections, and personal success.

Hardy lifestyle. A hardy lifestyle is a lifelong commitment to sound physical health. This commitment means regular, active exercise, not just seasonal activities; a steady diet that avoids large amounts of fat, sugar, and salt; regular checkups and monitoring of cholesterol, blood pressure, and weight; not smoking, or abusing alcohol or drugs; and being ever-vigilant about stress and all its symptomatic ills. Incorporating each of these prescriptions into one's daily lifestyle will provide the sustenance for pursuing total well-being.

Inner sense of control. In striving for health, people who possess a sense of control over their lives distinguish events they control from those they have little say in. Confident and capable, they are realistic about what they can achieve and where they may fall short. They know their weaknesses yet take responsibility for what they commit to. Although quite capable of making life decisions, they don't get caught up trying to change those who are resistant or uncompromising.

Maintaining a consistent posture is also a high priority, a consistency between who they are and what they say and do. Bolstered by a healthy sense of realism and practicality, people

Dr. Dean Ornish, a researcher and heart specialist at the University of California, San Francisco, has successfully treated heart-disease patients and lowered their percentage of clogged arteries by altering diets, lifestyles, and mental outlook. His recommendations include following a virtually vegetarian diet (except for egg whites, nonfat milk, and yogurt); limiting fat intake to 10 percent of total calories and cholesterol to five milligrams a day; eliminating caffeine and limiting alcohol to two ounces a day; practicing daily meditation, stretching exercises, and relaxation activities; and undergoing moderate exercise, such as walking, for thirty minutes three times a week.

with inner control take deliberate steps to ensure that their word matters, both to themselves and to others. While such people have strong relationships with others, they are masters of their own fate, blaming only themselves when things go wrong or illness strikes.

Healthy connections. Good health cannot survive in a vacuum; essential to an individual's well-being are mature, affirming relationships and strong commitments to family, friends, and work colleagues. Collaborative connections are nurturing, sustaining ties to other people that reaffirm such healthy values as harmony, decency, and mutual respect. Healthy connections include the ability to feel empathy with and appreciation of other people; valuing a relationship more than ego; and building win/win agreements, not competitive contests. In short, good health emanates from the intimate bonds a person forms.

The value of this bond has even been documented by health researchers, who have found that socially isolated individuals tend to be less healthy than people who have positive interpersonal connections. A study of 4,775 adults in California between thirty and sixty-five years old found that people with the weakest social ties (measured by marital status, contact with family and friends, and group affiliations) had a significantly higher death rate than those with strong personal connections. In fact, health experts have concluded that weak personal connections can be as hazardous to a person's health as is smoking.

Personal success. Health and well-being also derive from a much broader understanding of personal success: integrating career ambition into one's total personal landscape of success and achieving happiness on all fronts. Success at work is just one part of a larger scheme, a drive for meaning and fulfillment from all directions—family, job, community, friends, and spiritual sources. To achieve personal success, healthy people imbue their lives with humor, interject balance into personal and professional interests, and take time for their families as well as for themselves. Psychoanalyst Douglas LaBier describes them thus: "These new adults move away from the exclusive concern for position, power and possession toward a greater purpose, meaning and connection with others."

Medical evidence now indicates that people who feel alone in the world and are uninvolved with other people and their communities have a high risk of illness, including heart disease. People who are socially isolated are four times more likely to die from a second heart attack than people not isolated and not suffering from stress.

A national poll and census of more than eight thousand employees of the 3M Company found that those who rated themselves healthy— nonsmokers who exercise regularly and maintain normal weight—had a much more positive attitude toward work than less healthy employees. Morale was higher and personal job satisfaction greater. The report concluded that healthy employees equal happy employees, which equal better employees.

Attend to Your Vulnerabilities

You know your soft spots: eating that extra dessert, drinking a third beer before driving home, working ten days straight, ignoring the gym, or berating yourself with negative thoughts. Few people can attend to all these trouble spots at once. So the best way to bring them under control is to prioritize them, determining which give you the most trouble. Your emotional health sets the tempo and tenor for your physical health; thus, by gauging your natural weaknesses or traps, you strengthen your emotional muscles.

A good place to start is to figure out when or under what circumstances you begin to succumb to unhealthy habits. Stress is a good thing if it stretches us to new heights of competence and perspective, but it can stretch you so much that you snap. Like rubber bands, people are at their optimum strength when stretched just the right amount. Unfortunately, many of us push ourselves too far, and the rubber band weakens and breaks. So the critical question for each person is just how much stress or stretching is optimal.

Most people are sensitive to their stress thresholds, which often surface in such physical complaints as headaches, back pain, insomnia, loss of appetite, and eating binges. Stress can quickly spread into emotional areas like worrying, irritability, nervousness, or panic, with its sufferers growing despondent, dull, disinterested, and preoccupied.

Learn to identify stressful and potentially stressful situations and to handle and defuse them by anticipating and planning for stress. To manage stress, you need to know:

1. how to recognize it
2. how to control it
3. how to reduce its negative side effects
4. where to find help when it's overwhelming

Here's how some business people have taken charge of their stress.

▪ Retired CEO John Creedon of Metropolitan Life ran an hour on the treadmill every morning before work.

- Barbara Cherry, an attorney at AT&T, trains six days a week with weights. She varies her workout, each day concentrating on a different part of the body.

- Armand Hammer, the late chairman of Occidental Petroleum who lived well into his nineties, took 15-to-20-minute naps during the day.

- George Owens, managing director of Smith Barney in Boston, estimates that at least half the brokers in his office play squash three times a week—a practice he heartily encourages.

- James Ketelsen, CEO of Tenneco, Inc., runs for half an hour every day. Since double-bypass heart surgery in 1979, he has logged 7,500 miles.

- Winthrop Smith, Jr., a Merrill Lynch executive, is a devoted family man, cycles long distances with his wife on weekends, and volunteers for several philanthropic causes.

- Route drivers for Coca-Cola relieve back stress through a series of exercises they do before starting their shift.

- Milton E. Mohr, chairman of Quotron Systems Inc., escapes to a small room adjoining his office where he skips rope for half an hour every day.

- Executives at Hoover, Berg, Desmond, a Denver architecture firm, ease pressure in the office with a daily quiet hour—sixty minutes of mandatory silence every mid-morning.

It's the frame of mind that's important rather than the stress event itself. What matters is whether the stress leaves a person feeling helpless and out of control.

ALAN BREIER
Clinical Director,
Maryland Psychiatric
Research Center

Refine Your Type-A Qualities

Many managers fall into the category of personality called Type A: they are competitive, aggressive, impatient, critical, and results-oriented. Unfortunately, many people believe that the Type-A mentality is the catalyst for business success, because it appears to be effective and necessary for winning. However, researchers reexamining this classic personality have discovered that Type-A behavior is often confused with healthy energy and enthusiasm and that its frequent side effects, such as burnout and chaos, are usually overlooked.

Are You a Healthy Thinker?

Psychology teaches us that stress, depression, and anxiety frequently arise from misperceptions about our own abilities and the expectations of others. We create the source of our mental anguish by misconstruing people and events. Cognitive therapists call these thinking errors, and for some people they create personal problems and lead to intensive counseling. Even the healthiest among us possess some of these so-called mental tics that distort events and complicate how well we work with others. Do you recognize any of your mental tics here?

- *Overgeneralizing*—interpreting one negative reaction or failure as a regular pattern.
- *Obsessive thinking*—selecting one event or detail, dwelling on it, and amplifying it out of proportion.
- *Disqualifying the positive*—rejecting positive reactions and experiences, insisting they are isolated and don't count.
- *Jumping to conclusions*—forming negative interpretations with only a few facts or snap judgments about others' opinions.
- *Magnifying* or *minimizing*—exaggerating the importance or belittling the significance of problems or mistakes.
- *Emotional misperceptions*—assuming that negative emotional reactions accurately reflect the way things are.
- *Self-commands*—using thoughts of "shoulds" and "should nots" for personal motivation, as if a universal code of acceptable behavior existed.
- *Labeling*—ascribing to oneself broad labels from a single event or one person's opinion; for instance, interpreting a mistake into the label of being a loser.
- *Personalizing*—assuming inappropriate personal blame for situations or events.

The best way to identify thinking errors is by examining how you think and react in a time of stress. When a crisis or difficult situation arises, we assume our emotions, such as resentment, guilt, sadness, or jealousy, are the direct consequences of the crisis. What we fail to realize is that our thoughts—our interpretations of people and events—are what determine whether the crisis is upsetting or not. Try to pinpoint those thoughts about yourself and the people involved and break that automatic connection. It is likely one of these thinking errors is the culprit.

The Type-A personality becomes particularly unhealthy when it is coupled with negative emotions, such as anger (latent or overt), hostility, cynicism, and distrust. At their worst, negative emotions can predispose a person to heart disease. Says Redford Williams, a Duke University psychiatrist, "Of all the aspects originally described as making up the global Type-A pattern, only those related to hostility and anger are really coronary-prone." A hostile, cynical man (researchers consider these qualities to be more typical of males than females) is five times more likely to die before age fifty than one with a "trusting heart."

Four out of five human-resource executives report that at least half of employees' stress-related problems go undetected by coworkers.

Type-A behavior is not only potentially destructive but also contagious, wielding strong influences on the emotions of the work force. These personalities create an environment that forces coworkers to respond to their demands and false urgency, and thus they promote the same unhealthy characteristics in others: frenetic work pace, irrational expectations, mistrust, difficult deadlines, a low tolerance for mistakes, and a disregard for other people.

Type-A behavior can be all-consuming, but experts say that its unhealthy elements can be filtered out, specifically impatience and hostility. Psychologists have found that resentment and the obsession with time can be broken like a bad habit. They counsel people to reshape their behavior through exercise, not wearing a watch for a day, and eating more slowly, while they explore the real source of their anger and cynicism. Meyer Friedman, M.D., of the San Francisco Recurrent Coronary Prevention Project, offers Type-A patients these suggestions for controlling negative behavior:

- Announce to a close friend or spouse the intention to eliminate hostile attitudes.

- In a competitive or sporting situation, consciously play to lose some of the time.

- Smile more often and laugh at yourself.

- Relinquish unrealistic, perfectionist ideals.

- Give up feeling responsible for other people's actions.

- Keep a log of what makes you angry, and look for habits to break.

Not all managers have Type-A personalities. Dr. Manfred Kets deFries, professor at INSEAD, the European Institute of Business Administration in France, who studies unhealthy companies, offers this typology of related malignant behaviors:

- 💼 *Aggressive.* The aggressive person sees people as mistrustful, which justifies his or her aggressive, hostile stance. This manager is impulsive, dominant, and unpredictable and uses the bottom line to explain his or her behavior.

- 💼 *Paranoid.* Suspicious and concerned with others' hidden motives and agendas, this manager is guarded, deceptive, and secretive.

- 💼 *Histrionic.* Reactive, excitable, and easily distracted, this manager tends to steal the show and to devour people with tantrums and angry outbursts.

- 💼 *Detached.* Aloof, emotionally cold, and unable to engage in close work relationships, this manager is typically found behind closed doors.

- 💼 *Controlling.* Preoccupied with order, organization, and obedience, this perfectionist and judgmental manager has a strong need to control and avoid being controlled by others.

Regardless of the diagnosis, a malignant manager can spread illness and burnout in the office by venting his or her emotional troubles and unreasonable demands. In this atmosphere, employees feel no sense of cohesion or loyalty; self-confidence is low and their roles are conflicting; and there is typically little healthy supervision.

Warns professor Robert Golembiewski of the University of Georgia, employees tend to burn out in groups, generally under the same malignant manager, and it is not unusual for an entire group to suffer the same symptoms—headaches, heavy drinking after work, or chronic insomnia.

 ### *What the Manager Can Do*

Building a hardy work force requires avoiding actions that undermine people's health while promoting activities and attitudes that enhance it. A manager not only leads by example, offering a personal model of hardiness and well-being, but also by tending to problem employees and even confronting the most troublesome ones. This section contains ideas and suggestions for managing and boosting the level of health in your work group.

The state of your own health will necessarily determine how well you manage employees' health. Your ability to help others directly relates to your own self-awareness and your perception—can you recognize an employee with problems or do your personal preoccupations block your vision? Healthy managers readily recognize signals and symptoms in others, then decipher their meaning and personal impact. They apply sensitivity and compassion to understand the people they work with. These questions will help you uncover the emotions that affect how you deal with employees' personal problems. Use this scale to answer them:

For a long time, business took the attitude that health was a private matter. As long as people showed up at the right time for the right number of hours, the company had no interest in how they took care of themselves. But today when medical costs are so high, the health of employees becomes a bottom-line issue.

ANGELICA CANTLON
Director, Human
Resources, Avon

1 Never	3 Sometimes	5 Always
2 Seldom	4 Often	

1. Do you distance yourself from employees who have personal problems?

2. Do you encourage alcohol consumption at work by drinking at lunch, going for a drink with employees after work, or insisting office social events include alcohol?

3. Do you become overly resentful of nonproductive employees?

4. Do you believe that employees who seek mental-health counseling are exhibiting a character flaw?

5. Do you believe personal matters have no place in an office?

6. Do you believe that added stress sparks motivation?

7. Does your need to be liked make it difficult for you to confront employees who perform poorly?

8. Do you avoid confrontations or arguments?

9. Do you feel inadequate or unprepared when counseling a friend with a personal problem?

10. Are you uncomfortable talking about personal problems with friends and family?

11. Would you refuse to recommend a depressed employee for a promotion?

12. Do you think about transferring or firing someone who has personal problems?

13. Do you avoid job applicants with physical disabilities?

What Your Answers Mean

If you score between 50 and 65, you are wrestling with personal conflicts and areas of sensitivity that obscure your judgment about employees and interfere with your ability to manage them properly. If you score between 35 and 50, you can be objective much of the time but continue to harbor some personal biases that diminish your effectiveness. If you score between 12 and 35, you have managed to resolve most of your own personal conflicts and can compassionately help employees deal with their problems.

After counseling hundreds of managers, I have learned that many avoid dealing with unhealthy employees. Mostly, they are afraid of opening up a Pandora's box of problems, and they lack the insights and skills to deal with touchy, personal issues. Some managers skillfully rationalize problems away or find simpler ways of dealing with problem people—denial, transfers, terminations, or creating scapegoats. Once they have dismissed the problem, they convince themselves that their actions were right. Yet the problems do not go away, because they are often lodged as much in the avoiding manager as in the troubled employee.

Few of us enjoy dealing with others' personal problems; to broach them means opening yourself up to a closer, more intimate relationship. Wishing you could sidestep a problem is natural, but at work it is unrealistic. A manager cannot afford to avoid sticky personal problems or duck possible confrontations. You have to replace the instinct to ignore with the courage to confront.

Some managers believe strongly that personal problems should be kept out of the office and forget that people's problems cannot be isolated from their workday. Still others simply would rather sweep the problems under the rug because of their own need to be liked or to be seen as the all-knowing manager without personnel problems.

Another reason for avoidance may be an unpleasant personal

experience: a painful bruise or frightening experience that makes a manager skirt anything close to the subject. For instance, people who always had to be perfect as children are often the adults who are unable to accept anything but perfection from themselves and their coworkers. What happens when one of their employees suffers a depression? Imagine the manager who enjoys a weekend cocaine habit having to confront an employee with a similar problem. The manager's own denial may impede his or her management responsibilities.

The coping skills you have learned from solving your own personal problems will serve you well with employees. The first challenge is bringing to light any personal experiences that you have buried and forgotten. Furthermore, the fact that you have never experienced your employees' problems does not mean you cannot help them. While no one can fabricate experiences, you can educate yourself. Relatively few people, for example, have had direct experience with AIDS, but you can overcome your ignorance with reading and listening. Third, you need to understand a person's difficulties in the clearest light possible, totally separate from yourself. Guard against thinking that an employee's problem is somehow a reflection on you. Do not let your emotions color your response to your employees.

Finally, managers can easily lose perspective about the effects they have on employees' health. One way to break down these blinders is by surveying your employees, asking them to evaluate the healthiness of the office environment. Done anonymously, this survey offers a very useful outlet for employees who may feel pressured and unable to openly express their health concerns.

Citibank FSB in Illinois has formalized this process through its innovative Citibuilders program, which finds and recognizes healthy managers through an annual People Survey completed by the employees. The survey measures how effectively managers reward performance, manage change, and open up communication, and it enables the company to track healthy managers throughout the organization.

Present a Healthy Model

Although you may not be totally aware of it, employees watch how you take care of yourself, how you react to pressure from your boss, whether your actions match your words, and how you

A growing number of executives see the link between good mental health and high morale. Because of these changing times, we have culture clashes, poor morale, stress and more. The only way to turn things around is good personal relationships.

WALTER WRISTON
retired Chairman and
CEO, Citicorp

We need to get our managers to identify stress. But if I say to my manager, "Your secretary is under stress," he is going to look at me and say, "You're crazy, why should she be under stress? I give her a paper. She types it. It goes away." To a large extent, we have to educate people that stress doesn't have to do with my perception of how hard that job is, but with the perception of the person who is in it.

Human-resource manager

Are You a Narcissistic Manager?

According to Dr. Manfred Kets deFries, the narcissistic boss is a common and dangerous person—dangerous to the health of everyone around him or her. This person churns up stress, contention, and deep dissatisfaction. You may be sensing these qualities among your employees and not know why. If so, look hard at yourself.

- Do your priorities and goals always come before everyone else's?
- Do you feel you have special talents that need to be recognized and appreciated?
- Do you convey a sense of entitlement to exceptional treatment and deference?
- Are you ultrasensitive about employees' criticizing your ideas?
- Do you value employees according to what they can do for you?
- Do you avoid sincere personal interaction and keep people at a distance?
- Do you insist that your employees always agree with you?
- Do you always compete and need to win?
- Have people described you as haughty or arrogant?
- Do you turn the charm on and off depending on what you want?

---

manage your home life. Whether you like it or not, you are a role model, and your health and well-being can inspire or infect others. Here are ways to become a healthy role model:

Talk informally to employees about the value of their physical and mental health. Help them arrange a schedule that enables them to exercise. Discuss stress and how it can affect their outlook and productivity. Let them know what you do to stay in shape and reduce stress.

Avoid stigmatizing unhealthy employees. Firing, demoting, or ignoring employees who are ill does not improve your office health. It makes other employees angry with the way their coworkers are treated and afraid of what might happen should they get sick. When employees are ill, encourage them to stay home and take care of themselves. You might even send a card or flowers. If employees are out for a long time, call them regularly to keep them current on office events and to let them know they are still valued. However, remember to monitor closely those employees who abuse your good will.

Recognize the limits to your role. Sometimes being a health fanatic can alienate people, especially those who have difficulty staying healthy, such as the overweight, the sedentary, or relapsed smokers. Be sensitive to their personal situations, such as that of the obese employee who is trying to lose weight.

Be supportive of personal problems, but beware of slipping into the counselor role. Many managers are ill-equipped to be mental-health counselors. Learn to recognize when your title has shifted from manager to counselor so you can steer an employee to professional help.

Recruit other employees as health leaders and role models. At L.L. Bean, a switchboard operator teaches dance exercise, a marketing executive offers a runners' clinic, and a product manager leads a stop-smoking clinic. Enlisting the help of coworkers can broaden your influence and reduce the need for outside consultants.

William Kizer, chief executive at Central States Insurance Company, is one such role model for his people. He explains, "I am not a health nut and I am not an eccentric, and I don't practice all the rules I should, but when it comes to certain things, I'm careful. I once smoked, and I realized that was risky, so I quit. I learned there are ways to manage stress, and I started to listen to my own body. For whatever reason, I became interested in my own well-being, so I thought, if it's good for me, it might be good for other people, too."

Now Central States rarely serves alcohol at business lunches or company dinners and prominently displays soft drinks and fruit juices. "It's all part of creating a healthful environment," says Kizer. "People start to feel good about themselves, and the impact on morale becomes obvious."

With the workplace pool of potential employees shrinking, it makes real clear sense to try to rehabilitate employees rather than terminate them.

JACK ROSE
Lockheed Corp.

Central States Health & Life Company educated its employees by sponsoring a play dramatizing a manager's substance abuse and rehabilitation. This drama with a purpose was written and performed by employees, with the help of alcoholism professionals who educated them on chemical dependency. The play ran for four performances and triggered a spate of phone inquiries to a health counselor in the company.

Tend to Troubled Employees

Managing employees who go through serious health traumas is one of the most troublesome managerial jobs. A 1990 New York Business Group on Health survey of corporate medical and human-resource experts discovered that 32 percent of employees turn to their supervisors for help. From the addicted alcoholic to the neurotic hypochondriac, managers must spot and confront such employees, then steer them into treatment so they can resume work. Perhaps the most disturbing and costly problems are substance abuse, depression, and violence.

The Addicted Employee

Drug and alcohol abuse are the hidden villains in the workplace. Consider these statistics:

- A survey of small and large employers found between 6 and 15 percent of their employees have an alcohol or drug problem.
- A national cocaine hotline reported that 75 percent of callers used drugs on the job, 44 percent sold drugs to coworkers, and 18 percent stole money from coworkers to buy drugs.
- A study for the Office of Technology Assessment reports that alcoholism may be responsible for up to 15 percent of the nation's health-care costs.

The problem is that managers refuse to recognize substance abuse. A Mercer, Meidinger, Hansen survey of chief executives and human-resource experts from Fortune 1,000 firms reports that 88 percent said substance abuse was a "very significant problem" and likely to get worse, yet only 22 percent admitted it was a significant problem in their own company.

Detecting the signs of substance abuse is like reading Braille —the signs look random and meaningless at first until you learn the pattern. Telltale signs include erratic behavior; frequent, unexplained absences from work; changes in work habits; a spike in job-related accidents; or a drop in performance. Managers may assume that a certain age, ethnic, or economic group is more prone to abuse, but in truth, substance abuse crosses all lines. At times the victim will not be an employee but the relative of one. An employee living with a substance abuser suffers, too, and this spills over into work life. Here is what some companies are doing to tackle the problem.

Johnson & Johnson retired CEO James Burke established the long-term goal of eliminating substance abuse from its corporate culture. His arsenal included mandatory employee education, ongoing manager training, and a strong family outreach effort.

The Boston utility company Commonwealth Edison tests job applicants for drug use and give employees drug education, treatment, and rehabilitation. It aids anyone who asks for help but will fire an employee caught with drugs at work. Since the program began in 1982, absenteeism has dropped 25 percent, as has the number of job accidents.

The Association of Flight Attendants, comprised of 21,000 members from eleven airlines, uses peer review to spot and eradicate substance abuse. It has trained more than 100 flight attendants to recognize signs of drug and alcohol abuse among colleagues and to refer them for professional help.

The workplace is an easier place to deal with drugs than anyplace else. You have more control and you can build a supportive environment, which is sometimes difficult to do in the community.

JAMES BURKE
retired Chairman,
Johnson & Johnson

The Depressed Employee

During any six-month period, 10 million people, mostly between the ages of twenty-five and forty-four, are severely depressed. Spread out among the working population, this figure amounts to one in every twenty employees at your work site. Exacerbating the problem is that most depressed people—two-thirds—do not receive appropriate professional care.

Like alcoholism, depression is easily ignored and easily masked. Instead of exhibiting raw depression, people express it in emotional and physical symptoms, often behind closed doors. These include disinterest, boredom, indecisiveness, irritability, listlessness, fatigue, and an assortment of physical ailments, from nonspecific aches and pains to very real illnesses such as colitis.

Researchers say depression costs business more than $27 billion each year and is responsible for more days in bed and more physical pain than hypertension, diabetes, and back and gastrointestinal problems, according to a recent study by the Rand Corporation. The good news is that depression can be treated: up to 80 percent of even the most serious forms respond to the right combination of drugs and psychotherapy, says Isabelle Davidoff, spokesperson for D/ART, the public outreach effort of the National Institute on Mental Health.

The Violent Employee

Occasionally, an employee's personal problems explode. Every year there are about 1,600 homicides in the workplace, and this number is creeping upward. In the past decade, incidents of job-site murder have tripled.

According to James Fox, professor of criminal justice and co-author of *Mass Murder: America's Growing Menace,* the potentially violent employee stands out: "He is chronically disgruntled, seen as a troublemaker. He is quick to perceive unfairness, injustice or malice in others. When he does open up to someone, it's with a litany of gripes extending back months or a year. Even when people go out of their way to smooth things over, he sees that as some conspiratorial effort to keep him from getting what he deserves. And he doesn't take responsibility for his problems—it's always someone else's fault." In all three cases above, here is what you need to do:

> *Know the signs of mental-health and substance-abuse problems and how they affect job performance.* Pay attention to changes in employee personality, work habits, and work relationships. Treat these problems as you would any other business problem: gather the facts and educate yourself.

> *Start documenting job performance and attendance patterns as soon as you suspect something.* Trust your instincts. Many employees won't seek help without the prodding and encouragement of their supervisor. Inform employees about the problem, but do not try to diagnose, moralize, or counsel.

> *Don't get pulled into the problem.* Be prepared for denial, resistance, and even the threat of lawsuits. Be aware of your own anger and guilt. Focus on the job performance, not the personality. The best approach is to be strong and caring.

> *Don't wait for a crisis.* Untreated problems can lead to excessive absences, unnecessary accidents, deteriorating morale, and even litigation.

I know that good health is high on everyone's list of personal priorities. It is also a business priority because a healthy, growing and competitive enterprise depends on the health, vitality and energy of individuals.

ROBERT ALLEN
President and CEO, AT&T

Direct the employee to professional help. An employee-assistance program is most preferable. If necessary, threaten to fire a person who refuses to get help.

Manage the Troublesome People

Nothing is worse than the employee who actively sabotages your agenda and the environment of your department. Such people are most difficult to manage and require insight into yourself, their personalities, and the stressful effects on everyone else who comes in contact with them. Psychologist and author of *Coping with Difficult People* Robert M. Bramson offers these descriptions of difficult people and suggestions for managers who must cope with them.

The Sherman Tank. This person confronts others, using his or her physical presence to intimidate others. Exceedingly aggressive, such people never stop fighting or arguing and always need to prove themselves right. They readily roll over other people's self-esteem. Stand up to such people with statements like, "I disagree with you" or "You interrupted me." Do not fight with them; simply assert yourself.

The Sniper. This employee takes every opportunity to criticize you or coworkers, but he or she often does it surreptitiously or couches the barbs in jokes. Speak to such employees alone and confront their implied criticism. Tell them their jokes sound like thinly veiled digs and ask them what the real problem is.

The Exploder. This person swings wildly between calm moods and temperamental outbursts of insults and cutting remarks. His goal is to silence others and make them passive. These outbreaks are unpredictable and irrational, so others tend to treat the exploder gingerly, never knowing what will set him or her off. Do not react to an exploder's temper—neither shrink from it nor explode in response. Inform such employees that you will not listen to their tirades. Speak to them alone and ask the reason for the outburst, then work together to solve it.

The Complainer. This person whines constantly and feels powerless in the world. Be an active listener, paraphrasing his or her complaints and asking for suggestions on how to improve things.

Hostility is extremely destructive. I'd rather have ten people in the organization with heart disease than one person who is healthy but covertly hostile. Hostile people can tear your strategy to shreds.

JAMES RENIER
Chairman and CEO,
Honeywell, Inc.

Give such people specific tasks that help put their complaints in perspective, such as writing them out for a department discussion. Try to involve them in solving problems and respectfully question whether their complaints are legitimate.

The Negativist. This person is never happy and says no to everything. Such people want everyone to be as miserable as they are. Do not argue with them or allow yourself to be dragged into their negative mentality. Keep your statements and outlook positive. Discuss the consequences of all the negatives so such a person sees they aren't so horrible. Be decisive, thus showing the negativist that his or her nay-saying is inconsequential.

The Clam. This person is silent and unresponsive to requests for ideas, suggestions, or solutions. Begin discussions yourself, then leave large, silent gaps in your talk, encouraging the person to respond. Do not fill silence gaps—let them hang there until the person says something. Also, inform such people that their inability to communicate is creating serious problems.

The Bulldozer. Bulldozers overwhelm with facts and figures, trying to establish themselves as resident experts. They always have all the right answers and have little regard for others' knowledge. Paraphrase and simplify what such people say, letting them know that you completely understand their point. If you disagree, feign ignorance and ask for more information. As bulldozers spin out their ideas, their expertise will thin out.

Corporate Policies and Strategies

Johnson & Johnson

No company has woven the principles of health into its corporate culture like the giant personal products firm Johnson & Johnson. Through company-wide health assessments, education programs, and organizational changes, Johnson & Johnson offers a model for the rest of the country.

This New Brunswick, New Jersey firm has spent the last eleven years promoting healthful living to all its 35,000 U.S. employees through a program called Live for Life. The company estimates that this educational effort has helped it save $378 per employee per year by lowering absenteeism and slowing the rise in the company's health-care expenses. In 1989 it spent $93.5 million on medical costs, a rise of only 10 percent from 1988.

As Johnson & Johnson discovered, people are bombarded daily with news, information, and advice about health, which has become an American industry spewing out an array of sometimes conflicting facts about nutrition, fitness, medical breakthroughs, diseases, and treatments. This barrage of information creates an opportunity for employers, who can do employees a great service by distilling all this advice—guiding them toward information relevant to their lives and showing them how to integrate healthy habits into their jobs.

Employers, whether a large manufacturer or a small, family-owned retailer, are ideally suited to promote wellness. Because so many employees congregate in one place, companies can offer the right combination of practical incentives and advice to help people change their unhealthy habits. Corporate involvement helps to create wise health-care consumers and identifies the risks and remedies crucial for maintaining a healthy work force.

What a company endorses and what it ignores speaks volumes about the value it puts on health. In a healthy company, an active wellness culture is replete with activities and policies designed to improve the health of employees and reduce health costs. It spans seemingly inconsequential things like office decor that minimizes stress and healthy snack-food offerings to major programs such as preventative health benefits, exercise programs, and seminars. Healthy companies build a stronger work force and create an environment where people feel valued and important.

We believe that worksite wellness is going to be the hallmark of the 21st century corporation. It's one way to strengthen the fibers of a corporation like GM. We figure that for every $1 we've spent on treatment, $3 are returned in increased productivity over a three-year period. And, of course, there are dramatic reductions in time lost and on-the-job accidents.

ROGER SMITH
retired Chairman and
CEO, General Motors

Create a Wellness Culture

For your company to establish a healthy workplace, the first step is to tailor your wellness culture to the needs of your employees. A nationwide survey of employers identified these as the most pressing health concerns: prevention of chronic diseases, reducing alcohol and substance abuse, improving mental health, and controlling HIV infection and AIDS. Expect your program to take some combination of time, money, and resources, while remembering that leadership at all levels is most important. Here is some advice on how to get started:

An estimated 20 million American jobs are held by people who use illicit drugs like marijuana, amphetamines, cocaine and crack.

The *New York Times*

Form a partnership between the company and employees dedicated to promoting healthy habits and controlling health costs. Talk to employees about their needs and your costs. Ask for their participation and support. Emphasize that each individual is responsible for his or her good health and that the company will do all it can to bolster individual efforts. Indicate that the entire company—from the president to the receptionist—must be involved in the effort.

Set up a company-wide wellness committee with employees of different levels and backgrounds. Conduct interviews or surveys to assess what coworkers want, need, and will accept. Ask them about their primary health worries or about the existing programs they want expanded.

Identify your company's health-risk profile. How many employees smoke, wear seat belts, or do other things that harm or protect their health? Ask employees to complete a confidential health-risk appraisal to identify these risks. Attach costs to each risk factor and determine your total costs of unhealthy workers.

Check your records. Examine aggregate health-insurance claims, absenteeism, and disability absences to substantiate assumptions or proposals about health programs.

Designate company space for health promotion. Use bulletin boards, posters, pamphlets, and other sources of information. Information is readily available from organizations such as the American Cancer Society, American Heart Association, National Alliance for the Mentally Ill, and local hospitals and fitness centers. Announce and communicate the program with great fanfare. Use all kinds of communications, including paycheck memos, buttons, bulletin boards, posters, personnel policies, and newsletter articles.

Target your wellness programs to high-risk problems. Smoking, alcohol abuse, and hypertension are the culprits. Concentrate your resources on the minority of people who are likely to account for the majority of health-care costs. Keep the programs voluntary and the records confidential.

Put someone in charge who is energetic and enthusiastic. Make that person highly visible and clearly important to the company. Keep the program moving by revising and fine-tuning.

Encourage monitoring and screening of health conditions such as high blood pressure, high cholesterol, or cancer. Use preventive checkup procedures and screenings whenever possible. Consider sponsoring an annual health fair at work.

Provide financial incentives to employees who engage in healthy behavior. Consider reducing employee contributions for nonsmokers, seat-belt users, or avid exercisers. Offer health-insurance refunds for making cost-effective purchases; reward employees or departments for preventing workplace injuries. Discuss with your insurance carrier ways employees can reduce their contributions.

> *The health of our company is greatly influenced by the health of our people, and employee health is something we value.*
>
> H. W. BURLINGAME
> Senior Vice-President,
> AT&T

Here is how some companies have put these steps into action.

AT&T offers employees its Total Life Concept (TLC) health program, a comprehensive package of health-risk assessment, fitness classes, and courses for lowering stress, back pain, and cholesterol. Employees report feeling more enthusiastic about work, more pride in their jobs, and less stress. The company estimates the program will save more than $100 million over ten years. It also reports declines of 78 percent in absenteeism, 87 percent in disability absences, and 81 percent in on-the-job accidents.

King Broadcasting in Seattle, after dropping its Blue Cross coverage in favor of self-insurance, shares with its employees the savings that result from keeping health costs down. If the company spends less than it budgeted, the employees receive half the difference.

The First National Bank of Chicago believes that information is the key to managing healthy employees, so the company has developed an integrated health-data management system that keeps figures on health claims, short-term disability, employee-assistance plan use, nursing visits, wellness program participation, and health evaluations.

Quad/Graphics, a closely held printing firm in Wisconsin, opened a clinic to provide medical care to all 5,000 of its employees.

Promote Nonsmoking

While the smoke-free workplace is becoming legally regulated or the accepted standard in many states, some companies still do not aggressively discourage smoking. To do so, companies must apply a variety of tactics, from outright bans to attractive incentives. *Take action.*

- Hire only nonsmokers.
- Offer clinics or seminars conducted by employees or outsiders on how to stop smoking.
- Sponsor competitions or contests for quitters with tangible prizes.
- Offer financial incentives or bonuses to quitters and/or nonsmokers.
- Restrict smoking inside a company to limited areas and/or limited times of the day.
- Remove cigarette vending machines.

Provident Indemnity Insurance Company, a small Pennsylvania firm, instituted an array of nonsmoking practices, beginning with distributing literature about the dangers of smoking, then creating an employee committee to make recommendations on a company smoking policy. The committee suggested smoking be confined to the lunchroom. The American Lung Association presented weekly programs about smoking during working hours and invited spouses of employees. Employees who continued to smoke agreed to pay the extra insurance coverage for themselves and their spouses, about $300 a year. President Joseph Reese says that the program has helped reduce absenteeism and saved the company $15,000 to $20,000 in cafeteria damage and cleaning in the progam's first year.

Encourage Good Nutrition

To encourage good nutrition, employers can promote healthy eating at the work site: the company cafeteria, from vending machines, and around the office. *Take action.*

- Make sure the cafeteria fare includes a salad bar.
- Offer content information about food offered in the cafeteria, including the amount of fat, calories, sodium, and cholesterol.

- Supplement the company coffeepot with decaffeinated coffee and tea, soup, or other caffeine-free drinks.
- If offering breakfast, include fruit, muffins, and bagels.
- Replace vending machines packed with potato chips, candy bars, and sodas with fruit, popcorn, and mineral water.
- Offer nutrition clinics.
- Offer clinics on weight loss or contests among employees for pounds shed.

Here are some steps companies have taken to promote good nutrition.

In its cafeteria, Mattel Company displays information cards that compare foods' calories, sodium, and fat content in order to help employees reduce these in their diet.

Boeing Corporation instituted Rainbow Nutrition, a program to highlight recommended foods—foods that meet the dietary guidelines of the American Heart Association and American Cancer Society.

John Hancock Mutual Life Insurance Company holds an Annual Weight Loss Competition. Its first competition inspired 187 employees to lose nearly seven pounds each.

Workers at a Weyerhaeuser Company plant challenged another plant to a weight-loss competition, dubbed "A Ton of Fat." The winning plant shed 3,000 pounds, with average individual loss of five to eighteen pounds.

Offer Education

Whether healthy or not, all employees need an injection of information and advice to help them lead healthier lifestyles. The substance of this education depends on what employees want and need to know and what kind of expertise a company can marshal. Education can be presented in classes, written material, lectures, weekend retreats, and bulletin-board displays, and topics span the health-care and lifestyle spectrum. *Take action.*

- Offer classes, seminars, or lectures on AIDS, prenatal care, stress management, stroke and heart-attack prevention, cancer prevention and treatment, mental illness, nutrition, and work-site ergonomics.

If my employees are healthier than yours, I'm going to whip you. It's as simple as that.

DICK WARDROP
Director of Health Care Cost Containment, Alcoa

■ Give instruction or counseling in crisis trauma for accident victims, CPR, rape prevention and self-protection, avoiding back injuries, coping with divorce, finding child care, and ways to avoid surgery.

■ Start a health library with printed material, videos, resources for professional information, and access to knowledgeable health experts.

We have conceptualized wellness to the point where it is a way of life. We do not have a wellness budget because it's hard to budget an attitude.

GREG SCHERER
President, Scherer
Brothers Lumber Co.

The following is a sampling of programs being offered by various organizations:

The Franklin Life Insurance Company, Springfield, Illinois, offers employees prenatal education that includes nutrition counseling. After eighteen months, absenteeism among pregnant women has decreased an average 4.5 days.

The M&M Mars Company in Chicago educates employees about breast cancer by distributing literature and giving women free mammograms.

The Teamsters Health and Insurance Fund in Virginia offers health-promotion classes to spouses at the local union hall, because organizers have discovered that husband truck drivers learn about health best from their wives.

The American Federation of Teachers set out to educate members about stress in the classroom by offering workshops, creating a teacher-support network, and inaugurating a stress hotline staffed by volunteer teachers.

Southern New England Telephone's Reach Out for Health program includes individual screening for employees and a choice of courses on nutrition. These include an eight-week class on behavior modification for weight control, a six-week class on nutrition awareness, and short courses entitled Nutrition Potpourri, Pressure Cooker, and Nutrition Nonsense.

Levi Strauss & Company offers both education and support on AIDS. It gives lectures for managers, offers support classes for individuals with AIDS and their families and friends, has a video for home viewing, and publishes information updates in the company newsletter.

Push Exercise and Fitness

One of the lessons of America's fitness craze has been that regular exercise pays for employers as well as for exercisers. Peo-

An Idea a Minute

Here are some brief wellness tips from Timothy E. Glaros, health-promotion specialist at Control Data Corporation:

- *Dialing for Dollars.* Put a wellness hint on the company bulletin board. Randomly call employees and give prizes for the right answer.

- *Staywell Bake-off.* Ask your employees for healthy recipes for a company cookbook. Let the CEO do the tasting and determine the winner.

- *Holiday Weigh-In.* Weigh all your employees right before Thanksgiving and during the first week of January. Award prizes to employees who maintain their weight.

- *House Calls.* Take your doctor's bag and free blood-pressure kit around the office. Surprise your most resistant executives.

- *Congratulations Cards.* Catch someone engaging in wellness. Distribute cards that say "I caught you in the act of doing something healthy."

- *Wellness Grants.* Create a pool of money to be used by employees for office wellness activities.

- *Commuter Classes.* For those employees who leave together, place a health instructor in the commuter bus for the ride home.

- *Quiet Room.* Set aside a meditation and isolation room for employees.

- *Humor Fest.* Reserve a big room for Laurel and Hardy films in the middle of the day.

ple who are fit work better than their couch-potato contemporaries: they are more alert, mentally quicker, more energetic, and more productive. A company that values exercise and gives employees the time and opportunities to work out sends a message to all employees that it believes fitness makes a person a more valuable employee. *Take action.*

- Provide facilities, classes, and blocks of time for regular exercise.

- Help employees monitor their fitness with regular testing and screening.
- Sponsor sporting events and company teams.
- Subsidize membership to health clubs, or set aside a spare room for indoor aerobics and install a shower in employee bathrooms. Arrange for employee group purchases of athletic equipment at discounted prices.
- Institute flextime and rotating duties to enable people to exercise during the workday.

The following are some fitness programs instituted by various companies:

Bonne Bell, the beauty-aids company, goes to extraordinary measures to help its employees exercise seriously. For starters, it offers a fully equipped fitness center with exercise machines, tennis and volleyball courts, a track, and showers. Employees are encouraged to use the center by being offered an extra thirty minutes at lunch if they are exercising and, afterward, being allowed to wear workout clothes around the office. They also can buy running clothes and shoes at discount prices and bicycles at cost for riding to work. Employees who work out at least four days a week for six months are given a $250 bonus.

Goodyear Tire and Rubber Company sponsors walking, exercise, and folk-dancing classes for retirees.

At PepsiCo, employees have access to Nautilus machines, jogging trails, and dance floors. The company also has flextime and free laundry service.

Tenneco monitors employees' fitness performance via a sophisticated computer logging system that measures data about vital health and exercise habits. In return, employees receive feedback on achievements and new goals.

The fitness program at The Prudential Insurance Company of America includes physical exams, laboratory testing, exercise classes, and employee education. Major medical costs among one group of exercisers dropped almost 46 percent.

At McKee Baking Company, Collegedale, Tennessee, a 35,000-square-foot fitness facility is available to all employees and their families. Employees who use it have their life-insurance benefits increased and health-insurance deductibles waived and are eligible for cash bonuses.

The range of fitness programs at Sentry Insurance Company includes exercise classes for retirees, a parent-tot swim program, and prenatal clinics.

Stevens Real Estate in Lawrence, Kansas provides employees with mini-trampolines to use while listening to sales training tapes.

At Schwartz Meat Company in Norman, Oklahoma, employees, spouses, and children can earn up to two weeks of extra salary each year by doing aerobic exercises on their own time.

Townsend Engineering, Des Moines, Iowa, offers its 130 employees full use of the Townsend Recreational Athletic Center (TRAC), a 30,000-square-foot facility that includes health-education and fitness programs as well as recreation. Its health-education programs cover a wide range of subjects, from skin-cancer screening to weight-loss workshops, and its fitness offerings include a fully equipped gym, sports facilities, and complete locker rooms.

Organize an Employee Assistance Plan (EAP)

One step beyond the company wellness program is the employee assistance plan (EAP), an amalgam of mental-health programs coordinated and sponsored by a company. Originally, EAPs were designed as referral and counseling programs for people with drinking problems. Employers quickly discovered, however, that employees had an array of mental-health concerns—anxiety, eating disorders, compulsive gambling, child and sexual abuse, and depression—and developed larger programs to address an entire range of health concerns.

Today, EAPs usually encompass much more than counseling. Experts estimate that there are about 14,000 EAPs in the country and that 70 percent of Fortune 500 companies have EAPs, up from 50 percent ten years ago. For companies with federal contracts the programs are virtually mandatory, because the Drug-Free Workplace Act requires employers to adopt antidrug policies, including rehabilitation.

EAPs come in all shapes and sizes and are designed to handle a broad spectrum of emotional, psychological, and substance-abuse problems. They can be as simple as a referral hotline to outside counselors or as elaborate as on-staff psychologists offering family counseling and financial planning, and some programs include peer counseling—employees helping employees.

Confidentiality and open access are the cornerstones of an effective EAP. The most common route is self-referral. Employees with problems ask for help, hopefully early in the process; ward off more serious problems; and return to work after treatment. Other times, managers identify needy employees, make the referrals, and assist with their rehabilitation. The cost of these programs is usually shared by employee and employer, with the exact proportions determined by the individual offerings.

A manager's responsibility does not end after referral and treatment. He or she has to watch for relapses, which unfortunately are common among substance abusers. Health experts say that at least half the employees referred to treatment slip up at least once. Managers can help head off relapses through active follow-up, reassuring employees that their jobs will not be terminated and then giving them the same responsibilities after treatment as before. "It's one thing to send someone away for the cure and bring them back and forget about them. A good EAP is there long after an employee has left treatment and is struggling with the demon of relapse," declares Gerald Bunn of Owens/Corning Fiberglas Corp. EAP. EAPs are considered ideal mechanisms for establishing drug awareness, educating employees, and providing counseling and rehabilitation.

EAPs can be costly, but a mentally unhealthy employee is even more expensive. Pacific Northwest Bell reports that it costs as much as $40,000 to replace a key employee, while it pays $3,000 to $4,000 to put a worker through its EAP. Illinois Bell's EAP led to 31,806 fewer disability days, 60 percent fewer accidents, and a greater than 50 percent decline in absenteeism. And at McDonnell Douglas, an analysis of 20,000 employee medical claims and absentee records shows that over four years, employees who used the EAP for chemical dependency missed 44 percent fewer workdays, had 81 percent lower attrition, and filed $7,400 less in claims than those who did not use the EAP. The firm expects its EAP to save $15.1 million over four years.

HEALTH IS ALL AROUND YOU

As you have probably discovered, health in the workplace extends far beyond questions about employee sick days and insurance coverage. Health concerns are reflected in every aspect of an employee's working life. Genetics, mental well-being, family history, lifestyles, and personal relationships all contribute to an employee's health and how well he or she performs at work. Physical and mental health cannot be separated; the two are so tightly intertwined that managers must learn new ways of managing the whole person.

There is another element of health, however, that this chapter has not discussed, and that is the effects of environmental stressors that can raise or lower a person's health and productivity. The work site is an especially powerful influence on individuals, and the next chapter focuses on how jobs and the work setting can strengthen or weaken people.

Sick Jobs Sabotage Long-Term Investments

SALLY WORKS FOR A small insurance company as a clerical analyst, sitting at a keyboard, filling out forms, and plugging in numbers. She is responsible for one section of a claim form, which passes through a number of hands before it is completed. In an average day, Sally spends about 5½ hours in front of her video display terminal underneath bright fluorescent lights. Everyone in her department has the same type of work station. She has added a pillow to her chair to adjust the height but it is still not right, and sometimes her wrists and elbows are sore from tendonitis. When her tendonitis flares up, she makes keyboarding errors. On one particularly painful day, she transposed numbers and cost her company $12,000.

Jay is a reservation and sales representative for a national hotel chain. He works at an electronic console, fielding hundreds of telephone inquiries and using a computer to find rate and room information. His supervisor randomly monitors Jay's calls to ensure a uniform description and pitch among all representatives. Knowing he may be monitored and that he should handle at least 100 calls a day, Jay is frequently annoyed and disgusted with management. When he suspects he is being monitored, he gets even by being curt, impatient, and sarcastic

The elements of an office—people, work, and the environment—exist as a system. When one of these factors changes . . . something else must give. In the past, the element which most often has been forced to change has been the people rather than the environment.

CECIL WILLIAMS, et al.
The Negotiable Environment

While management may
increase productivity in the
short run by creating narrow,
specialized jobs designed
around the capacities of the
system, in the long run this
approach can carry considerable costs as decreased
employee satisfaction, resentment, and stress lead to
unacceptable levels of error
rates, absenteeism, turnover
and ultimately, reduced
productivity.

ALAN WESTIN
Professor, Columbia
University

with callers. He finds such monitoring insulting and an affront to the hard work he is putting out.

Jeff is an editorial aide in the newsroom of a metropolitan newspaper. He helps reporters check facts, runs errands, does research in the paper's library, and sometimes helps write stories. On a daily assignment basis, he has no single boss but helps many reporters, who often fill his "In" box with scribbled requests for items they want as soon as possible. His office is the newsroom, a large open space where over twenty employees talk on the phone, gossip, type, and read. Because the windows are sealed closed and the building ventilation system is ancient, the atmosphere in the newsroom is often stuffy and noisy. Jay hates enclosed spaces, so when the newsroom gets crowded and the air sickly stale, he disappears and runs errands outside the building. Sometimes he misses deadlines and reporters must scramble to cover for him.

Gary is a finance manager at an accounting firm. Layoffs over the past two years have shrunk his department from five to two people. As a result, he must prepare and process twice as many quarterly budgets as before, as well as attend the meetings former colleagues used to cover. A typical workday for him begins at seven-thirty A.M. and ends around six-thirty P.M. unless he has a dinner meeting, which happens two or three times a week. The toll from Gary's workload pressure shows: he is on medication to control his blood pressure and his wife has suggested a trial separation.

Susan is an assembly-line worker for a farm-equipment manufacturer. She is on her feet all day fitting parts into tractor cabs. The work is strenuous because of the constant, repetitive twisting and stretching. To ease her sore back, Susan sees a chiropractor regularly, even though her insurance doesn't cover the cost. The most discomforting part of her job is the shift rotation every ten days. While she usually knows her schedule weeks ahead of time, it occasionally changes quickly if orders fall off or pick up. Around three A.M. one evening on a back-to-back shift she hadn't planned on, Susan slipped and wrenched her back. She is filing for disability payments.

A STEW OF SICK JOBS

Few employees possess the perfect job or toil under ideal conditions. For years, people have accepted the discomforting, boring, aggravating, stressful side of earning a living. Working people have always been expected to fit into their jobs—to mold their bodies to the furniture, tools, and surroundings of their employment and disregard the physical toll of this molding. But now we are learning that some occupations, working environments, and even psychological situations literally make us sick.

In certain workplaces, the dangers of becoming sick or injured are so well known they are movie material. Coal miners, police, and fire fighters regularly risk life and limb, accepting physical danger or long-term illness as part of their job. But less glamorous occupations in which people labor in noisy factories, with dangerous tools or chemicals, or simply in badly ventilated, dimly lit offices have only recently been suspect as hazardous.

Today, the definition of sick jobs has evolved far beyond the usual image of installing asbestos tiles without proper clothing or manning a jackhammer without earplugs. Like nineteenth-century explorers who discovered that mosquito bites were more than annoying and deposited deadly diseases, health experts have found that many kinds of work stress bring illness.

A sick job has spread to encompass a host of psychological and emotional pressures: persistent, unremitting stress; lack of control or power; boredom; repetition; social isolation; skewed shift work; lack of privacy; constant demands to perform; climates of constant crisis populated by workaholics; and more.

And when it comes to unhealthy conditions, factories have nothing over offices. Modern technology and changing work attitudes are beginning to reshape offices and factories to resemble each other. Computers and high technology are standard tools on many factory floors. And many offices have sweatshop atmospheres, designed on an open plan devoid of privacy or with managers and employees toiling in identical, windowless cubicles that isolate and exert relentless pressure to produce.

Treating these sick jobs is complicated, because it is sometimes difficult to identify a single cause and the most effective remedy. In some instances, the unhealthy aspects of a job are hidden, disguised as productivity, or are slowly cumulative, identifiable only after months or years.

Sick jobs poison both people and companies. They lower productivity, eat away at morale, and jeopardize corporate survival. Their outgrowths are higher absenteeism, illness, and accidents and steeper disability and workers'-compensation costs. A company that consciously or unconsciously promotes sick jobs is

The basic issue is how to design the job around auto-mation so you don't make the office job of the 1990s into the factory job of the 1930s.

JEANNE STELLMAN
Founder, Women's
Occupational Health
Resource Center

Here are the ten worst jobs in America according to Tom Juravich, Associate Professor of Labor Studies at Penn State University: data entry, electronic-assembly worker, garment worker, janitors and maids, food-service workers, meat packers, migrant farm-workers, telephone salespeople, booth sitters, and civil-service workers.

The more advanced our machines become, the more humane our treatment of people must be. . . . if you serve a machine instead of the machine serving you, you have cramped your style as a human being and have limited your opportunity to share your individual gifts with others.

PEHR GYLLENHAMMER
Chairman, Volvo

also behaving unethically, abdicating its responsibility to the people who give it life and make it run.

The damage from sick jobs spills beyond the confines of a company and its employees into the community and environment. Jobs that pollute the working environment typically let loose on the community air pollution, noise pollution, toxic or hazardous substances, and water contaminants. The poison in a sick job cannot be contained within a company—it seeps outside, destroying natural resources and threatening public health. Although environmental hazards are beyond the scope of this book, they are an extension of sick jobs and are the responsibility of employers sincere about curtailing the damage their companies can do.

Lastly, employees are rejecting jobs and companies that jeopardize their health. People who once tolerated positions that gave them ulcers or bad backs are leaving those spots. In today's shrinking labor market, no organization can survive with a reputation as an unhealthy place to work.

This chapter is about sick jobs—what they are and who is vulnerable to their dangers—and how managers and companies can turn them into healthy ones and reverse their impact on a business.

Diagnose Work-Induced Stress

Work stressors come from all directions—people, machines, and situations, as well as from inside yourself. These stressors affect everyone differently, depending on individual physiological and psychological make-up. Some employees literally feel sick in a job over which they have no control, while others prefer formal, rigid structure because it does not demand much independent thinking. Although every task imposes some degree of pressure, an intolerable pace to one person may spell boredom for the next. Even people with the same titles and similar responsibilities do not respond in the same way to a job.

Some job stressors are acute, others chronic. The acute strike suddenly, throwing you into immediate decline. They are situations such as a crisis with a very short deadline and little administrative support or a lack of physical support in carrying heavy boxes, causing you to throw your back out.

Chronic stressors are those insidious situations or demands that steadily chew at your health and outlook. Such stressors may be a steady diet of thirteen-hour days, with only Sunday off, month after month, and a feeling of never getting the job done. They may take the form of a factory area that is a safety worry because it is always messy with greasy floors and loose cables, or they may be the knowledge that supervisors are monitoring any telephone call, looking for wasted time.

After a while, chronic stressors, especially if there is a conglomeration of them, reach critical mass. Building up gradually until their number and intensity reach a person's breaking point, they eventually explode. The sickness becomes visible: a person feels exhausted and may show symptoms such as persistent headaches or constant battles with viruses. He or she loses interest in work, accomplishing less and less, and may make mistakes and cause hazardous accidents. Affected employees may start to dislike their job and employer and grumble about bosses and working conditions. And they lose their sense of professional responsibility, calling in sick and/or reducing their productivity for the smallest reason. Overstressed employees also infect others; their diminished capacity makes it difficult to maintain effective, cooperative relationships with coworkers and customers.

While the previous chapter discussed teaching employees to reduce their own stress, managers and companies equally need to eliminate or reduce work-induced stress. Stressors originate from four sources, and the most unhealthy, unpleasant jobs are tainted by all four and will eventually make an employee sick.

Job stressors. Stresses associated with actual work tasks or responsibilities.

- repetition, monotony, boredom, and dead-end jobs
- excessive demands, chronic overload, and deadline pressure
- piecework
- excessive red tape, paperwork, and bureaucracy
- insufficient resources
- physical demands such as lengthy sitting, standing, stretching, or twisting
- unhealthy shift work

A poll by Louis Harris and Associates, Inc., reveals that 70 percent of workers surveyed feel "it is very important to have the right kind of physical office environment in order to do as much work as they reasonably can." Another conclusion from the poll: "top management tends to underestimate the value workers place on the office environment."

Psychological stressors. Stresses associated with unhealthy relationships or invasion of personal territory.

- lack of privacy
- absence of control and autonomy
- performance monitoring
- multiple supervisors
- confusion about goals and responsibilities
- conflicting demands and responsibilities

The National Safety Council has estimated that every American worker must produce $380 worth of goods or services per year to offset the cost of work injuries.

Environmental stressors. Conditions in the physical work area that create stress.

- confining space
- crowding
- constant, loud, distracting noise
- bad lighting or wrong air temperature
- cigarette smoke
- uncomfortable chairs, desks, and work tables
- presence of chemicals, gases, fumes, or dust

Technological stressors. Stresses from working with machines, tools, or equipment.

- work pace determined by a machine
- inadequate training
- outdated, poorly maintained equipment or tools
- absence of the right equipment or tools
- unsafe or poorly designed equipment or tools

The worst combination, according to employment experts, are jobs where employees are pressured to constantly produce, have little control over their tasks, and receive little support from management. The ideal job, in contrast, consists of more than the absence of these stressors. It entails a series of challenges a person feels well suited and sufficiently skilled to meet, mixed in with a reasonable dose of decision-making authority, regular feedback and support, occasional pressure and intensity because of the importance of the job, and enough variety and stimulation to be interesting.

Managers need to gauge and calibrate stress levels and evaluate how individuals are reacting to them. The simplest and most direct way would be to perform each employee's job for a day. At Service Master, all corporate personnel spend time working at their MerryMaid Services. HealthTrust, a hospital chain, requires their executives to work inside the hospital for two weeks to experience firsthand what a hospital worker goes through. But not all managers have the temperament or time to do this, so perspicacity and talking with employees about their daily stresses must often suffice.

If observant, you can detect signs of extreme pressure and pace. Here are some clues:

Psychological disorders have become one of the fastest-growing occupational ills of this decade. Compensation claims on average draw $15,000—twice as much as those for workers with physical injuries.

National Council on Compensation Insurance

- Do employees take long lunches or wolf something down at their desk? Arrive late or leave early, or work into the evening? Always seem to be scrambling, persistently frantic with work to do? Or walk the halls and read a lot of magazines and newspapers?

- Do you hear complaints or faint grumbling about work loads, company management, or how things are done? Do people complain about the smallest addition to their responsibilities?

- Do people complain about crowding, noise, the inability to make a private phone call, or being cut off from fellow workers?

- Has the number of accidents, mistakes, or days of non-specific absenteeism risen? Take a look at your disability or worker's-compensation claims. You may find a pattern that points the finger at a specific boss or department.

- Are employees constantly interrupted? Do they work for long, monotonous stretches on a single assignment? What kinds of deadlines do they have? Do people feel they have some control over how their jobs are managed?

Stress Claims

These stories will send a chill through any manager:

- The president of a worldwide machine manufacturer claimed the pressure of managing a bankrupt company caused his alcoholism. He successfully sued for compensation.

- A Florida switchboard operator became depressed after being robbed at work by a gunman. She successfully sued for compensation.

- A New York advertising executive had a nervous breakdown after being asked to retire early. He successfully sued for compensation.

- A Michigan assembly-line worker unable to keep up with the production line and so frequently criticized by his supervisor suffered a psychological breakdown. He successfully sued for compensation.

Successful claims for mental stress and suffering associated with work are becoming commonplace. The National Council on Compensation Insurance says that stress accounts for 14 percent of all occupational disease claims, up from 5 percent in 1980. Few employers are immune from employee suits alleging a variety of forms of mental distress. Courts allow three kinds of stress claims:

1. *Physical-mental*—an emotional reaction to a physical injury.

2. *Mental-physical*—mental stress that causes physical injury.

3. *Mental-mental*—emotional disability without physical injury.

To head off these suits, companies are offering employees stress-management programs that include instruction in muscle relaxation, meditation, and even biofeedback. They are also soliciting employee attitudes about stress on their jobs and trying to alleviate their anxieties.

Armstrong Transfer & Storage Company in St. Paul, Minnesota polled employees and learned that many were concerned about unsafe working conditions such as worn loading equipment and were confused about which supervisor to report to. The company repaired and replaced the equipment, held weekly meetings with employees so they could vent their anxieties, and distributed clear chain-of-command charts to everyone. A survey after these remedies showed people under much less stress, and accidents in a three-year period were down from sixty-five to ten.

Soothe the Stressors

Stress is not all bad—all workers need at least a modicum of stress to push them to excel or be productive. As a steady diet, however, it can be brutalizing. The goal is to determine the right amount of pace and pressure for each person. Depending on what kind of stress is prevalent around your workplace, here are five tips to help you alleviate high-level stress and reach an optimal level. Some of these suggestions will eliminate your personal stress, while others point to specific policies for relieving stressors for your employees.

1. REDESIGN JOBS TO ADD VARIETY. Underwriting services needed improving at Northwestern Mutual Life Insurance Company, so the company focused on the tasks of policy analysts. It discovered that individual employees handled only a tiny segment of underwriting or policy-owner services and so did not truly understand what they were trying to accomplish.

To correct this, Northwestern redesigned their jobs. It eliminated the numerous small tasks and trained people to undertake much broader, core jobs. In one department, it telescoped sixty job functions into six. During this reorganization, to relieve any stress or anxiety about positions being eliminated, the company made a written promise that no one would lose his or her job.

2. ROTATE EMPLOYEES IN REPETITIVE JOBS. At Fisher Price, production-line workers move to a new position and new machine every two hours in order to avoid monotony. Engineers also rotate: newly recruited engineers shift every eighteen months through plastics, product development, and manufacturing engineering.

Employees of G.S.I. Transcomm Data Systems Inc., Pittsburgh, are closely watched for signs of boredom and offered the opportunity to move around in the company when their interest flags. For instance, the company controller devotes a couple of days each month to demonstrating for customers the company's financial software program.

3. AVOID NEEDLESS HOURS AND WORK LOADS. In the early years of building up her business, Carol Osborn, founder of a San Francisco public relations firm, became accustomed to sixty-to-seventy-hour work weeks and assumed her employees felt the

Boring supervision, boring management pep talks, boring control systems, boring looking offices, boring memoranda, and boring bureaucracies have unintended consequences. The bored and alienated person comes almost to welcome disaster, unsettling surprises, stupid leadership acts—anything to break the monotony of keeping a tight mouth and doing as you are told.

D.W. EWING
former Managing Editor,
Harvard Business Review

same urgency to produce. "I thought I was an inspirational leader," she recalls. "Whenever I gave a speech on the goals of the company, I noticed everyone worked harder." Then one day, employees rebelled. "I wasn't inspiring them," she realized. "It turned out they were afraid of getting fired."

Recognizing the pace and pressure had become too brutal, Osborn eased up considerably, paring everyone's hours to forty a week and encouraging people to take vacations and paid mental-health breaks such as a walk or an afternoon movie. The work load was dramatically cut by letting go half the clients. As a result, business boomed. Employees felt more creative and productive, existing clients got first-class service, and profits increased by 20 percent.

In other innovative moves, Red Lobster fights so-called brain-fade, the syndrome that occurs when you work too much, by monitoring managers to make sure they aren't requiring employees to put in long hours simply as a show of commitment, stamina, or toughness. And when employees of BurJon Steel Service Center, Springboro, Ohio, work long hours, the CEO supplements their overtime pay with flowers and coupons for dinner at a local restaurant.

4. **SURVEY EMPLOYEES ABOUT THEIR JOB STRESS.** Maids International, a franchised house-cleaning service, has tried to eliminate stress and boredom by first watching its employees clean a home. It then asked them about boring and tiring tasks and accordingly organized cleaning teams and parceled out individual jobs so that employees were not asked to do too much or become stuck in dull activities.

5. **AVOID THE ILLS OF SHIFT WORK.** At Argonne National Labs, workers avoid the physiological and social stress of shift work by following company guidelines on chrono hygiene, a management technique for balancing employees' internal and external clocks —their daily habits for certain activities—with job responsibilities. Applying chrono hygiene, workers carefully schedule meals and leisure activities, light and dark (night and day) cycles, diet, and their daily rest and activity patterns.

While managers must be observant and sensitive to stressors affecting employees, employees themselves are the more insight-

It is not the bosses but the bossed who suffer most from job stress. The most common problem is not executive stress but stress among low status workers who bear equally heavy psychological demands but lack the freedom to make decisions about how to do the work.

ROBERT KARASEK
stress researcher

The introduction of new technology in an organization as large as Honeywell presents employees with a dilemma. On the one hand, they have opportunities to expand their professional horizons. . . . On the other hand, many feel threatened by the new technologies, which introduce the stress of change, insecurity, reorganization, and possible technical obsolescence.

ARNOLD KANARICK
Vice-President, Human Resources Planning and Development, Honeywell

ful source of ideas for alleviating tension in their jobs. Only they know the minute details of their work—what they enjoy and feel competent doing, what they loathe, and what makes them ill—so employers would do well to listen to their complaints and solicit their ideas for solutions.

Make Safety Everyone's Responsibility

It is the end of the night shift at a plating company, workers are eager to get home, and the company is short of clean-up personnel. A relatively new employee climbs into a chemical storage tank to finish cleaning it. He hasn't been trained for the work, nor does he wear any kind of respirator. Overcome by poisonous fumes, he faints and dies on the vat floor. Four coworkers who try to rescue him are overpowered by hydrogen cyanide gases and die.

Admittedly, this is an extreme example of an unsafe workplace, and the company involved was fined for safety violations. Yet everyone was to blame here, because no one took safety concerns to heart.

How many times have you walked through your office or plant and seen a worn electrical cable, a jerry-rigged machine, or a turned-up corner of carpeting and thought, "Someone else will fix that up"? Multiply that by the number of employees in your company and you know what happens in most work areas to cause accidents: no one takes responsibility for safety.

Costs from unsafe working conditions are a major drain on businesses, both in dollars and human resources. Safety—or, more accurately, the absence of it—costs this country billions every year in disability, accidents, and workers'-compensation costs. Since 1950, industrial injuries have tripled, with the average cost of an accident reaching $10,000 and days lost reaching seventeen. In 1986, the industry price tag for industrial accidents topped a staggering $35 billion, according to the National Safety Council, and total workdays lost hit 75 million.

The problem lies at everyone's feet. Employees cut corners, choosing which habits and regulations to follow and ignoring the seemingly trivial things that ensure safety. This creates accidents waiting to happen, affecting not only individuals but everyone working around them. The National Institute of Occupational Safety and Health echoes this potential disaster by reporting that

Studies show that shift work upsets the body's circadian rhythms, leading to fatigue, increased accidents, poor job performance, worker dissatisfaction, and increased health problems. Other studies indicate more sleep, mood, and digestive disturbances among shift workers and that shift workers are more susceptible to noise, vibration, radiation, and chemical agents such as fumes, gases, and dust.

One million workers a day are absent from work because of stress-related disorders, and 40 percent of job turnover is due to stress, according to the Bureau of National Affairs.

There were 284,000 cases of occupational illness and 6.3 million job-related injuries among workers in private industry in 1989, according to a Labor Department report.

In 1987, more than 80 percent of workers who suffered head injuries were not wearing hard hats and more than half the eye injuries occurred without eye wear, according to the Labor Department.

Allstate®

Safety in Belts

The statistics are unequivocal: seat belts save lives and reduce injuries. Every year, motor-vehicle accidents kill about 2,100 on-the-job workers while some 48,000 people die on the highways. In the workplace, car accidents are the leading cause of lost work time, and businesses spend $40 billion in lost productivity, insurance claims, and death and disability payments.

Some companies have recognized the importance of using seat belts and have instituted incentives and penalties to encourage buckling up. Here are examples of how such programs work:

- ▪ At Westlake Community Hospital, Melrose Park, Illinois, any employee who is injured in a car accident and is wearing a safety belt receives 100-percent payment for any emergency care, and all deductibles and co-payments are waived.
- ▪ Allstate Insurance Company offers free child-safety seats to its employees.
- ▪ At Nalco Chemical Company in Naperville, Illinois, not using a seat belt can lead to losing company car privileges. To receive a company car, you must pass a safe driving class; even those having a preventable accident must take the course.

---

nine out of every ten industrial workers are not adequately protected from exposure to harmful industrial substances. Employers also sidestep safety by selectively enforcing safety conditions. Or they might adhere strictly to the minimum regulations while ignoring common sense and direct observation. For instance, few employers require employees to use vehicle safety belts despite the overwhelming evidence about their safety effects. Furthermore, when they turn a blind eye to the environmental hazards they produce, they also jeopardize everyone's safety and health.

In short, no one is taking responsibility for his or her own safety. We leave it to coworkers, employers, unions, government, laws, and regulations. It is *in loco parentis*—we trust someone more knowledgeable and with more authority will make us safe. Both employees and employers have become comfortable and accustomed to abrogating responsibility, denying that a problem or threat truly exists, and feeling someone else is watching out for them. The child in all of us prefers to defer to a parent, whether real or imaginary, who will eliminate danger and make the world safe.

Every manager must take responsibility for workplace safety into his or her own hands. This is the time to be selfish, to think of yourself—your eyes, your lungs, your arms, your well-being. This way, you will be safe and healthy, and so will your employees.

Dupont Chemical Company aggressively enforces safe practices at its work sites, and employees at its plant in Chattanooga, Tennessee hold the National Safety Council record for longest string of injury-free workdays: 2,490, or nearly seven years. To achieve this, Dupont administers a strict safety program at all its plants. The program is based on these principles:

- All job-related injuries and illnesses can be prevented.

- All managers, from chairman of the board to first-line supervisors, are responsible for preventing injuries and illnesses.

- Safety is a condition of employment. Every employee must act safely.

- Safety is as important as production, quality, and cost control.

- Training is an essential element for safe workplaces. Managers must take the lead in teaching employees about safety.

- Managers must audit safety performance to see how effective facilities and programs are and to look for areas that need improvement.

- Safety problems must be corrected promptly.

- All unsafe practices, problem areas, and injuries must be investigated.

- It is good business to prevent illness and injury.

- People are the most critical element in the success of a safety program. Employees and their suggestions play an important role in keeping workplaces safe.

All the equipment, controls, and procedures in the world will not make a plant safe unless they are used properly. Statistics show that more than 95 percent of all accidents seem to involve human error. So plant safety is, in large part, a people problem.

JOHN LUTNESS
Safety Manager,
DuPont

Other businesses put similar philosophies into practice every day. For example, top officials from all of Philadelphia Electric Company's divisions, stations, and shops meet monthly solely to discuss safety. The utility trains every employee in first aid, CPR, and safe handling of hazardous chemicals and equipment. For managers and maintenance staff involved in dangerous work, it conducts special programs. Superintendents run safety audits every month, while shift supervisors run daily audits.

Similarly, managers at the Canadian railroad CP Rail know that employees look to them as safety role models, so they regularly don the proper gear—boots, glasses, hard hats, and leg bands. To get the safety message across to every employee, CP Rail managers meet monthly to talk about safety with employees who work by themselves.

The Black and Beech construction firm requires all workers to put up safety nets and tie on safety harnesses whenever they work more than twenty feet off the ground. Anyone who breaks this rule three times is fired.

And safety-conscious employees of Peavey Electronics, Inc., in Meridian, Mississippi, participate in a bingo game at the end of each accident-free day, with the winner receiving a $100 U.S. savings bond.

Cure Sick Buildings

A couple of years ago, hundreds of Eastman Kodak employees at two offices in Rochester, New York, suddenly developed allergic reactions. While doctors diagnosed their condition as an inflammation of the lungs (hypersensitivity pneumonitis), the source of the allergy was a mystery. Extensive testing of the plant and everything surrounding the employees revealed that a fungus had invaded the ventilation system. More than 1,000 employees were exposed to it and 115 became sick. Kodak spent millions trying to defeat the fungus and eventually had to replace the entire ventilation system.

As Kodak managers discovered, not all safety hazards are as apparent as an unbuckled safety belt or not wearing protective eyeglasses. Sometimes office areas are inherently sick—in what is now called Sick Building Syndrome (SBS). While SBS is a newcomer to medical dictionaries, office workers have been aware of it for decades. According to the World Health Organization, one-

A study of three thousand employees in seventy-one plants by DuPont found fewer accidents in plants where employees believe that management's commitment to safety is unwavering than in less committed plants.

third of all new and remodeled commercial buildings are sick from indoor air pollution, and other sources report that more than 20 percent of U.S. office workers report symptoms of illness from poor air quality. SBS is a collection of sicknesses and health complaints caused by indoor air pollution and spawned during the 1970s energy crises when building contractors and owners sealed windows and working spaces to lower energy costs.

Now these air-tight buildings are making us sick with an assortment of troubles from respiratory ailments to memory loss. The *Journal of the American Medical Association* reports a 45-percent higher incidence of respiratory infections among occupants of new buildings than among people who work in older ones. Air-tight offices trap air-borne chemicals such as formaldehyde, asbestos, and particulates from cleaning materials; make us breathe tobacco smoke; and breed viruses, bacteria, and molds. As much as half of all worker absenteeism is attributable to upper respiratory problems, which are common symptoms of a sick building. To make office buildings safer:

- Test office air for pollutants.

- Watch for dysfunctional working habits, such as employees becoming drowsy every afternoon or people insisting on breaks outside the building.

- Keep a record of complaints about itchy eyes, congestion, scratchy throats, headaches, asthma, and allergies.

- Install air filters and humidifiers to adjust air circulation, and design windows to open when possible.

- Service and maintain efficient ventilation, heating, and air-conditioning systems.

- Use indirect lighting or task lighting whenever possible.

- Provide smoke-free work space.

The EPA estimates that the economic cost of indoor air pollution totals tens of billions of dollars annually in lost productivity, direct medical care, lost earnings, and employee sick days. Sick-building suits could rival those that have proliferated over asbestos.

Technology well applied should enrich jobs for people, should liberate them, should make them more masters than servants, should make the job more interesting and increase ambition and eagerness to develop with the job.

PEHR GYLLENHAMMER
Chairman, Volvo

Match People and Their Machines

People are forming closer and closer relationships with their machines, an alliance that is both liberating and laced with dangers. We are surrounded by an agglomeration of hardware, tools, furniture, and fittings that can make us remarkably productive, incredibly speedy, and highly informed. Yet these innovations

Put a worker in a bad chair in a noisy stuffy office, require that worker to perform a dead-end job for low pay on a video display terminal with a dirty screen made worse by the harsh glare from fluorescent lights, add a dash of pressure—and you've got an explosive situation.

JOEL MAKOWER
Office Hazards

The president of an ergonomic consulting firm, T.J. Springer Associates, says that reducing glare on terminal screens adds 3 to 5 percent in performance; sitting in good chairs adds 4 to 6 percent; and adding furniture that can be moved or adjusted adds up to 24 percent.

can also chisel away at our health and our lives, so they must be managed with keen sensitivity to people.

After visiting hundreds of offices, I have noticed that the best organizations place people ahead of their machines. And they are always on the lookout for ways to adjust the machines to the needs of their employees.

Ergonomics—the relationship between people and their machines—is the backbone of these healthy workplaces. Ergonomics may entail small adjustments, such as the numbers on a telephone or adding machine, or may encompass the refitting of an entire assembly line. When the ergonomics are right, with employees and their tools fitting well together, good health and productivity follow. But when the fit is skewed and a person must constantly adjust and strain his or her body and mind to do the work, then something must give—usually the employee. Eventually this adjustment causes an assortment of disorders that go directly to the bottom line.

The best workplaces manage their machines for compatibility and flexibility whether in an office or a factory. Compatibility means machine and tools adapt to you, not vice versa. They are designed and constructed not just for function and efficiency, but for people to use. Their shape, size, and operation take into consideration the human form and how human beings move and work.

Flexibility recognizes the inevitability of change in the workplace—people, jobs, machines, and tools change. Few people do the same work year in, year out, and the equipment and environment are constantly updated and improved. So people have to be flexible and adapt to new technology, and existing technology must be flexible enough to accommodate different people.

At Mazda Motor Manufacturing (USA) Corporation, ergonomics and operations are meshed together like a synchronized drill team. Running a high-quality assembly line generates special human problems for managers. The assembly line can move at an erratic pace and work stations are usually designed for function, to complete a task, so people sometimes have to twist, stretch, and crawl. "The most efficient way of production is for each person to do the same thing over and over," explains a manager at Mazda. "But that's the worst thing for humans."

To make itself ergonomically sound, Mazda anticipates and

redesigns jobs that could produce injuries and ferrets out and corrects mismatches between workers and machines. To head off problems, the company inaugurated a formal ergonomics program that studies jobs and people, listens to complaints, and recommends changes. Much of its attention is focused on the fifty-two jobs that pose the most ergonomic risk because they involve repetition and extreme bending, reaching, and lifting. So far, the program has made these changes:

- altered tool designs to reduce repetitive-motion injuries
- rotated workers in the most repetitive jobs every two hours
- rebalanced the assembly line by having workers do a couple of tasks rather than only one

Furthermore, in the trim and final shop, the line tilts thirty degrees so employees can work underneath the cars without bending, crawling into pits, or stretching. It has a pneumatic lift to move instrument panels so workers do not have to maneuver or hold them. And the overhead conveyor line moves at different heights depending on which point of the car an employee is working on.

Statistics confirm that Mazda's ergonomics programs have improved employees' health and costs. In one year, overall repetitive-motion injuries dropped 27 percent, while such injuries in its largest department, trim and final, plunged 40 percent. At the same time, workers'-compensation costs have begun to decrease even though the company anticipated doubling these expenses because of higher production levels.

Establish a Computer-Friendly Environment

While the science of ergonomics originated on the factory floor, it has spread to the computerized office. Employees who sit at computers for long stretches face myriad health risks, some proven and some suspected. The proven hazards include carpal tunnel syndrome, a pinching of the nerves in the hand and wrist, and tendonitis, inflammation of the tendons of the lower arm and elbow. These are the disorders with medical names, but other, less specific ailments lurk: lower back pain, sore neck, eyestrain, headaches, and fatigue.

Our field study confirms the judgment of thoughtful supporters and critics alike that office technology is a two-edged sword, an opportunity and a danger, and a Jekyll-and-Hyde force. Managers have a critical role to play in seeing that wise choices are made between these alternative outcomes. This is what managing for excellence in the office environment will mean in the next decade.

ALAN WESTIN
Professor, Columbia
University

Other suspected dangers swirl around news stories of pregnant VDT users reporting unusually high numbers of miscarriages and birth defects. People are worried about the low levels of radiation that are emitted from the sides and backs of VDTs. To make VDTs healthier, take a walk around the office and take the following steps:

Repetitive motion disorders accounted for most of the increase in 1989 in the nation's job-related illnesses, which rose by 43,000.

The *Washington Post*

- 💼 Limit daily use per employee to no more than four hours.
- 💼 Talk to employees about fears of cataracts, miscarriages, and long-term health effects. Research the subject and share information. If requested, reassign pregnant VDT users.
- 💼 Eliminate screen glare and make screen position adjustable.
- 💼 Use high-resolution VDTs in detail work.
- 💼 Allow frequent and regular breaks from keyboarding. Let employees manage their own breaks.
- 💼 Ensure that the keyboard is at the optimal level and tilt for each user.
- 💼 Make sure source documents are easy to read by providing document holders.
- 💼 Provide a shield between the back and sides of computers and workers within two feet.
- 💼 Offer regular eye exams at company expense.
- 💼 Teach people exercises they can do at their desk to relieve strain.
- 💼 Ensure proper training for both hardware and software.
- 💼 Keep records of ailments and pains.

In one recent case, Pacific Bell decided to spend roughly $8 million over four years to upgrade its office equipment throughout California. The company estimates that repetitive-stress injuries already cost it about $2 million per year. Its safety director, James Stout, believes Pacific Bell may achieve increased productivity in the range of 3 to 5 percent, but even a 2-percent increase would "wash the cost of what we're doing over a three-to-five-year period." Pacific Bell's decision is in response to the 1991 San

Francisco ordinance requiring businesses with more than fifteen employees to invest in ergonomically sound work stations (including lighting, furniture, and equipment) for employees who spend more than four hours per day at a computer terminal.

Privatize and Personalize Work Space

People need the right kind of space to be productive—a balance of privacy and group interaction. When employees have no visual or auditory privacy, they feel pressured and distrusted, and their cramped quarters create antagonism and discontent. People in this situation feel like livestock. At the other extreme, working alone, people feel little connection to the organization. Eventually, these unhealthy conditions gnaw at them and so push up absenteeism and benefits costs.

Uncomfortable, ergonomically unhealthy surroundings can be found in even the most seemingly well-furnished places. While office spaces are generally designed to look attractive, not enough attention is paid to the practicalities of daily work. Work spaces are often put together piecemeal with no overall design scheme in mind, and the question of how employees fit and use their furniture becomes an afterthought. As a result, chairs don't match desks, lighting systems are too dim or glaring, and where employees' work suits the furniture, not the people. To make work spaces healthier:

- Consult with employees or outside experts on how to make these areas more comfortable and more efficient.

- Ensure that every employee has enough privacy— acoustical (privacy from distracting noise) and visual (privacy from being constantly on view).

- Ensure that chairs, desks, and work tables are flexible and adjustable.

- Ensure lighting levels and positioning are adjustable.

- Eliminate crowded offices, desks, and work areas.

- Eliminate noise that is too loud or distracting.

- Adjust the ringing level of loud telephones.

- Give headsets to employees who are on the phone a lot.

- Allow people to decorate their own work space. Their office is their home away from home.

Dr. Stanley J. Bigos, professor of orthopedic surgery at the University of Washington, found after questioning 1,569 Boeing Company employees that those who don't enjoy their jobs are 2.5 times more likely to file back-injury claims as those who like their work; workers who reported high emotional stress were more than twice as prone to file a claim.

- Provide an array of group spaces—formal conference rooms, rooms for informal team meetings, areas for relaxation breaks, and kitchens.

Data Bank

- *VDT workers complain more than other workers about eye irritations and back, neck, and shoulder discomfort.*

- *A study sponsored by the National Institute for Occupational Safety and Health has found that 75 percent report aching or burning eyes; 79 percent report neck and shoulder pain; 81 percent report backaches; and 66 percent report fatigue, exhaustion, or irritability.*

- *NIOSH also reports that 15 to 20 percent of workers in construction, food preparation, clerical work, production, and mining are at risk for carpal tunnel syndrome and other cumulative trauma disorders.*

- *A 1990 NIOSH study indicates that employees subjected to electronic performance monitoring have an elevated heart rate and blood pressure.*

A Prescription from Federal Express

It is hard to imagine a company more vulnerable to a plague of sick jobs than the overnight delivery service Federal Express. Every day, this company of more than 90,000 employees handles 1.2 million packages and documents and 297,000 phone calls and drives approximately 1.8 million miles. This remarkable activity is accomplished through an elaborate network of information technology: computerized tracking systems, electronic terminals in courier vans, portable mini-scanners for deliverers, and on-line photographic scanning for coding packages. The core of this system—the hub where all its information enters and exits—are its approximately 100,000 video display terminals spread around the country in service centers, offices, and relay stations.

From its inception, the company has recognized the importance of a healthy, productive relationship between its employees and advanced technology. Yet, as computers and their terminals became an integral part of FedEx operations during the 1970s and early 1980s, little attention was paid to how they interfaced with employees. In 1983, amid public controversy about the possible health effects from VDTs, the company became aware of safety concerns among employees and so created a task force to examine VDT use.

Composed of twenty participants and chaired by the company's director of safety and health, Fred Rine, the task force began meeting in mid-1983 and continues to meet. It first defined the scope of its investigation and its goal, formulating a three-point position statement: (1) the VDT issue is not a narrow ergonomics issue limited to equipment and furniture, but requires rethinking job design, work-group relations, work quotas, performance supervision, employee education and participation, and manager education; (2) the task force will identify what other companies are doing and consult with outside experts; and (3) the resulting policies must be formulated and institutionalized with strong support from the company CEO.

In order to accomplish all this, the task force began to gather information from a number of sources. It reviewed scientific literature, visited other large users of VDTs, and studied the demands of its technology in light of the company's daily high-pressure environment. For instance, an industrial psychologist on the task force examined proposed data-entry

Ergonomics is everywhere. It demands that every manager make sure that jobs are tailored to people and that people are not twisting and stretching themselves all the way to the medical department.

jobs for a new operation and concluded the jobs, as designed, would be too monotonous. To solve this problem, he proposed combining the VDT data-entry jobs with non-VDT tasks.

A recurring theme in its investigation went beyond issues related solely to VDT use and centered on job design and performance evaluation. Through personal interviews and focus groups with customer-service agents and line managers, the company discovered that VDT users were angry, frustrated, developing severe musculoskeletal ailments, and fearful of complaining. The mandatory short-response time made agents feel they were sacrificing service to beat the clock.

In addition, working conditions were inconsistent by using a number of different vendors and thus acquiring a variation of furniture and equipment. Employees used a collection of chairs and consoles that were uncomfortable and unadjustable, and, in the case of some computer work stations, required training that was never offered. In short, the employees felt that the company was abusing technology and driving its people to illness.

The task force, which reported its findings to executive management as it went along, proposed corrections to individual problems as it encountered them. In 1984, the company adopted guidelines in seven areas: (1) equipment and work-station design, (2) image quality and display design, (3) lighting and reflections, (4) general work-station environment, (5) job design and organizational factors, (6) conclusions about radiation hazards, and (7) eye care. Two years later, FedEx took additional steps to improve VDT-user jobs, spending $500,000 on new ergonomic chairs, providing training on all new computer terminals, distributing to employees videos on healthy use of VDTs, and instituting a stretch-and-flex exercise program for users.

The VDT task force reaffirmed the company's founding people-technology philosophy. The company officially committed itself to "systematically incorporate human factors, ergonomics, and job/task design criteria with the development or modification of electronic technology applications." In short, it acknowledged its dependence on technology while insisting that people come first.

Source: Professor Alan Westin, Columbia University and Federal Express.

Research by the Buffalo Organization for Technological and Social Innovation (BOTSI), a nonprofit research and consulting firm, found in a study of eighty companies that the two most powerful influences on job performance were how much enclosed space employees had and whether their work space was arranged to support the job they did. Results from a study by BOTSI indicate that the economic benefit of planning and designing the office space can easily equal 2.5 percent of each employee's annual salary and can be higher if the office is a perfect fit for the work.

A poll of office workers by Louis Harris, Inc. found these four factors to be the most important: good lighting, a comfortable chair, good air circulation, and the right temperature.

Who Are the Disabled?

- 💼 *44% have physical disabilities*

- 💼 *13% have sensory impairment*

- 💼 *6% have mental illness*

- 💼 *33% have other serious health conditions, e.g., heart disease, cancer, diabetes, or epilepsy.*

Decide Between Disabled People or Disabled Jobs

Tom Tufano, director of laboratory research in photographic science at DuPont, is nearly blind. He lost his vision around age eleven to Stargardt's disease and now can see only directly in front of him. While Tom has successfully adjusted to his disability on his own, earning a Ph.D. in chemistry from the University of California at Berkeley, DuPont has ensured that his job fits. The company has provided him a closed-circuit television that enlarges printed material and a computer program that magnifies text on the monitor. About all his work, Tom remarks: "I don't dwell on the number of things I can't do. Instead, I concentrate on enjoying what I can do."

The disabled in this country number 43 million. With the passage of the Americans with Disabilities Act (ADA), which prohibits employers from discriminating against them and mandates reasonable accommodations at work, they are certain to become more prominent in the workplace. However, companies have been too slow to make adjustments for disabled workers. Injured employees stay away from work longer than necessary because they are discouraged, and the system prevents their easy return. Those with chronic physical ailments are written off as casualties for the long-term disability rolls. And employers are often not eager to bring a disabled person back to work, fearful that he or she cannot perform. Now, the legal compulsions as well as the economic realities of the value of skilled disabled workers should push business to reexamine its jobs and benefits. The problem is not the disabled person, it is the disabled jobs, evidenced by these Washington Business Group on Health figures:

- 💼 Short-term disability costs frequently run from 2 to 4 percent of total payroll, and long-term disability benefits can add another .5 to 1 percent. For every $1 million of payroll, $50,000 is spent on disability alone.

- 💼 The payoff to business and society for rehabilitating people with disabilities is between $8 and $10 for every dollar spent.

Here are some principles for accommodating disabled workers and company programs that put them into practice:

1. KEEP TRACK OF DISABILITIES—ON AND OFF THE JOB. The absenteeism program at Alcoa includes early contact with the absent employee by both the manager and a medical professional and weekly plant meetings to review absences. And at Aetna Insurance Company, every time a disabled employee visits a medical practitioner, that person reports to Aetna the substance of the visit, whether the employee will continue to be absent, treatment recommendations, and how long the absence should last. This information is fed into the computer, which then estimates the expected disability period.

2. OFFER INSTRUCTION FOR AVOIDING DISABILITIES. The Mississippi Power Company offers a Back Accident Prevention Program taught by the Gulf Coast Physical Therapy Group. Before the program, workers had thirty-one back accidents, 170 lost days, and four surgeries. Since the program, only one person has injured his back.

3. CHANGE COMPANY STATEMENTS TO ELIMINATE SUBTLE DISCRIMINATION. Change "Cannot lift over 40 lbs." to "Can lift up to 40 lbs." and "Cannot sit for long periods" to "Can sit for moderate periods." Other positive approaches include changing "Must use wheelchair" to "Is very mobile with wheelchair" and "Must take frequent breaks" to "Can work for extended periods with breaks."

4. BRING THE DISABLED BACK TO WORK AS SOON AS POSSIBLE. The furniture manufacturer Herman Miller, Inc. has a transitional work center to bring restricted workers—employees injured or disabled—back to work quickly even if they cannot return to their old jobs. The company matches the employee to a job that meets his or her medical restrictions, with the same pay as before. If necessary, the company provides training. For instance, an employee who permanently injured her wrist cutting and packing wood veneer was retrained as a full-time projectionist in the company's audiovisual department.

5. REDESIGN JOBS TO FIT THE DISABLED. The Adolph Coors Company rehabilitation center has helped 1,800 workers with temporary medical problems and 166 workers with long-term disabilities return to work. For instance, a construction worker who

Data Bank

- *The disabled population is growing younger, constituting a potentially very productive group of employees.*

- *A survey of companies employing the disabled reports that more than half the firms had no extra costs associated with accommodating them. About 18 percent spent less than $100 on special facilities or equipment.*

- *The biggest obstacles to a disabled person seeking work are employers' and managers' attitudes, not physical limitations.*

fell from a thirty-foot platform and suffered multiple back injuries was retrained as an administrative coordinator for a company construction group.

6. IDENTIFY EXISTING JOBS FOR THE DISABLED. Boise Cascade Corporation, headquartered in Idaho, constantly identifies jobs that
disabled workers can perform. In a two-year period, it reassigned
about 200 disabled employees. For example, an employee with a
back injury was assigned a clerical and administrative job tracking pumps. To identify jobs for the disabled, managers should ask
these questions:

- Are the adaptations acceptable to the employee?
- Can the technology, job, or space be adapted for the
  disabled?
- Are disabled employees included in discussions and decisions about accommodations?

7. MAKE SURE WORK SPACE IS FLEXIBLE FOR THE DISABLED. Sprague
Electric Company instituted a return-to-work program for disabled workers that involved modifying people's work space and
flexible work schedules. As a result, its annual workers'-
compensation costs dipped from $350,000 to $40,000 in two
years. Similarly, several Hewlett-Packard Company sites have Enabling Committees that assess the needs of disabled employees
and make recommendations to management. For people in
wheelchairs, they suggested installing mirrors on ceilings and
windows in the bottom half of bathroom doors so people can see
better.

8. WATCH FOR TOOLS THAT MAY AGGRAVATE DISABILITIES. A
telephone-assembly plant with a high incidence of carpal-
tunnel-syndrome injuries examined specific tasks and found that
most sufferers used vibrating air screwdrivers that required repeated grasping, squeezing, and clipping motions. The company
modified its tools by adding sleeve guards and changing task
positions to minimize hand and wrist stress. Thus, over two
years, injuries dropped by nearly two-thirds and lost and restricted workdays dropped 80 percent.

9. BE SENSITIVE TO DISABLED WORKERS FEELING IGNORED. Bell Labs has regular Disability Awareness Days when it rents equipment used by the disabled and for a day, everyone assumes a particular disability. For instance, on Hearing Impaired Day, employees use electronic mail, sign language, and other nonauditory means to communicate.

10. REWARD MANAGERS WHO ACCOMMODATE DISABLED EMPLOYEES. These rewards can take different forms: kudos in company newsletters, plaques, recognition at company events, or financial bonuses. At Bank of America, managers receive special attention through the in-house newsletter.

CURING SICK JOBS

Many organizations cited in this chapter have cured sick jobs. Yet unlike a broken arm or a heart condition, unhealthy work conditions cannot be permanently remedied with a slab of plaster or bypass surgery. People, jobs, and technology constantly change, and today's solution to a sick job may not work tomorrow. Companies must continually adjust and be sensitive to the human and technological evolution of workplaces. Only employers and employees who contend daily with the demands of their work can determine, together, the ideal fit between a person and a job.

Yet, as many employers have discovered, curing sick jobs is more complex than just recognizing a problem exists. Many companies are leery about taking decisive action to remedy unhealthy environments because of legal fears—fear that in doing so they are admitting to their responsibility and liability for employee illness. For example, a company was recently sued by pregnant employees who objected to their employer excluding them from high-paying jobs that could expose them to dangerous chemicals. But if you wait too long, legislation may force the change, as happened in San Francisco, where a 1990 ordinance mandated that VDT workers be provided regularly scheduled rest breaks, adjustable chairs, and adequate lighting.

The next chapter is an examination of the various kinds of people, rather than their diverse jobs, that must be accommodated in a healthy company.

Research shows that work overload is associated with increased hypertension, heart attacks, job dissatisfaction, anxiety, depression, drinking, absenteeism, decreased self-esteem, and family difficulties. The greatest physical and mental-health difficulties occur when work overload is combined with underutilized skills.

Our Strengths Lie in Celebrating Differences

"ONE OF THE UNUSUAL THINGS about the 1990s is that most of the growth in the marketplace will be among women, minority persons, immigrants, people with different needs, different perspectives, different ideas," declares Darlene Siedschlaw, the aptly titled director of diversity for the Denver-based telecommunications firm U.S. West. While Siedschlaw's observations are true for all businesses, the daily reality at her company illustrates how the composition of the American work force is growing increasingly diverse and what a company can do to accommodate its multifaceted employees.

Despite its dependence on sophisticated technology, U.S. West tries to operate by the maxim "People are our most valuable asset." The philosophy is not public-relations copy, but reflects a very practical reality inside the company. "We're a big company, deeply involved in the worldwide growth of the Information Age," explains Siedschlaw. "That requires a lot of resources, a lot of leading-edge technology. But the plain truth is every company has access to the same technologies. The only competitive edge we can hope to gain is through ideas, energy, strategic planning.

Today the melting pot is the wrong metaphor even in business, for three good reasons. First, if it ever was possible to melt down Scotsmen and Dutchmen and Frenchmen into an indistinguishable broth, you can't do the same with blacks, Asians and women. Their differences don't melt so easily. Second, most people are no longer willing to be melted down, not even for eight hours a day. Third, the thrust of today's nonhierarchical, flexible, collaborative management requires a 10- or 20-fold increase in our tolerance for individuality.

R. ROOSEVELT THOMAS, JR.
Executive Director,
American Institute for
Managing Diversity

In short, through our *human resources.* Tapping all available human resources is the key to our corporate survival."

For example, the chairman of U.S. West, Jack MacAllister, cultivates his reputation as a people person who encourages employees to contribute ideas about managing the company. So when a group of employees made a formal request to meet with him, he was eager to listen. The employees who appeared at MacAllister's office were a group of black and Hispanic women, not unusual considering the company has 69,000 employees, including a healthy slice of women and minorities. Their numbers, however, were not the point of their visit—their future was.

Armed with statistics about the hierarchy at U.S. West, they presented a disconcerting picture. In their company, a woman of color had almost as little chance of reaching upper management than she did of winning a lottery. Their numbers were undoubtedly comparable to figures published by the New York firm Catalyst, which shows that women comprise fewer than 5 percent of the senior managers in the top 1,000 corporations in the country and that the percentage of minority women in that small group is infinitesimal. That day, U.S. West acted to improve those odds: it created a new organization within the firm called the Women of Color program.

The Women of Color program became another of a number of programs at U.S. West to address the special needs of its employees and made everyone part of a larger corporate strategy. The company describes this strategy as pluralism, a far-sighted philosophy for managing employees, enhancing careers, and surpassing the competition. Siedschlaw believes developing the talents of the diverse U.S. West work force will "lead to greater creativity, more flexibility in responding to change, stronger commitment and better cooperation within heterogeneous work teams."

Around company headquarters and throughout its fourteen-state service region, pluralism is embodied by numerous resource groups like Women of Color. Most of the groups emerged in the late 1970s as mutual-support and advocacy groups. They were a way for nonwhite and female employees to learn the company ropes, to find a mentor, and to air complaints. These groups are still active, though their mission now leans more toward sharing information among themselves and with the rest of the com-

pany than establishing their identity within the company. For instance, SOMOS, a Hispanic group, recently held a regional business conference to discuss sales and marketing techniques; the
Black Employees Association has organized a special management course for itself; Voice of Many Feathers conducts workshops entitled The American Indian at Work; and the Single Parent Economic Independence Demonstration Project is helping
employees cope with raising children and managing their jobs.

The groups do not operate in a vacuum, but are closely followed by senior managers, who meet quarterly with a coalition of
the resource organizations. The managers also learn about their
varied employees by attending mandatory training sessions and
the workshops Leading a Diverse Workforce and The Value of
Human Diversity. Every month, the Pluralism Council—senior
managers from operations in all fourteen states—meets to discuss policies, strategies, and programs. Siedschlaw describes
Council activities: "We've got Black History month, we've got the
month of recognizing women, the month of the child, gay and
lesbian, veterans, religion, American Indian. We've added Pacific
Asian so that the major groups are covered in the calendar."

The resource groups, training sessions, and pluralism philosophy are tightly woven into the fabric of U.S. West; they are not
special efforts of the Employee Relations department dusted off
every few months for a pro forma meeting. They are part of people's daily working lives. Siedschlaw declares, "Concerning ourselves with human resources is not taking time off from running
the business—it is the business."

A KALEIDOSCOPE OF FACES

As U.S. West knows, the American work force is quickly losing its
homogeneous complexion to become a kaleidoscope of faces.
The clique that has predominated for so long, white Anglo-Saxon
men, is giving way to workplaces dominated by no one group but
populated by a diverse citizenry of men and women of various
races and ethnic groups, among them seniors and the disabled.

In 1988, white men comprised 45 percent of the work force;
between 1989 and 2000, they are expected to shrink to 22.3 percent. At the same time, the percentage of female workers will

grow from 45 percent to almost 64 percent and the percentage of nonwhite workers will leap from just under 14 percent in 1988 to almost 40 percent.

In every office, factory, and shop, managers and employees are surrounded by people unlike themselves—people who look different, speak different languages, and grew up in different countries. Some differences are obvious: coworkers may dress in unusual clothes, possess varied family customs, or practice unusual religions. But the unseen differences are even more important: they may have widely different notions about the value of punctuality, about aggressiveness and affiliation at work, or about heeding authority figures. Workplace diversity extends beyond gender, race, ethnic origin, and nationality to encompass people who differ in terms of their age and generational influ-

When I asked a white male middle manager how promotions were handled in his company, he said, "You need leadership capability, bottom-line results, the ability to work with people, and compassion." Then he paused and smiled. "That's what they say. But down the hall there's a guy we call Captain Kickass. He's ruthless, mean-spirited, and he steps on people. That's the behavior they really value. Forget what they say."

R. ROOSEVELT THOMAS, JR.
Executive Director,
American Institute for
Managing Diversity

A Man's World

Men occupy more than 90 percent of all executive positions in this country, so it is no surprise that most companies are institutional personifications of the white male psyche. Their philosophies about success, business strategy, relationships, and families are woven into the fabric of organizational life.

As little boys, males learn to suppress emotions and weakness—to "be a man." By age five, sex-role stereotypes are firmly in place, as boys are told to deny pain, hold back tears, and disregard signals from their minds and bodies of disease and discomfort. For them, the weakness and dependence that comes with illness or admitting mistakes means being helpless and passive.

As they grow into young men, they are taught a myriad of lessons, many of which become part of the male vernacular: "Don't let anyone push you around . . . take it like a man . . . keep a stiff upper lip." A constant theme is to stay in charge, to control and dominate, and not to rely on others.

The lessons are learned well. Studies show that boys and girls seek help from others at the same pace until age twelve, at which point there is a dramatic drop in the rate at which boys seek help. In the fifteen-to-twenty-one-year age range, male visits to doctors diminish, dropping by more than 3 million per year.

By the time they go to work, men are conditioned to fight. Their aggressive, rational, tough-minded outlook suits them well in a competitive

ences, sexual preferences, lifestyles, religions, physical abilities, and education. It is a pluralism that embraces a wide spectrum of origins, values, and traditions.

A CLASH OF VALUES

While this kaleidoscope of faces is quickly becoming a reality, the workplace is not yet prepared for its rich diversity. For decades, offices and factories have been operating according to a collection of narrow values advocated by a white American male power structure. Despite this country's tradition of welcoming immigrants and celebrating pluralism, corporate attitudes are still biased by ethnocentric assumptions, and these attitudes are

The subjects of racism, sexism, and other differences among employees are so threatening to many people that even the best managers find themselves "walking on thin ice" when these topics are discussed. . . . Embarrassment about cultural differences often stems from a perception that employees who are different are inferior.

LENNIE COPELAND
Producer, *Valuing Diversity* film series

---

work world of triumphs and conquests. Their role models—cowboys and quarterbacks—have taught them to be strong and independent. Their success is measured by the amount of money they make and the prestige they acquire.

As they age, men pay a dear price for the lessons they have learned about manhood:

- On the average, men die eight years earlier than women.
- Men have much higher rates of suicide, fatal motor-vehicle accidents, cirrhosis of the liver, and respiratory diseases associated with cigarettes.
- Men are six times more likely than women to suffer disabling injuries on the job.
- Men are three to six times as likely to become heavy or problem drinkers.

It is sad that many men don't learn about feelings and fears until it is time to retire. As they enter their late fifties and sixties, something happens inside. They become more aware of physical limitations, of gaps in achievement, and of years left to live. They discover their health, a sense of purpose, and their families. Business success, for them, is not necessarily a ticket to successful living. They finally learn to challenge the male stereotype, but for many it is too late.

on a collision course with the multitudinous values and cultures now sweeping through business.

The culture that has dominated business, which is grounded in the beliefs and aspirations of white American men, is founded on the premise that men are in charge and have an insatiable drive to subdue, dominate, and control. It is the spirit of Marine Corps commercials and the daily manifestation of the Protestant work ethic. These values are embodied in the emphasis on competitive male sports and all that they require, such as fairness, physical challenge, a desire to win, and an abhorrence of losing.

Other qualities inherent in these values surround the notion of independence and self-sufficiency. White American men have promoted the idea that people should be able to take care of themselves, be invulnerable to (or, better yet, stoic about) pain, and possess an indomitable will to strive and succeed.

These white male cultural values have become institutionalized in the workplace, with most companies using them to define what is desirable and good for all employees. They are the silent rules, defining policies, practices, and promotional opportunities. Yet many of these values are at odds with those of today's multifaceted employees, producing a great clash of aspirations and attitudes and generating widespread fear, dissension, and antagonism.

A 1991 Department of Labor study of promotion practices of nine Fortune 500 companies shows that invisible barriers, sometimes called "glass ceilings," block women and minorities at a much lower level than previously thought. Out of 4,491 executive managers (assistant vice presidents and higher,) only 6.6 percent were women and 2.6 percent were minorities.

A GROWING XENOPHOBIA

Surrounded by unfamiliar appearances and new ways of thinking, managers and employees cling to their own traditional values and experience a sharp xenophobia—a fear of strangers. They tiptoe through the corporate hallways fearful of those who are different, reluctant to confront the perceptual and institutional barriers that separate people, while harboring long-standing prejudices. Explains corporate-diversity expert David Dyer about the effects of the clash: "We wind up with people feeling very uncomfortable or self-conscious and maybe hostile toward another person or group of people, and they tend to spend a lot more time thinking about that situation rather than what their work assignment may be or how to do better on the job."

The clash between these traditional values and those of the minority work force begins the day any female, nonwhite, or non-

American employee starts work. Many companies make few efforts to culturally integrate such employees into the mainstream, assuming that they will somehow learn to fit in. Few employers build networks or foster mentoring programs for them and instead keep a tight fist on job assignments, training, and advancement opportunities. The employees don't help matters by clinging to insecure attitudes about their cultural background and deep-seated resentment toward the white male majority. The clash persists long after different cultures have met, sending permanent reverberations throughout the workplace.

The clash of values shows up in subtle and blatant discrimination, and while laws exist to curb obvious discrimination, less clear forms of it are common. Your office is probably splintered by discrimination among employees. Cadres of various groups—blacks, Hispanics, lesbians, or whoever—lunch together, swap company gossip, share a special vocabulary or language, and keep to themselves. Their cliques may simply reflect personal preference. Clannishness, per se, is often harmless. We all prefer to be around people like ourselves, to work with and socialize with those who reaffirm our values and preferences. Intentional separateness, however, may be isolation created by subtle discrimination and rejection, a reflection of outsider status in the company.

Robert Kleeb, an equal-opportunity manager at Mobil Corporation, offers this illustration: "Look at our executive dining room. Do you ever see four blacks sitting together? You see four white males all the time. Why is that? Because blacks would feel that everyone is thinking, 'Why are they together? Are they plotting? Are they being exclusive?'"

These are some typical acts of subtle institutional discrimination: company publications written in sexist language; ignoring holidays important to a group of workers, such as Muslims, Hispanics, or blacks; sponsoring social activities aimed only at football fans or married couples; and not considering older workers for promotions. Discrimination based on values may be apparent in a company denying an employee's request for extra training; in highly critical performance evaluations or minimal pay raises; in insisting on certain personality types for prized jobs; in limiting the seniority of employees who insist on time for families and personal lives; and in demanding standard forms of communication based on a white, middle-class Ivy League college education.

As a white woman dealing with my racism, the best I'll ever be is a recovering racist. It would be easy for us to push it off on the white male and say well, the white male is the problem. We all carry our baggage and we all have to address it.

DARLENE SIEDSCHLAW
EEO/AA Compliance Manager, U.S. West, *Valuing Diversity* film series

QUELL THE CLASH, MANAGE DIVERSITY

Data Bank

💼 *In 1988, 3.7 million Americans worked for foreign subsidiaries in the United States. That number will rise to 4.6 million in 1991, according to* Business Week.

💼 *A 1988 Commerce Department report cited these percentages of U.S. employees at foreign-owned companies located in the U.S.: British, 20%; Canadian, 19%; Japanese, 11%; German, 10%; Dutch, 8%; French, 7%; and other countries, 25%.*

The clash between traditional corporate values and a heterogeneous work force is inescapable, yet it must be quelled if a company is to function and advance. Companies can no longer avoid hiring varied groups of employees; and in fact, in most businesses, a heterogeneous work force adds talent, creativity, and productivity.

One of the most compelling reasons for hiring a diverse work force is the shrinking labor pool and the increasing competition for quality employees. Experts estimate that by 1995, the pool of potential employees will drop 7 million, or 24 percent, from 1980. A 1990 study by employment experts Towers Perrin and the Hudson Institute reports that already 65 percent of companies say they are experiencing labor shortages. This same group reports that the new ethnic and racial mix among their employees is a significant concern to management.

As the United States' demographics shift to include more immigrants and growing numbers of nonwhite and female workers, employers will increasingly need to hire all sorts of minorities. Already, women and nonwhite workers account for almost two-thirds of the new entrants to the work force. According to the Bureau of Labor Statistics, between the mid-1980s and year 2000, the bulk of new entrants—82 percent—will be women, non-Caucasians, and immigrants. Thus companies already are not only seeking out diverse employees, they are competing for them.

A diverse work force gives a company a competitive edge in the marketplace. Employees who speak more than English, know the customs and cultures of other countries, and have experience with different nationalities are a great boon to companies operating in an international arena. Even in domestic markets, a diverse cadre of employees helps a company understand and better serve its customers, the great American melting pot. Furthermore, companies where a multi-ethnic employee roster is not only encouraged but considered a valuable asset are sure to attract talented, committed job applicants from diverse cultures.

Business, in limited ways, has tried to quell the culture clash. Its first response to the diverse work force was formal, relying on the legal system and government to ensure equality and fair treatment. Like rounding up the creatures of Noah's Ark, many businesses pursued two of everything. However, following equal-opportunity laws, regulations, and quotas to the letter of the law does not alter the spirit of the workplace. "Aside from equal opportunity being the law," asserts Pacific Gas & Electric president George Maneatis, "there's also a need to make it the spirit of business."

Managing diversity, which has become a personnel necessity for all healthy companies, requires accommodation and assimilation. Companies need to make accommodations for *all* employees, taking into consideration not only ethnic and cultural backgrounds but also personal, lifestyle differences. Simultaneously, managers must help create a corporate culture broad enough to encompass diverse values and then assist employees in assimilating into the culture. Lastly, employees themselves must make efforts to integrate their beliefs and customs into the prevailing company culture.

This chapter offers suggestions for learning how to accommodate and assimilate. Beginning with an examination of your own personal attitudes toward strangers, it goes on to identify what managers and healthy companies can do to manage diversity and reap its benefits.

Studies show that students and trainees taught by different people (e.g., men/women, black/white teams) learn better. In genetics, hybrids are stronger and more resistant to disease. Alloys are stronger than pure metals.

LENNIE COPELAND
Producer, *Valuing Diversity* film series

INSIDE OUT

Where Are Your Prejudices?

Each of us possesses a unique collection of prejudices and stereotypes acquired since childhood from parents and friends, then magnified or shrunk according to our experiences. Some of these automatic thoughts are so ingrained we are not aware of them and only close, honest examination will bring them to light. These questions will help you explore not only the content of your special biases but also take stock of the memories and experiences that engendered them. Score your questions:

1 Never	3 Sometimes	5 Always
2 Seldom	4 Often	

1. Have you ever felt uncomfortable visiting a foreign country where you were considered different?

2. As a child, were you ever expected to be seen but not heard?

3. Do you resent people who live in this country but whose English is imperfect?

4. Do you discount opinions of people who are female, over fifty, short, have a Polish name, speak in a Southern accent, have brown skin, or different from you in any other respect? (Use just one score.)

5. Are you annoyed by women who swear?

6. Do you react negatively to men who wear jewelry?

7. Are you afraid to bring up racial issues with acquaintances of a different race?

8. Do you believe older people are inflexible and unable to learn new technology?

9. Do you believe you know who is gay in your office?

10. Do you think black women are emotionally stronger than black men?

11. Do you believe disabled people would rather not work?

12. Do you find successful women to be pushy and abrasive?

13. Do you resent the special opportunities given to minorities?

14. Do you tell a lot of ethnic jokes?

What Your Answers Mean

If your score is between 56 and 70, you harbor a number of cultural biases and tend to be xenophobic; a score between 35 and 55 indicates that while you possess some biases, you also try to avoid stereotypes and regard people more or less equally; and if your score is less than 35, you are remarkably free of ethnic or cultural taints and judge everyone individually.

The underlying goal of many of these questions is to ascertain your familiarity with and acceptance of people unlike yourself. Stereotypes and biases are usually fabricated from a small amount of material or gathered secondhand—from a vague acquaintance, a single conversation or meeting, listening to outspoken parents or friends, or seeing someone in an advertisement, a commercial, or a movie. Most people are woefully ignorant about each other and fill their knowledge vacuum with gross generalizations and stereotypes.

Prejudice is the result of stereotypes left unchecked. Everyone is prejudiced to a greater or lesser extent; I have confronted my own prejudices throughout the writing of this book. Prejudice is a natural emotion that starts early in life in our relatively isolated families and neighborhoods. We often attend segregated schools, play in racially or ethnically unmixed schoolyards, and socialize with friends who look like us, while our stereotypes germinate and grow. Acquiring prejudices is a sifting process that identifies the person who is different and thus not understood and sometimes feared, who may even pose a threat to our beliefs. To protect ourselves and all that is important to us, we maintain a distance from strangers, who may hold dear other beliefs.

At its most fundamental, our rejection of unfamiliar people is based on ignorance and insecurity. We conclude there are two worlds: our safe, known sphere and the outer world populated by threatening strangers. Strangers produce a full regalia of emotions—including fear, envy, admiration, revulsion, and insecurity—not because they are inherently ferocious or worthy of envy but because of what they reflect about ourselves.

To overcome your prejudices, you need to separate opinion or emotional reaction from hard facts:

Step 1. Distill your own cultural and family roots—the deep-seated assumptions, mores, heroes, and messages that are part of your upbringing. What are the common generalizations people make about your background? Ask yourself whether these stereotypes are based on fact or fiction.

Step 2. Carefully watch how you ascribe personality characteristics to other groups. Observe your emotional reactions when you are around them. Do you feel a sense of resentment, deference, insecurity, or disrespect? Do you exclude them in overt and subtle ways—from your eye contact to lunch invitations to whom you gossip with?

Step 3. Now ask yourself why you have these feelings and what assumptions are behind these stereotypes. Take apart each generalization and ask yourself whether there is sufficient evidence to

The responsibility is always the individual's to find out at some level, "How do I feel, what do I think about people who are different from myself, how do I react when I find out that the man I'm talking to is gay? What goes on inside of me, what do I do and how do I behave? And how does that behavior affect him? What do I do when I talk with someone who has cerebral palsy—am I frightened or am I uneasy? Do I close down? What goes on inside of me?

LARRY WALLER
Director of Pluralism, U.S. West, *Valuing Diversity* film series

warrant such a conclusion. Can you link your assumptions to a dinner-table conversation you heard as a child, a playground experience, or your parents' employing a black housekeeper in the home? The assumptions probably circle back to your upbringing and have little to do with the truth about others.

Step 4. Try to imagine what life would be like in someone else's shoes. The next time you interact with someone from one of these groups, look for individual differences before you impose your generalization. Discriminate between real cultural differences that need to be respected and stereotypes that need to be rejected. If you open your sphere of interest and shrink your world of strangers, in time you will feel less defensive and more comfortable.

 ## What the Manager Can Do

Managing diversity is a step-by-step process of personal and organizational change, involving two kinds of activity to harness your work force into a compatible, productive team. The first is understanding people in a deeper way; the other is to better utilize the diverse talents around you, learning to be more culturally sensitive and adept in nurturing differences among groups of employees.

Most companies are familiar with the fundamentals of managing diversity: equal hiring procedures; promotion goals that include all minorities; and fair treatment in assignments, training, and rewards. They talk about equal pay for equal worth, issue press releases about minority members on their boards of directors, and position female role models in visible, key spots.

Nevertheless, the consequences of mismanaged diversity continue to plague managers, because people are not backing their words with deeds. Managers must close the gap between the talk and bromides for equal opportunity, aggressive hiring, fair treatment, and genuine action. Without decisive steps, the rhetoric simply gets longer and deeper, employees are no better off, and companies waste valuable talent.

Here are some ways to master the complexities of your diverse work force. These steps are sequential, starting with an

It's in the best interest of each and every one of us to do the personal growth work that valuing differences is about. If we can reduce the social distance, then we will find ways in which we can become interdependent, work together more productively. We will be more synergistic, we will share power, we will be more collaborative, we will be more creative, and at that point, we'll make more money.

BARBARA WALKER
International Diversity Manager, Digital Equipment Corporation, *Valuing Diversity* film series

overall audit of the cultural qualities of your workforce and moving to ways to manage specific, individual employees and tackling the cultural clashes that can tear an office apart.

Conduct a Cultural Audit

You may believe your employees are all the same and that you treat them alike, but odds are, they are not, and you do not. Regardless of how insightful you are about people, you probably underestimate the rich diversity in your office. Survey the people in your immediate work circle to discover what you have been missing:

Demographics. Your audit of characteristics should cover not only gender but also race, cultural origins, primary language, generation designation, regional influences, and physical infirmities.

Personal characteristics. Get a sense of less obvious attributes, such as number and ages of children or parents living with them; family influences (for example, a spouse who is mentally ill); and personal interests and ambitions.

Working styles. Consider how people design their working lives and how they interact with coworkers. Some people are natural team players; others prefer working alone. Employees differ in their desire for independence, need for flexibility, and willingness to take lengthy business trips. Some people are natural nesters and enjoy quiet family life, whereas single employees may rely on the office for socializing.

Lifestyle values. Lifestyle values encompass much more than moral or ethical beliefs, translating on a day-to-day basis into a predilection toward such qualities as neatness, practicality, a sense of adventure, creativity, loyalty, tradition, a sense of humor, or spiritual tranquillity. Such values prioritize our lives and influence how we spend our time.

People want to be treated as individuals, with unique interests and capabilities, so your goal is to know the exact composition of your work force and to pinpoint what makes every person special. To analyze your audit, list employee characteristics and discover the wealth of talent you never knew about. Use this information to initiate personal, informal conversations. As you walk around the office, watch how people's behavior, including your own, responds to these individual differences. Allow your employees to talk freely among themselves about what is important to them. Spending a meeting discussing interests and values is one way to get started.

Armed with a thorough cultural audit and a sense of the real demographic patterns, you can take the next step by digging deeper into the needs and concerns of your diverse work force.

Recognize the Faces of Diversity

Although managing diverse clusters of employees requires an understanding of individual psychology—the what and why of people's thinking—there are several groups that share common attitudes about work. In managing these groups, one should be sensitive to their shared psychology, keeping in mind the need to respect differences among individuals. Here is a brief overview of the concerns of various groups of employees often considered outsiders, as well as statistics that reflect and even reinforce the validity of their beliefs.

Women: Battles on All Fronts

Women are at a pivotal point on the road to being full partners with men in the work world. Although corporate America has opened its doors, management isn't letting women climb the career ladder as quickly as they would like. Women continue to experience pay inequities, special tracks for working mothers, and daily struggles to balance work and family needs. Still perceived as outsiders, women remain confused about how to manage and conduct themselves as healthy, successful people in today's organizations.

Women earn, on average, $16,232, or 70 percent of men's wages. Regardless of their numbers in the workplace, women often feel like second-class citizens. Cited studies by Supreme Court Justice Sandra Day O'Connor indicate that women make up only 6 percent of all partners in the nation's law firms, only 16 percent of all doctors, only 7 percent of engineers, and only 6 percent of news-media executives.

One reason for this disparity is that women often feel forced to choose between success at work and raising children. According to *Business Week,* less than 5 percent of U.S. companies provide child care. Most working women hold two jobs, being responsible for the upkeep and cooking at home as well as an outside job. Women devote an average of eighty hours a week to home and office, compared with men, who devote an average of fifty hours.

Women also must contend with coworkers who believe they are unable to have a business relationship and are emotionally weak. A Swain & Swain survey of managers at Fortune 500 companies reports that 50 percent of the men believed they worked well with women, while only 34 percent of the women believed that. Half of the men also believed they accept women as peers, while only 33 percent of the women shared that belief.

Women feel they must conform to white male working styles, being tough-minded and unemotional, or risk losing their place. Studies have shown that if they don't conform, women are labeled independent, a troublemaker, or simply unsuitable for a company. Women say they cannot afford the luxury of sometimes producing mediocre work, because the male world demands that they be exceptionally skilled and competent, and so must log superior performances simply to stay even with male coworkers.

Too much work, too little time and control describes the life of today's clerical worker. Like the blue-collar counterpart, those at the lower rungs of the office ladder are most at risk for stress-related problems. And there is a gender bias here: the majority of all female workers are still employed in traditionally female jobs, including those of secretary, data-entry clerk, and sales clerk. Not surprisingly, women are the major users of hospitals and doctors.

Almost every woman encounters sexual harassment at some point in her working life yet often feels helpless in combating it. Ninety-five percent of all women and men who report sexual harassment fear retaliation and a loss of privacy, according to Mary Rowe, special assistant to the president of MIT. They also feel that it is pointless to complain. *Working Woman* magazine reports that sexual harassment costs a typical Fortune 500 company $6.7 million a year in absenteeism, employee turnover, low morale, and low productivity.

However, good news is on the horizon. An International Women's Forum report shows that a new wave of women is making its way into top management, not by adopting the style that has proved successful for men, but by drawing on the skills and attitudes they developed from their shared experience as women. As leaders, they are more interactive and empowering and have learned to be more sensitive to the needs of others. These women are likely to be married and make the same amount of money as their male peers.

Ethnic Minorities: The Sting of Stigma

Blacks, Hispanics, Asians, American Indians, and all other ethnic minorities know the sting of stigma in the workplace. Regardless of their qualifications or education, they begin the race with a handicap behind Anglo-Saxon coworkers. Caucasians tend to see minorities not as individuals but as representatives of a group, and minorities feel they must assert their personal identity while combating their ethnic stereotypes. Equal-opportunity and affirmative-action programs have produced personal and professional stress, because minorities feel their skills and experiences count for less than their ethnic classification. Furthermore, they feel coworkers' resentment of them for the special treatment.

Minorities feel frustrated, stressed, and deceived, knowing the promises of equal opportunity by corporate America contain limited substance. "Minorities no longer need a boarding pass—they need an upgrade," declares diversity expert R. Roosevelt Thomas, Jr. Less than 1 percent of Fortune 500 senior executives are minorities, according to the recruiting firm Korn Ferry International. The Bureau of Labor Statistics also reports that the wage gap between whites and blacks from 1979 to 1989 showed black men made very little progress in closing the salary differences.

To be a minority in the workplace means to be regularly scrutinized—noticed and highlighted when hired and then perpetually evaluated by bosses and coworkers. Years of such close examination undercut self-confidence, making minorities question their competence and confidence. A survey of black managers by a minority recruiting firm reports that 43 percent believe they have less opportunity now to move up the corporate ladder than they did five years ago.

There's a myth afoot that equal treatment is the desired objective for management. No one treats anyone equally, whether in personal or public relationships. And I would go beyond that: anyone who does treat equally is not a very analytical person. I adjust myself to the individual so that I will treat each individually, mindful that some of the ways that person reacts are conditioned by an ethnic or other culture.

SANTIAGO RODRIGUEZ
Director of Multicultural and Affirmative Action Programs, Apple Computer, Inc., *Valuing Diversity* film series

Older Workers: Daily Indignities

Everyone grows older; our minds and bodies slow down and wrinkle through no fault of our own and despite monumental efforts to stave aging off. Older workers bristle at the indignities and unfairness of old age, waging a two-front battle against age discrimination and the perception of declining powers.

Older workers, despite their growing numbers, often feel as if they are either invisible or elaborately disguised, like actors from an ancient Greek play. Younger workers first notice the infirmities and limitations—the slower gait, a trembling hand—or simply the gray hair. Older workers' healthy, vigorous side is barely acknowledged. Yet by the end of the century, only 39 percent of the work force will be under age thirty-five, compared with 49 percent now. The number of workers between fifty and sixty-five years will grow twice as fast as the general population.

Older workers are always braced for the reaction their age may trigger, and they know their positions are tenuous because of their age. They must prove themselves every day, struggling especially hard against the preconception that they are inflexible and unwilling to learn. Nevertheless, because of their experience and maturity, they are often superior employees. A Yankelovich survey of 400 companies reports that 71 percent rated the performance of older workers as excellent or very good. Other ratings were 86 percent for punctuality, 82 percent for commitment to quality, and 76 percent for practical knowledge. However, "older employees of large companies continue to receive low ratings on a critically important issue—the ability to cope with new technology," found a survey by the American Association of Retired Persons.

Older workers focus more on the job at hand than on future concerns like promotions. Unlike the ambition of younger co-workers, theirs is a desire to perform well and to be recognized and appreciated. They seek satisfaction today, not tomorrow or next year. Seven out of ten workers over age sixty-three say the chance to be of service is the main consideration in a job, according to a Gallup Poll.

Older workers know that many employers are not as loyal to them as they are to younger employees. An AARP survey of top corporate managers reports that only 25 percent voiced a commitment to older workers, versus 33 percent five years ago.

Older workers also worry about health-care costs—about losing their jobs and coverage, possibly because employers fear costly liabilities. They know that employers consider them a burden on health plans, one more reason why they are forced into early retirement. However, a recent study by AARP found that insurance costs for older workers compared favorably to younger workers, because the elders had fewer dependents.

Younger Workers: A Hidden Minority Struggling for Identity

At first glance, younger workers do not look like a minority. To many, they are the mainstream, the competition—and the enemy. Demographers call those born after 1964, when birth rates started to decline, the baby busters. But their relatively small numbers make them a special-interest group with pressures, fears, and feelings different from older coworkers. Younger workers possess unconventional values, aspirations, and work styles. Raised in a time free of war, economic pressures, and political uncertainty, they have developed unique philosophies and goals about what they want from their life's work.

The young employee expects more from work than simply money or financial security. He or she wants meaningful assignments, access to decision-makers, and the freedom to balance professional demands with personal interests. One in three workers under age thirty consider self-development their first priority, according to a survey of 3,000.

Impatient about their jobs, younger workers feel little necessity for simply putting in time or paying their dues, and they want to see signs of success immediately. In a survey of 1,000 college students by the Roper Organization, starting salary ranked sixth in importance and opportunity for promotion ranked first.

Job security means little to younger workers, because they are confident that their skills will always be in demand. In their hierarchy of needs, security falls below such goals as a healthy work environment, time for self-development, and a sense of purpose. "There's no sense of real emotional security. Their whole outlook is, 'I gotta keep learning and developing to be independent and marketable,'" according to Michael Maccoby, author of *Why Work? Leading the New Generation.* Among Harvard Business

School students, 90 percent hope to own or manage their own business someday, compared to 60 percent ten years ago.

Younger workers tend to reject authoritarian management styles. They are more questioning, more demanding of explanations, and more pragmatic in their solutions. If they follow directions it is because an idea makes sense, not because of the source of the idea.

Eliminate Cultural Clashes

Once you have understood the complexity of human psychology, you must identify the cultural clashes at work and take aggressive steps to eliminate them. In truth, few people seek out cultural confrontations; they are more typically the result of misperceptions and misunderstandings and are exacerbated by a general reluctance to discuss these issues at work. You need to confront this reluctance head on. Eliminating the resistance usually requires examining routine encounters, fostering open dialogue among employees, and identifying the assumptions that are creating the clash.

At the computer company Intel, relations between American and Israeli employees grew tense because the foreigners did not express themselves the same way as the others—the Israelis raised too many questions and objections. Intel's manager of diversity finally brought the contending groups together and discovered that "Israelis believe that if you don't argue, it's not fun."

At times, untangling beliefs based on ethnicity demands probing, because people may try to keep their cultural uniqueness tucked away in their personal lives. A vice-president of a manufacturing company describes such a situation:

"When I worked in Canada, the first-line supervisor came to me and said, 'Look, I've got an employee who's a North American Indian and he hasn't come to work for three days and our policy says we should fire him because we haven't been notified. But he's a real good worker and I don't understand what's going on. He's never done this before!'

"So I called him at home and said, 'Well, what's the problem?'

"And he said, 'My son's sick.'

" 'Oh, you mean both you and your wife work and you don't have anybody to take care of him? Maybe we can make arrangements,' I said.

What we're bringing into the workplace is what we see around us every day in society when you ride the subway, when you walk the streets. What we're trying to create is an easiness about how people can come together in the work environment. What we're about is trying to have a sense of understanding about the inherent and fundamental dignity and worth of each individual as a person.

DON MILLER
Vice-President, Employee Relations, Dow Jones, Inc., *Valuing Diversity* film series

Apple Computer, Inc.

"And he said, 'No, you don't understand: my son is sick. My wife's home, but my son is very important to me. He carries on the family heritage. I can't come to work until he's better.' "

While some cultural conflicts are unavoidable, a manager has to air them and seek out a compromise that allows people to maintain their cultural identity while also making adjustments for accepted standards of behavior. Explains Santiago Rodriguez, a manager of multicultural and affirmative action at Apple Computer: "It's rude in East Asian cultures to answer a question in the negative. People will tell you yes even when they mean no. So we need to train people not to ask binary questions that require a yes-or-no answer. . . . In Hispanic cultures, modesty is in-grained. If you're good, someone will know about it. You never talk about yourself. To single out an Hispanic and praise him or her publicly could be terribly embarrassing, especially if ethnic peers are in the group."

As this manager discovered, you never can fully manage di-versity. What you can learn, however, is to acknowledge the dif-ferences around you, talk openly about them, and accept the fact that each person sees the world through his or her own special pair of glasses. Regardless of their gender, race, or lifestyle, peo-ple just want to know that you understand their unique feelings and fears about life.

 ### *Corporate Policies and Strategies*

Company culture is like a television signal: the transmission is invisible, but the pictures received are very clear. For instance, your signals may be pointing to aggressiveness or outspokenness as signs of intelligence; people's willingness to work overtime as a sign of loyalty; eye contact as a sign of deference or antagonism; or the ability to write formal memos as an indication of people's education and vocabulary. Without being aware of the signals, you may inadvertently be pushing employees to mimic the main-stream corporate culture.

I learned about these subtle influences some years ago when consulting simultaneously with two communications firms. One company was a hard-charging, competitive East Coast public-relations firm with a long history and culture of powerful leaders and a tough, critical work environment. Managers achieved status and scored points by pointing out flaws in others, staying on the offensive, and being critical about new ideas. To get ahead, managers had to cultivate an air of superiority and to truly want to win, no matter how it was done.

The other company was an advertising agency where the primary topic among managers was what the company was doing to make customers more satisfied and employees' lives easier and more productive. Of interest were programs such as flextime for employees with children, awards for promoting minorities, and workshops on positive customer relations.

The employees of the two firms even dressed differently—at the first, in yellow power ties, gray suits, and suspenders, while at the other, managers wore whatever was appropriate for that day, coats and ties for client meetings and blue jeans for days spent at the drafting board. Not surprisingly, the turnover at the first company was a major headache; the firm could not attract and retain enough people to fit its mold. The ad agency, which had no mold, had a fat file of unsolicited résumés and job applications.

Build a Culture Sensitive to Diversity

Like people, organizations come in all shapes and sizes; and like people, they can promote or undermine diversity. Reading your company culture requires picking up clues from how people act and talk. Here are questions to ask yourself:

- What are the norms in your office for acceptable behavior and attitudes?

- Do people feel pressured to dress like those in power positions?

- Are people rewarded for being agreeable? For being aggressive and expressing opinions? For being conservative and risk-averse?

- What is the mood of your workplace—informal, with a lot of camaraderie, or quiet and serious?

- How do people address and talk to coworkers, managers, and senior executives?

- Do people feel comfortable talking about their personal lives at work?

Management will tell you that everybody gets along wonderfully and that's the way it is here. They don't have racial problems and they don't have sexual harassment. But the truth of the matter is, when you sit down with the individuals, you find a different story. You'll find small little things that might bother them and might have bothered them for years.

KAREN KENNEDY
Production Manager, *Wall Street Journal, Valuing Diversity* film series

- ▪ Do employees talk about their disagreements and misunderstandings, or do they remain silent and sweep them under the rug?

- ▪ How flexible are company policies affecting personal lives? For instance, does the company allow for everyone to observe their religious holidays, and does the company cafeteria cater to vegetarians or kosher diets?

These questions are the beginnings of a litmus test for determining how open your company is to individual cultures. Company cultures that are insensitive to their employees tend to be rigid, hierarchical, and formal. In such a workplace, disagreement is discouraged; nonconformist opinions are shunned; people are encouraged to look and act alike; discussion of personal topics (which help people affirm their individual identity) are avoided; and there is clear delineation of classes or levels of employees.

In contrast, the culturally sensitive workplace encourages spontaneity, nonconformity, sharing of conflicting ideas, and independent thinking. In short, in this office, employees' individual differences are not only valued, they are encouraged and supported.

One company determined to stimulate a broader corporate culture is Corning Glass Works, which a few years ago faced the dilemma of losing talented minority employees. Chairman James R. Houghton explains the situation: "We do a good job at hiring but a lousy job at retention and promotion. And it's not good enough just to bring them through the door." Statistics highlighted his point: Between 1980 and 1987, one in fourteen white male professionals left the company, while one in six black professionals left.

The company tackled the problem head on, a formidable task. Says a company consultant, "Corning is committed to change but they're working against the backdrop of a culture that's insisted for years and years that only white men could run the business." Chairman Houghton told male managers that their own promotions depend in part on helping women and minorities succeed in the company. It rotated jobs every eighteen months for newly employed blacks to give them a range of experience and open up opportunities; it conducted workshops on tough issues, including racism; and it shared with employees unflattering figures about the promotion rates of white males in the company. Houghton declares: "Anyone who can't adapt to these management changes won't be around here long."

Some features of a prevailing company culture are easy to identify. Most managers recognize the influences of their white-male-Protestant analytical/hierarchical offices, and most of them are sensitive and smart enough these days to avoid insisting employees conform to this mold. But other, much less obvious standards may be imposed, so look carefully at the more subtle norms and expectations that influence people's relationships at work.

Root Out Institutional Bias

Everyone is responsible for eliminating discrimination, from the chairperson to the overnight desk clerk. Keep a log for one week, writing down what you see, hear, and read around your office that suggests a blindness to diversity. Take a hard look at your company's policies and practices, as well as your own.

You may be doing things that are unfair and offensive simply out of tradition or habit, such as assuming John, an Asian-American, wants to stay in the lab rather than move up the management hierarchy, or avoiding letting Bob, a Hispanic, meet with a senior vice-president, who is female, because you are afraid a Hispanic man cannot deal with a female authority figure.

Study how you and your company communicate with employees. Do you assume they possess the same education and verbal skills as you? Listen to people's vocabularies, especially the slang and jargon, and the tone of voice. Watch the nonverbal communication, such as body language and gestures.

Here are some offenders you might encounter: signs and manuals in English for a bilingual work force; ignoring important cultural holidays, such as Martin Luther King Day, Rosh Hashanah, Chinese New Year, or Cinco de Mayo; limited facilities or access for handicapped workers; social events for mainly married couples; boring assignments and insufficient training for minorities; conformist dress codes; company support of male sports, as by offering only tickets to football games; executive dining rooms and bathrooms; recruitment programs limited to certain types of colleges; an all-female secretarial staff; and harsh pregnancy policies.

Whether it's on the athletic field or in the workplace, the same rules apply: the teams that win are teams that play together, the teams that complement one another, and whenever you find a situation where people who are of a different sex or a different color can't play together on a team, that team doesn't win.

JOHN SIMS
Vice-President, Digital Equipment Corp.

Fifty-five percent of companies worry about supervisors' abilities to motivate diverse groups of employees; 41 percent are concerned about differences in values and cultural norms; fewer than 25 percent of companies educate supervisors about diversity; 25 percent say their corporate culture is not open to diversity; and 15 percent say discrimination is a problem, according to a study by Towers Perrin and the Hudson Institute.

Institutional bias became the unintentional subject of a leadership conference for managers at DuPont Corporation, which had already instituted a number of programs to understand and support its minority employees. However, during this conference, one of the company's vice-presidents closely watched the group dynamics, noticing that when either of the two black women made a suggestion or interjected an idea, she was met with silence by the white males. It was as if she had not spoken; her words were ignored, and the discussion resumed as if she weren't there. "I had never really appreciated the problem before," vice-president Tony Cardinal recalls. "I started to get the very early inklings of what blacks and women live with every day."

Conduct Diversity Programs

A healthy company should also inaugurate specific programs aimed at its various groups of employees. Before you proceed, however, remember that when you turn the spotlight on special groups in your office and start opening doors for them, you may witness a backlash from mainstream employees with complaints about reverse discrimination and promotions for less-qualified minorities. These clashes generally take time to subside and will require commitment from all concerned parties.

The word *programs* is used loosely here, because these gatherings can take many forms—they may be focus groups, retreats or regular conferences, small clusters of employees meeting monthly, teams of select employees conferring weekly, language classes, supervisory training about your harassment policy, specialized mentoring programs, or standing support groups. Regardless of their shape, though, such programs all have two qualities: they are encouraged and sanctioned by the company and their sole purpose is to confront issues and problems related to cultural diversity. Here are a few examples of healthy company diversity programs in action:

Partners in Progress. The publishing company Gannett is addressing the needs of employees through its Partners in Progress program, which promotes advancement of women and minorities in its broadcasting and advertising operations. A clear sign of the program's success is Gannett's board of directors, which includes four women and two members of minority groups. In fact, of the seven black daily newspaper publishers in the United States, five work for Gannett papers.

Supporting Vietnam Veterans. Southern New England Telecommunications Corporation has created a program for a very select minority, Vietnam veterans. Through an employee network, veterans talk about how their war experiences have changed their jobs and home life. The network publishes a quarterly newsletter, offers counseling, and has assembled a veterans' library.

Quad Squads. Dow Jones, a 100-year-old company at the heart of the traditional male bastion of finance and investing, has created an elaborate mentoring program for minority employees. Called Quad Squads, the program consists of teams of four people: a senior-level manager with one white male, one woman, and one minority. The senior manager meets with and counsels squad members about how to advance in the corporation.

Core Groups. DuPont Corporation offers numerous programs, including Core Groups, that mix top executives with blacks, women, and other minorities from different departments and meet once or twice a month. A company task force, the Committee to Achieve Cultural Diversity, first conducted focus groups among employees, then helped the firm institute mentoring and career-development programs, as well as changes in the performance evaluation system.

Bilingual Operations. Pace Foods in San Antonio, Texas, with a work force that is about 75 percent Hispanic, anticipates hiring even more Mexican-Americans, so its white male president has created a bilingual company, with staff meetings and employee handbooks routinely translated into Spanish.

Awareness Week. American Telephone and Telegraph Corporation has had a nondiscriminatory policy since 1975, yet only 400 employees belong to League (Lesbian and Gay United Employees), its gay support group. Extrapolating from studies indicating that 10 percent of the population is gay, Stephen F. Mershon, the League's president, estimates that at least 25,000 of AT&T's 254,600 domestic employees are gay. So the company decided to designate a week this year as Gay Awareness Week.

Put Someone in Charge of Diversity

Ideally, the chief executive is also the chief diversity officer. As David Kearns, former chairman of Xerox Corporation, notes: "It is absolutely clear that we have to manage diversity right now,

---

"Walk the Talk" at Procter & Gamble

The expression is a little odd at first, but at Procter & Gamble, "walk the talk" is almost a company slogan. And while they don't take credit for coining the expression, they have given it special meaning.

Lynwood Battle, the company's manager of corporate affirmative action, explains: "We use it a lot. It says in a very few words what we expect to be happening—that you don't say one thing and do another. It's very easy to run a week-long seminar on managing and valuing diversity and go back to your organization or department and do absolutely nothing but put the training manual on the shelf to collect dust. There has to be reinforcement. When top management sees good examples of the types of attitudes and behaviors that we're talking about, it reinforces these with rewards and recognition."

So how does Procter & Gamble walk the talk? First, it formed a Corporate Diversity Strategy Task Force to closely examine its diverse work force and devise strategies for managing it. One result of this was the creation of an Engineering On-Boarding program, which brings together from the engineering division bosses and employees—men and women, including all minorities—to talk specifically about how everyone interacts. It also helps to introduce new employees and ease their way through the company.

The task force also prompted the sponsorship of the film series "Valuing Diversity," an extensive training program that P&G shares with thirty other major corporations. Other diversity programs include multicultural advisory teams, minority networking conferences, diversity seminars and training programs, and mentoring programs for black and female managers.

---

and much more so in the future. We will not be able to survive because those are the demographics. No choice. The company that gets out in front managing diversity, in my opinion, will have a competitive edge."

However, CEOs alone cannot change a company's attitude about diversity. You need leaders at every level organizing seminars, creating networks, and arranging mentoring programs for minorities. These diversity officers translate the company culture for a new hire, make sure new minority employees are given opportunities to advance, ensure that assignments and rewards are fair and equitable, hear grievances, and bring people together. The diversity chief must be a true believer—someone whose instinctive thinking and behavior reflect genuine respect and appreciation for employees from all backgrounds.

This position may have many names. At Digital Equipment Corporation, it is director of valuing differences; at Honeywell, director of work-force diversity; and at Avon, director of multicultural planning and design. Regardless of the title on the door, this person should not be confined to a single department or a particular level of management, but be able to interact with everyone, from the top executive to line workers.

One of the toughest things in dealing with diversity is getting people to understand what's going on inside their own minds when they make decisions about people.

KIM BREESE
Chief Administrative Officer, Dow Jones, Inc., *Valuing Diversity* film series

BEYOND MANAGING DIVERSITY

The whole issue of managing diversity is based on respect for individuals and the belief that all people should be treated fairly and equally. Companies and managers who recognize and celebrate these cultural differences will find that managing diversity is simply an extension of their core healthy-company values and philosophy. Nowhere is this issue more pronounced than when we manage people and their families, the topic of the last chapter.

CHAPTER EIGHT

Work and Family Are Partners for Life

THE ADVENT OF DUAL-CAREER couples in the 1980s has forced businesses in the 1990s into finding ways to help employees better integrate their work and family lives. For instance, Linda Frost, a chemist for the pharmaceutical firm Merck & Co. and mother of two small children, was having difficulties juggling career, maternity leave, and child-care pressures and had a hard time persuading supervisors into letting her work part time.

Like hundreds of other companies, Merck was forced to pay special attention to the family concerns of its employees. Companies that are taking care of family business are instituting a host of programs and policies, from sensitivity training for managers to extensive services for relatives and even unmarried partners of employees.

Family concerns among Merck employees were brought to the forefront in 1984, when researchers from the Work and Family Life Study Group of the Bank Street College of Education surveyed the company's employees and managers. They found that fully one-third of employees were having trouble balancing work and family responsibilities. In one division, the Bank Street re-

When people feel successful in the rest of their lives, they're more apt to be successful in business.

ANDY PLATA
CEO, Computer Output
Printing, Inc., Houston

searchers discovered that many managers were unaware of employees' family dilemmas, especially those affecting female employees. When the researchers tallied their surveys of employees, they concluded that 41 percent had a great deal of work and family conflicts, 36 percent had some conflicts, and only 21 percent few or none.

The feelings of Merck employees were probably more a sign of the times than a reflection on the company, for this firm of 35,000 has long been a leader in family programs. And while the experiences of its employees have been typical for the times, its efforts to expand company programs to better address family concerns offer an exceptional model for all companies.

Merck has had an active maternity-leave program for more than thirty years, and over this time it has gradually refined the program to meet employees' changing family needs. For instance, all its benefits (including six weeks' leave with pay, an eighteen-month leave of absence for biological or adopting parents, and continued medical benefits) have recently been extended to fathers. Also, the company has gone beyond the usual corporate route of sponsoring or supporting a child-care center to funding a company-wide child-care referral program.

A significant sign of the times at Merck was the inauguration in 1985 of a series of workshops on family matters, focusing on specific problems such as child rearing, teenage substance abuse, and caring for elderly parents. Originally conducted after work at the child-care center, these workshops now meet during lunch at Merck headquarters and other company locations. Another step in the evolution of its work-and-family activities was its support of a spouse-referral career service in the form of a computer-based job bank through the Home Buyers Assistance Corporation. Through this service, spouses of employees can plug into a job network that covers the northern New Jersey-New York metropolitan area; they also can turn to Merck for help in preparing résumés.

As times change and employees continue to seek more personal and family time, Merck will undoubtedly refine its family programs. Over the years, it has learned what many companies are only beginning to realize now: supporting employee family life programs not only builds a more loyal work force but, over the long run, lowers operating costs. Declares Merck's senior director of corporate planning, J. Douglas Phillips: "Pro-family policies can be profitable. Given high turnover costs, avoiding turnover for just a few employees will yield excellent paybacks. But when you describe the economic value of these programs, you have to talk to management in the terms they want to hear—that it makes pre-tax income go up, and increases value for shareholders."

PORTRAIT OF THE AMERICAN WORKER

The portrait of the traditional American worker is fading fast, yet the frame still hangs on the walls of American business. It shows a middle-aged, married man with a couple of kids and a wife who doesn't work. He puts in a five-day week, more or less from nine to five; leaves his work at the office; and rarely lets family matters impinge on his workday. Although he is years from retirement, he is looking forward to getting out around age sixty-five so he and his wife can travel.

Now meet the modern American worker: You. Odds are close to even that you are a woman, and chances are you do not work a standard nine-to-five work week at the office. Also, there is a good chance your family is not the traditional nuclear one: you may be a single parent, or part of a couple without children, or perhaps you live alone. Retirement may be a quaint notion to you. You may have plans to take a sabbatical, then return to work, or hope someday to go into business for yourself and never stop working.

Unfortunately, many businesses have clung to the faded image of times past. By acting as if employees match the antiquated portrait and not recognizing the true nature of their family lives, business has been mismanaging and alienating its most valuable asset.

Three qualities distinguish the modern employee: diverse family and personal lives; blurred boundaries between work and home life; and a sizeable choice of personal and career paths. Each of these realities creates crises or opportunities, depending on how they are managed. Here is a close-up look at the issues surrounding these qualities and how they affect people and employers.

There are still a number of men who believe their people have traditional families waiting for them at home. But the workplaces are filled with single and divorced parents and dual-career couples who want a balance in life.

BARRIE SANFORD GRIEF
organizational psychiatrist

The Diversity of Family Living

The traditional family has disappeared. The bulk of American homes are not occupied by a married couple and two children but a potpourri of people: single parents; gay parents; couples without children; children and stepparents; adopted children and parents; unmarried couples; grandparents and grandchildren; and households with no relatives by blood or marriage. The following statistics highlight the diversity among families:

Massachusetts Mutual Life Insurance Company surveyed 1,200 adults, asking for their ideas about what constitutes a family. Just 22 percent picked the legal definition, "A group of people related by blood, marriage, or adoption." Almost 75 percent opted for a much broader concept: "A group of people who love and care for each other."

- According to the *Wall Street Journal,* fewer than 10 percent of the population lives in the classic family headed by a single male breadwinner, and only 26 percent of American households consist of married couples with children.
- More than 25 percent of middle-aged Americans are not married, and Americans living alone constitute 24 percent of households.
- More than half of all marriages end in divorce.
- Stepchildren comprise 20 percent of all children of married couples.
- There are more than 2 million gay mothers and fathers.
- Unmarried heterosexual couples living together total more than 2.6 million. People living with nonrelatives make up the fastest-growing household type, showing a rise of 46 percent in the 1980s.

Why haven't we done more as a nation to help working parents face the stresses of family life? We seem to be dominated by a bias left over from our pioneering ancestors: Families should be self-sufficient. If they're not, they should suffer for it.

DR. T. BERRY BRAZELTON
child-development expert

Today's family has evolved far beyond groups of people related by blood or marriage; it has grown into an emotional entity—a milieu for sharing, caring, self-expression, personal growth, and commitment. But when companies refuse to recognize these emotional foundations, the result is resentment and alienation.

Companies may think that they support people's families. However, their benefits and attitudes respond to only the most traditional arrangements. Consider these true situations:

- A devoted unmarried couple living together and both working at the same company in Boston are told that the man is being transferred to San Francisco. The company makes no provisions for moving his partner, so the employee is forced to quit.

- A single woman decides to adopt a child, but her company provides maternity leave only to married women. In an attempt to deceive her employer, she presents bogus evidence of a marriage in order to qualify for benefits. The story hits the city paper.

- A father receives custody of his two small sons but finds it difficult to arrange for child care. While parental leave and flexible schedules are officially available, he knows that male managers who take time off are not serious contenders for promotion.

- A gay executive discovers his live-in partner of fourteen years has AIDS. Submitting health claims to the company is out of the question, because it would jeopardize his position in the company. Although the executive is not infected himself, he worries constantly about his friend and his work suffers.

- A computer scientist working in a small consulting company is about to have her first child. Because the company is largely male, with most of the female employees being secretaries, it does not have a paid maternity-leave program.

I have a great family existence. I have eight children; they range in age from 34 down to five months. I try to keep a perspective on what is really important. Work is certainly an important part of life and you should aspire to do a good job and be successful. But it isn't everything.

JIM RENIER
CEO, Honeywell, Inc.

Companies that disregard employees' families create heartaches and headaches for all. Employees deeply resent the belittling of their family demands and feel little loyalty toward an employer who neglects or disparages, either through official policy or unofficial attitudes, the importance of their families.

Blurred Panorama of Work and Home

A person's work life and home life once were separate, with very little overlap. Today, the white picket fence between them has collapsed. People's discrete existences have become blurred into one demanding, sometimes chaotic, usually complicated, collage of work and family. These statistics tell the story:

- According to a survey of hundreds of managers by *Management Review* magazine, 85 percent work at least forty-five hours a week; 63 percent work through lunch once a week; 65 percent work at least one weekend a month; and 47 percent work at home three hours or more a week.

Husbands, wives, children are not getting enough family life. Nobody is. People are hurting.

ARLIE HOCHSCHILD
The Second Shift, quoted in *Newsweek*

- Leisure time has dropped from an average 26.6 hours a week in 1973 to 16.6 in 1987. At the same time, the average work week is longer: for professionals it is up to 52.2 hours, and for the owners of small businesses, it is 57.3 hours.

- A survey of employees at thirty-three companies found that 55 percent of the women and 50 percent of the men were interrupted at work because of responsibilities to care for relatives.

- About 20 percent of U.S. employees toil during the evening or night hours or rotate through day, evening, and night duty. Many are sleep starved and are out of sync with their families.

- Thirty-five percent of working men and women with young children have told their employers that they will not work shifts, relocate, travel extensively, or put in a lot of overtime, according to research by Work/Family Directions, Inc.

- A Boston University survey of 1,600 employees at a large public utility and high-technology company found that both mothers and fathers felt a lot of stress in balancing work and family life.

Two powerful currents are blending work and family lives: the American woman's exodus out of the home and into the marketplace, shedding the role of primary child raiser; and men's growing attention to their children and families, in conjunction with exploration of new roles as father, homemaker, coach, and confidant. The demise of the sexual stereotypes of breadwinner and homemaker epitomizes these trends.

As work and family mingle more and more, stress emerges: a father who devotes long hours at the office is unhappy because he is missing his son's swimming career; a single mother worries about not having enough available leave when her daughter is sick; an ambitious woman is quietly put on the so-called mommy track because she plans to have children; and a salesman who frequently travels discovers his marriage is crumbling.

Without help in managing these dilemmas, people feel torn and overwhelmed. They curtail career-advancing activities to spend time with children, and then feel resentful; they neglect children to devote energy to work deadlines, and then feel guilty; and spouses are so busy catering to jobs, kids, or each other that they forget about themselves.

These stresses have produced enormous headaches for employers, too, who must pay the price of ignoring employees' family concerns with higher costs from lost productivity, accidents, and premature turnover. These statistics indicate the cost of family stresses among employees:

Data Bank

- *Forty-five percent of all workers are women.*
- *Fifty percent of all mothers work.*
- *One-third of all small businesses are owned by women.*

- The average employee with latchkey children at home misses thirteen days of work a year, compared with nine annual absentee days among workers without school-age children.

- Forty percent of 1,200 working parents surveyed by Honeywell said their ability to concentrate was often affected by family worries.

- An employee survey at AT&T found that 77 percent of the women and 73 percent of the men take time away from work for their children—talking to them on the phone, seeing them for lunch, or attending school activities.

- An *INC.* magazine survey of parents of children under age two found 89 percent of the women and 62 percent of the men reporting child-care difficulties.

- Some 35 percent of children of executives undergo outpatient care for psychiatric problems or drug abuse every year, compared with 15 percent of nonexecutives in the same companies, according to the Ann Arbor, Michigan health-care information company Medstat Systems.

Multiple Life Paths

Like the traditional family, the linear career is a thing of the past. A person's neat progression through school into the early twenties and the working years from the twenties to the sixties, culminating in retirement and more leisure time around age sixty-five, has been discarded for more individual, practical approaches. Instead of a succession of predictable stages in our lives, we are moving along increasingly diverse paths.

Education has become a lifelong event for many, with people enrolling in part-time programs or interrupting jobs for a solid chunk of education toward a new career. Work years now may stretch far beyond so-called retirement years or may be abbreviated by weary employees temporarily relaxing in their midlife years. And leisure interests, whether they be sports or antique collecting, are no longer relegated to weekends, vacations, or evenings. In short, there is no average adult life. Consider these statistics:

. . . when companies hire employees, families and all of their home life headaches are taken on as well. If little Suzy goes off to day care with a cold, Dad may fret about it at the office all day. If Mom suddenly has to work late, there may be no one to pick up Suzy and give her dinner. And if Grandma falls and breaks her hip, that budget report due tomorrow just doesn't seem so important anymore.

Time magazine

- Eighteen million Americans work part time.
- Fourteen percent of American companies offer some type of sabbatical program.
- Only about 27 percent of workers want to stop working entirely at retirement age.
- The average age of evening students in community colleges is thirty-eight.
- People change jobs on average every three years.
- Tomorrow's employee will have to be retrained up to thirteen times in a lifetime.
- Children are born to parents whose ages range from thirteen to fifty.

These multiple life cycles present new choices and dilemmas for people who, free of the straight-line, programmed life, see many paths. Yet without employer help and understanding, they may find themselves locked into unwelcomed situations in which job constraints and company attitudes are inconsistent with their life cycles. Women may decide to postpone having children because their employers reward only single-minded dedication; managers may forgo returning to school for new skills because their job schedules are too inflexible; workaholic employees may burn out because their company gives only lip service to the benefits of relaxation; and older employees who want to remain active and working may be forced into retirement and years of sedentary life.

Talent is lost when organizations misjudge the life cycles of their employees. These organizations lose out when working parents leave a company for their families, when skills are not developed, when older workers are shelved, and when employees look elsewhere for more enriching jobs as they prepare for their next stage of life.

THE MYTHS OF WORK AND FAMILY

Business has largely overlooked concerns among employees about family life and personal development. Many companies have stubbornly held fast to a collection of myths and outdated assumptions that have enabled them to discount the importance of people's personal lives. Until business understands the fallacies of its mythical thinking, employees will feel the uncomfortable tugs of conflicting loyalties to work and family, and companies will continue to suffer the effects. The following is an examination of these myths and assumptions.

Working mothers who feel confident and fulfilled in their jobs bring those feelings home to their children, according to a study by Lois Hoffman, a professor at the University of Michigan.

Myth 1: Family is a women's issue, and work is a men's issue.

The myth that family and personal concerns are women's issues is oppressive, because it has given rise to the assumptions that women are less interested in careers and that men are less interested in families. Beneath this myth are several faulty assumptions.

Young mothers should not work. The economic realities overshadow any philosophical question here: many mothers must work to help their family survive. And the notion that a child's health suffers because a mother is absent during the day is patently fallacious. Given quality child care, socialization with other children, and supportive parents, a young child can grow up healthy and strong. The most significant influence is quality parenting, not a mother around every hour of a day. Furthermore, a working mother provides a worthwhile role model for children.

Fathers are not interested in families. Men suffer quietly from their lack of family involvement and as they grow older, it becomes more difficult to acknowledge their stress and guilt. But a man who has just had a heart attack, has received a call from his infirm, dependent mother during the workday, has heard complaints from his daughter about lack of child care, or has just become a grandfather suddenly becomes a convert and very willing to talk seriously about work and family. It has been said that no

You have your job, and you have yourself and your family. Time spent away from the job is becoming increasingly important, even at the upper management levels. Today's manager is not willing to spend an 80-hour week on the job.

Human resources
director, diversified
manufacturing firm

Many women are still battling corporations' preconceptions of their collective career commitment. At the same time, many women are experiencing tremendous burnout as they struggle to balance work and family. These pressures, combined with the lack of widely available, affordable child care and of corporate support for men's growing involvement in child rearing, are real and troubling.

FELICE N. SCHWARTZ
Catalyst

man reflects on his deathbed, "I wish I had spent more time at the office." But evidence shows that family concerns extend far beyond women's issues.

Two studies at DuPont found that men's family-related problems nearly doubled from 1985 to 1988. When the company asked 3,300 male employees about their attitudes toward child care, it found 33 percent were interested in part-time work to meet child-care needs, 48 percent want sick-leave policies that include time off to care for a child, and 26 percent want to take leave after the birth of a child.

Of 500 men polled by Robert Half International, more than half said they would be willing to cut their salaries by as much as 25 percent to have more family or personal time. About 45 percent said they would probably turn down a promotion if it meant spending less time with their families.

The mommy track is the optimal solution. Some experts suggest companies should design two career tracks—one for working mothers and another for female executives. (One study suggests that the mommy track is already in place: it reports that two-thirds of women under forty who are top-level executives in large companies are childless, while virtually all male executives are fathers.) This idea presumes that for women, work and family are mutually exclusive; it also implies that corporate policies regarding advancement and benefits should tilt to the presumably more dedicated, non-mommy-track employee.

Myth 2: There is no such thing as a balanced life.

Many companies treat the idea that you can have it all—a good job, a healthy family, and time for love and leisure—as a fantasy. This too is based on many faulty assumptions.

Workaholics are the best performers. The corrosive effects of workaholism amply illustrate the flawed assumption that extra time spent at work is valuable. Still, people persist in believing that working harder and longer means working better and smarter. In 1989, almost 25 percent of working Americans labored forty-nine hours or more a week, an increase of 18 percent over 1970, according to the Bureau of Labor Statistics. But employees compulsively dedicated to long hours at the office are often less productive than the nondriven worker, and consciously or not, they destroy the personal and family portion of their life. Workaholics are notorious for sour marriages, health claims and stress problems, and disorganized, inefficient management.

Time spent away from work is a sign of laziness. Taken to its limits, this belief forms the underpinnings of much workaholism. This mentality not only penalizes the family person, it also limits taking time for creativity, relaxation, and recuperation. The best evidence that this idea is flawed is the many successful business people who have shown that time taken for family and personal interests has enhanced their thinking and performance, not diminished it. Managers who do seize time away from work find they become more creative and more productive when they do work. Such was the case with Apple CEO John Sculley, who took a summer sabbatical in Maine for studying photography, designing a barn, and boating. "I found my sabbatical a way of reacquainting myself with the fact that I'm a mere mortal," Sculley says.

In theory, most employees and employers recognize the necessity of balancing their lives, yet in practice, they have a hard time meshing the two halves. Complicating the balancing is that all facets of one's life must be in harmony; a successful, respected executive cannot build a healthy life if the other half is represented by a neglected spouse, ignored children, or the absence of any interests outside of work. Part of the difficulty is that people are not always sure how to align them, and organizations are similarly handicapped by a lack of perspective and confidence about how to design the right environment.

Everyone is multidimensional, with interests, intellects, and dreams forming overlapping layers of their personalities. But when these layers become uneven and misaligned, when people do not allow for the fullest expression of professional and personal dimensions, or when one layer dominates all others, mediocrity, unhappiness, and poor health follow. Insists James W. Rouse, founder of a very successful, innovative real estate development firm and the Enterprise Foundation, "A full life is not achieved through one's material well-being but by dealing with the whole of life wherever one is."

Employees need to cultivate both work and family skills, for

[The superwoman] is dead of stress and exhaustion, and [now believes] that her career was cheating her out of forming and enjoying the most important relationships of her life.

ARLENE CARDOZO
Sequencing

these two spheres are complementary, with one enhancing the value of the other. For instance, at work, delegation, deadlines, and teamwork are fundamental skills that teach people to master discipline, scheduling, and organization management. In the personal arena, many families could benefit from the application of such skills. Conversely, who knows better how to manage chaos and uncertainty than the typical parent, who is an expert in delegating, sharing, cooperating, and balancing the needs of different family members? Tolerance, love, and respect are cornerstones of healthy parenting that could serve a person well at work.

To balance these two identities, you must first learn to recognize them in yourself and then find ways to manage them effectively. The remainder of this chapter offers ideas and suggestions for building balance in your life, managing with flexibility, and creating a responsive, family-friendly organization. It is intended to help you as an individual come to grips with your conflicting family and work demands, to help you as a manager acquire the flexibility needed to enable your employees to become optimal workers, and to help your company create an environment that reinforces healthy family values.

Corporations are going to have to do more to get good skilled people and to keep them. To do that, we will have to start looking at the whole person, and work on strengthening our understanding of the employee-family relationship.

ROBERT BECK
Executive Vice-President, Human Resources, Bank of America

Researchers say that two out of every five employees are having problems managing the conflicting demands of jobs and family.

ELLEN GALINSKY
Cofounder, Families and Work Institute

INSIDE OUT

How Well Do You Juggle?

We all juggle work and family concerns to a degree, but some of us are more adroit, others more clumsy. Portions of our lives may fit together seamlessly while others constantly tug and tear, creating enervating tension and stress. Our juggling talents are the result of upbringing, childhood experiences, age, gender, emotional make-up, and intellect. These questions will help you explore the personal ingredients that determine how well you manage work, family, and personal life. Score them:

| 1 Never | 3 Sometimes | 5 Always |
| 2 Occasionally | 4 Often | |

1. Does your spouse complain about your work hours?
2. If unmarried, does work keep you from meeting someone special?

3. Do you feel guilty about not spending enough time with your children?

4. Does your work interfere with necessary household chores?

5. How often do you cancel leisure activities or events with your family because of work?

6. Is inadequate or unreliable child care a major problem in your life?

7. When your child is sick, do you feel guilty that you cannot take off time to care for him or her?

8. Have you put off learning something new because work does not allow you enough time?

9. Do you miss work or have to interrupt your normal routine to care for an elderly parent?

10. Is a problem at home—such as a troubled teenager, divorce proceedings, or money worries—distracting you from work?

11. Do you feel depressed or bored when you're not working?

12. Are household tasks one-sided and divided according to traditional sex roles?

13. Do you work on the weekends and holidays?

14. Do you have breakfasts or dinners with clients instead of family or friends?

15. Do you take regular vacations?

16. Does your travel schedule at work create friction at home?

17. Is your manager insensitive to your work and family conflicts and concerns?

18. Does your employer make decisions about your job—such as to change hours, transfer you, or send you on trips—without consulting you?

19. Are you impatient with coworkers who have family and personal priorities?

Teenagers these days don't get pregnant in motels and cars at ten at night. Sex happens at home at three in the afternoon while mom and dad are at work.

PROFESSOR THOMAS LONG
Catholic University

What Your Answers Mean

If your score is between 19 and 30, you have learned to balance the demands of your life, devoting sufficient time and emotional energy to balancing work, family, relationships, and outside interests. If you scored between 30 and 75, something is unbalanced; and the higher your score, the closer you are inching toward the dysfunctional. Perhaps you are too absorbed in your work; your children need to spend more time with you; you are dissatisfied with your company's family benefits; your spouse isn't pulling his or her share of the work; or you are nearing retirement but don't want to stop working. If you scored between 76 and 95, your life is dangerously out of kilter and this imbalance, if it persists, will undermine your health and your productivity.

Finding your healthy balance sometimes requires a few small changes, while at other times what is needed is a total reshaping of your life, a process that requires forming new attitudes, knowing your desires and capabilities, and taking charge. The following suggestions will help you take the steps to fashion a healthier, more balanced life.

Arrange Your Trade-Offs

Trade-offs between work and family are inevitable. Every day you sacrifice one aspect of your life to plow your energies into another endeavor. The big trade-offs are obvious: you might relinquish caring for your child during the day so you can earn a better living, refuse a promotion and transfer because your husband cannot afford to leave his job, or refrain from enrolling in law-school night classes because your wife needs help at home. The smaller trade-offs are no less difficult or painful: they might include working through the dinner hour and missing a child's birthday party, skipping an important meeting at the office to help an elderly parent move, or going to work with the flu in order to save sick days for when your child is ill.

To adjust and align trade-offs, you need to know the priorities in your life and then be true to them. Arrange the contenders in order of importance to you: job or career, money, spouse or partner, children, special interest or hobby, education, and so on. Decide which are more or less important, and make your time and

---

Data Bank: The Home Front

■ *Seventy-five percent of wives reportedly do most of the housework.*

■ *Sixty-one percent of men do little or no housework.*

■ *Only wives who earned more than their husbands did less than half the housework.*

ARLIE HOCHSCHILD quoted in *Newsweek*

energy allowances accordingly. Here are examples of how people have arranged their priorities:

- An audit manager for an accounting firm reduced her work load from one very demanding, large client to several smaller, less insistent clients so she could spend two afternoons a week at home with her new baby.

- A lawyer picks up his son from day care, goes home to eat dinner and spend time with his family, then returns to his office at night when they have gone to bed.

- A magazine editor arranged with his employer to work at home as a freelance editor so he could be with his handicapped son.

- A divorced CEO of a fast-food chain gets home by five-thirty three nights a week so he can prepare and eat dinner with his teenage children.

- A successful graphic art designer goes on a half-day schedule to play in national senior tennis tournaments.

- A fifty-year-old small-business owner sold his company and, with his son, started a new business.

In two-thirds of American households with children, both parents work.

Dodge the Dangers of Workaholism

In many professions and for many people, workaholism has become the norm. Preoccupation with getting ahead, fear of failure, and a low tolerance for mistakes are common workaholic traits. Sometimes workaholism is forced upon them by the nature of their jobs; other times it is accelerated by a perfectionist boss. And occasionally, it is an escape from an unhappy marriage or deteriorating relationship. But most often, it is the result of self-imposed, unrealistic demands, and many people are not even aware they are workaholics until carefully quizzed about their working habits.

Workaholism appears to be spreading. According to organizational consultant Diane Fassel: "Workaholism is the most socially accepted of all addictions. But it is a progressive disease, just like alcoholism and drug addiction." This addiction makes workaholism a hard habit to break, so here are suggestions for curbing obsessive work habits:

It's clear to me that I squandered large parts of my twenties and thirties in needless, completely neurotic work. I got tangled up in the myth of the "hard charging, hard working, we'll-stay-here-till-they-drop" entrepreneur. That's a very destructive attitude. It's unnecessary. It's unhealthy. It's not the best way to lead your life and not a good example to set for your company.

CHRIS WHITTLE
Whittle Communications

- Know the physical signs of overwork, including such stress-related illnesses as headaches and peptic ulcers, or the unhealthy personal habits that accompany it, such as drinking too much, overeating, or not exercising.

- Be disciplined about taking time away from work. Don't postpone or cancel vacations, family dinners, Saturday bike rides, or pursuing special interests.

- Learn to say "No" to work colleagues, so that your work load is not overwhelming. Respect your right to relax and spend time with your family, and don't feel guilty.

- Make working evenings or weekends the exception, not the rule.

- Examine your workaholic behavior and the reasons behind it. Are you afraid you will lose your job or influence at work if you do not put in long hours? Are you using it as an escape from something painful outside work? Can these fears be confronted in better, less stressful ways?

High Five

Walter Kiechel III, managing editor of *Fortune* magazine, offers ten reasons for leaving at five o'clock:

- It will cause you to become a more efficient manager.
- It will encourage your boss to act like a manager.
- It will shape up your subordinates.
- It will force you to clarify your values.
- It will help you establish independence from your organization.
- It will make those exceptional occasions when you do stay late more enjoyable.
- It will keep you out of the burnout cycle.
- It will permit better use of your leisure time.
- It will enable you to be healthier.
- It will enable you to be more loving.

Refine Your Family Skills

The emotional needs of those closest to you—children, spouse, partner, or parents—can unbalance the most stable life. Growing children need constant guidance and attention, spouses and partners need companionship and intimacy, and aging parents sometimes need care-taking. But sometimes your ability to meet these needs weakens. The signs of waning family skills are unmistakable: young children who are discipline problems; rebellious teenagers who have problems in school or use drugs; repeated separations or divorces; and complaining, unhappy elderly parents. These suggestions may help shore up your ability to meet your family's needs:

A Boston University study of women at two high-tech companies found that the average working mother devotes eighty-four hours to her job and home responsibilities, while married men with children devote seventy-two hours.

- Give young children your complete attention when you get home from work. Their egocentric world does not understand your bad moods. The key to producing healthy adults is to teach children the right values, self-esteem, and independence while they are growing up.

- Maintain strong lines of communication with latchkey children (school-age children who are home alone in the afternoon). Ask them to call you as soon as they get home. Talk about what they can do and help them plan activities to avoid their getting bored, feeling unwanted, or getting into trouble.

- Encourage teenagers to become involved in after-school activities, such as sports, drama clubs, part-time jobs, or community service. Be aware of the warning signs of problems: isolation, irritability, deteriorating grades, or bad friends.

- Be sensitive to your child's growing pains. Listen to your children's troubles. Don't nag, but give positive encouragement. Avoid criticizing their styles or fashions, remembering the fierce peer pressure they are under.

- Schedule special time to spend with a spouse or partner, a time when nothing else intrudes. This can be for a candlelight dinner, a weekend getaway, an evening walk, or a quiet lunch.

- Be a true partner in household chores. Forget tradition or how you have normally handled responsibilities in the home, and make sure no one is devoting a disproportionate amount of time to laundry, errands, cleaning, cooking, yard work, or paying bills.

■ If caring for elderly parents, be aware of their concerns about growing old. Are they safe, and do they have access to the right medical attention? Make sure they have emergency numbers to call, have adequate medical insurance, and are receiving whatever social security benefits they are entitled to.

A Bureau of National Affairs employee survey found that 14 percent of job holders were caring for elderly relatives, that 75 percent of these employees were women, and that 31 percent also tended to dependent children.

 ## What the Manager Can Do

As a manager, your awareness of your own personal work and family issues provides insight to help employees deal with similar concerns and express their multiple identities. In business, this means being sensitive and flexible; instead of applying formulas to employees, you must accommodate each person individually. You must allow for employees' diverse family lives and varied interests and recognize their unique life cycles. And you must shed any myths you have about women, age, and sexual roles by assessing their individual needs and talents.

No single corporate policy can address the range and complexity of problems you probably face. The real challenge is to create a sense of family among your work group—an atmosphere in which personal concerns are treated with the same seriousness as worries about work and where people feel free and have the time to devote to both. Managers who are caring and understanding allow employees to grow personally and professionally, and they instill great loyalty and commitment.

Manage Along the Life Cycle

Each stage of life brings new realities, new trade-offs, and new passions. What is important to pregnant mothers in their twenties differs greatly from what is important to retiring fathers in their fifties. A manager has to be sensitive to these stages and life events, while recognizing that employees experience them in different ways.

The secret to becoming a flexible manager is recognizing age-related patterns while allowing for individual variations. Here in broad outline are the life stages that many employees experience:

Ages 20 to 30. Young people have a mandate from parents and friends and are under enormous pressure to start a lifelong career, find a mate, start a family, and formulate a life's dream. Many are eager to become part of the adult world and show more interest in professional advancement than personal or leisure activities. This is a time, not unlike the teen years, when people feel pressed into conforming and imitating rather than developing personal styles.

Ages 31 to 40. As they enter their thirties, employees evaluate their work commitments and start families. Many women, as well as some men, may drop out of the work force or work part time to care for young children, and men may feel guilty about not being more involved in child-rearing. Employees are deep into their work, while fiercely dedicated to their families. At the same time, unmarried or childless employees may resent the attention and benefits given to coworkers with children. In these years, employees may be pulled in many directions with children beginning school, women returning to jobs, and older parents asking for help. As a manager, you need to be sensitive to the family pressures among your employees and make sure your demands and timetables are not creating even more conflicts for them.

Studies at the Families and Work Institute show that employees who perceive their supervisors as flexible and supportive with family concerns report lower levels of stress and fewer stress-related health problems.

Ages 41 to 50. This is a time for more thoughtful evaluation of careers, accomplishments, and trade-offs with family life. The psychological clock ticks loudly as people wonder about time lived and time left. This is a period of great gains and great losses. Some people begin thinking of slowing down or retiring. With the specter of fleeting youth and certain middle age, these employees seek experiences outside of work, wanting sabbaticals, longer vacations, or new careers. For others, it is time to become invigorated and grasp one more chance to pursue a lifelong dream.

Ages 51 to 60. During these years, many people begin to slow down physically. They have peaked, in terms of either professional or personal accomplishments, and acquire a certain realism about work and personal dreams, becoming more comfortable with who they are and what they have done. Energies now can be invested in mentoring and in taking care of aging parents. With children off at college, couples may take a hard look at their relationships. Others in their fifties are charging forward, still curious and restless, and striving in their careers or searching to begin a new one.

People should have a lifelong opportunity to work. Businesses have found that, with mandatory retirement, they have thrown away many irreplaceable skills. But the answer is in the workplace. If you humanize the workplace, restructure it around flextime, around mentoring, people will be less eager to retire. Personally, I want to die in an airport, briefcase in hand, mission accomplished.

MAGGIE KUHN
Gray Panther leader

Age 60 plus. People in this age group face retirement, part-time work, or, at the least, slowing down, and interests and activities away from work move to center stage. Some people may follow intellectual pursuits and go back to school, while others fulfill dreams of travel. Family members and time with grandchildren become more important than the small victories at work. People become more nurturing and giving, eager to make things easier for others or to share some of their good fortune.

The flexible manager understands these stages as guideposts, not stereotypes. They watch what is happening in their employees' lives without being intrusive or judgmental. Managers uncertain about employees' family demands should first survey employees, asking about the configuration of their families, the nature of dependent-care arrangements, and their current work–family stresses. Focus groups are especially helpful for learning about employees' feelings concerning company policies and attitudes regarding family life. Begun as a discussion about how benefits and working hours match people's needs, focus groups can easily be broadened into personal and family concerns that affect work and how you as a manager can help them.

Arrange a Flexible Work Environment

The possibilities for rearranging a company environment in terms of when and where people work are endless. Some of the more common programs are flextime, part-time work, voluntary reduced time, job sharing, peak-time work, shift work, the compressed week, flexiplace, and sabbaticals. Instituting flexibility requires trust and commitment from manager and employees. Managers must bear in mind that accomplishing things is more important than putting in time. Suppress fears about employees working less, machines idling, or communications between co-workers breaking down, and give flexibility a chance to work.

Maintaining flexibility will be hard for a manager operating within a rigid, mistrustful organization. A flexible manager cannot defy company policies or institute impractical programs but can usually find enough latitude to create a degree of freedom among his or her work group. The programs described below show how managers can put flexibility to work.

Flexible time. Flextime, which includes variable schedules by job, department, person, or company, is slowly becoming the norm in American business. A 1990 Hewitt Associates survey of 259 employers found that almost 50 percent offer flexible scheduling, and 59 percent of the human-resources executives stated that flextime would soon be an important feature in recruitment. Flextime can entail shifting schedules according to hours, days, or months; the key is to establish a clear contract that both employee and employer can accept. Consider the following questions before introducing flextime:

- Could employees work a schedule other than nine-to-five? What problems would the new schedule help solve?

- What are the core hours of work, and how often could people change flexible hours?

- Could a flexible schedule help reduce stress or strain either at home or on the job?

- Could a flexible schedule reduce on-the-job accidents, absenteeism, or insurance claims?

- What effect could a flexible schedule have on administrative costs, department expenses, other expenses, or revenues?

For daily flextime to work, a company must first establish a core period when all employees need to be at work. Sometimes this is the middle of a shift, or one of two segments: ten in the morning to noon or one to three in the afternoon. Another alternative is weekly balancing, letting employees set their own hours each week as long as they log in the minimum weekly requirement. Here are examples of companies that have instituted flextime:

- At the Transamerica Occidental Life Insurance Company in Los Angeles, 90 percent of the employees participate in flexible scheduling, with many parents using it to solve early-morning or late-afternoon child-care complications. Employee turnover dropped 45 percent in the nine years after flextime was implemented.

No employee who has to leave a sick child or an elderly parent at home without adequate care can be expected to be your most productive employee. It is clearly in our best corporate interest to find ways to help employees address these problems.

FRANK SKINNER
President, Southern Bell

TRANSAMERICA
LIFE COMPANIES

Employees lose five days a year on average because of problems caring for family members, according to Michael Creedon, Director of Corporate Programs, National Council on the Aging.

- At DuPont headquarters in Wilmington, Delaware, employees arrive anytime between seven and nine-thirty and depart between three-thirty and six o'clock.

- A big user of flexible scheduling is Apple Computer in Cupertino, California, which has no strict time requirements for any employee as long as the work gets done. Employees are lent computers to set up at home and hook into the company communications network, called Applelink.

- A variation on flexible hours is Levi Strauss & Company's summer-hours program. During June, July, and August, employees can work extra-long days and leave work on Friday afternoons.

- To give employees more discretion in managing their paid time off, Hewlett-Packard Company instituted in 1982 a policy of flexible time off. Employees earn personal time off that can be taken for any purpose, including illness in the family, sick leave, and vacation. For those who need time off to handle significant personal situations, leaves of up to one year can be requested.

Job sharing. Job sharing is growing and represents a viable alternative to overstaffing, understaffing, or sudden changes in workforce size. In job sharing, two people split one full-time job, taking on related but separate assignments. This works best with stressful work for which two heads are better than one, although the two heads must be compatible and able to communicate. Here is how some employees are sharing jobs.

At Bank of America in San Francisco, two mothers with young children work in strategic planning and analysis and share one job. One woman works Monday, Tuesday, and Wednesday, and the other on Wednesday, Thursday, and Friday. On the overlap day, they coordinate their work.

Steelcase, a Michigan-based office-furniture manufacturer, has at least seventy employees who share thirty-five jobs, including management tasks, clerical positions, and production assignments.

Juggling motherhood and investment banking is rough. That's why two vice-presidents at Dain Bosworth, a Boston investment house, chose job sharing. After selling the idea to their partners, they agreed to a six-month trial period during which time they had to answer three questions: (1) Are the clients happy? (2) Did the job-sharers produce revenue for the company? (3) Did others end up doing their work? In the end, both parties won: the company kept two committed employees and two mothers were able to balance their work and family lives.

At Rolscreen, job sharing is limited to workers whose jobs consist of repetitive tasks—factory and clerical workers. Average absence rate among the 100 participants dropped from 4.5 percent to less than 0.4 percent.

Patagonia's 450-member work force in Ventura, California enjoys the benefits of a totally flexible work environment. For instance, two avid mountain climbers fill the same position during alternating three-month periods of the year.

Off-site employees. Allowing people to work at home can boost employee morale and productivity while helping them manage family lives. Managers have found that the best off-site employees are those who require little supervision, possess solid communication skills, and are motivated enough to make the arrangement work. Working mothers, older workers, and the disabled are especially well suited.

For telecommuting to be successful, managers have to be comfortable letting go of some control over people's work habits and daily routines while continuing to link them to the office. Linking telecommuters to the office, both socially and technically, is critical to give them a sense of belonging and purpose. Here are some examples of off-site arrangements.

Johnson & Johnson prefers telecommuters for special research assignments. Although these people cannot attend all meetings and may be simply a voice from a box during group consultations, the company found no decline in communication or exchange of data between telecommuters and office-bound employees.

Before employees at U.S. West in Denver begin working at home, they spend a day in training, where they learn what is expected of them. Following training, the off-site worker meets with a supervisor at the home office, to review expectations and responsibilities.

Companies are afraid of part-time work. They don't know how to approve it. They're afraid to open the dam, that if they allow one person to work part time, everyone will want to.

BARNEY OLMSTED
Co-director, New Ways to Work

I announced that 80 percent of the women in the work force will be of childbearing age and that 90 percent of them will get pregnant. One CEO jumped up and said, "Well, I just won't hire them!" I said, "You are not going to have a choice, since (and then I gave him the third statistic:) two-thirds of the new entrants in the work force will be women."

DANA FRIEDMAN
Cofounder, Families and
Work Institute

Costs and Benefits of Flexible Work Schedules

FLEXTIME

Company Costs: reluctant supervisors, additional time-keeping costs, labor-union opposition, higher overhead costs.

Company Benefits: increased productivity, reduced absences and lateness, less turnover, less overtime pay, easier recruiting, better use of production facilities.

Employee Costs: less overtime pay.

Employee Benefits: increased job satisfaction, easier commuting, more and better family time.

JOB SHARING

Company Costs: higher fringe benefits, problems locating compatible partners, problems with coordinating and office communication.

Company Benefits: reduced absences, less overtime pay, improved work coverage.

Employee Costs: possibly slower career advancement.

Employee Benefits: continued pay and fringe benefits.

COMPRESSED WORK WEEKS

Company Costs: more difficult supervision, labor-union opposition.

Company Benefits: reduced absences, less turnover, lower overhead.

Employee Costs: more difficulty with weekday child care, greater fatigue.

Employee Benefits: more personal time, less commuting.

FLEXIPLACE (WORK AT HOME)

Company Costs: difficult supervision, benefit inequities, equipment transfer, office tension.

Company Benefits: improved recruitment and retention, improved productivity, reduced office-space costs, better use of employees.

Employee Costs: isolation, less supervision, family conflicts.

Employee Benefits: convenience, less commuting, more personal time, fewer interruptions.

Source: Working Hours Flexibility, Graham L. Staines, U.S. Department of Labor, Commission on Workforce Quality and Labor Market Efficiency.

At Aetna Life & Casualty, 1,200 employees work part time or telecommute. Some telecommute to the office, staying in touch via computers, faxes, and telephone; others share jobs and so work only part time, sharing salary and one set of benefits.

Sabbaticals. Sabbaticals are becoming increasingly popular as hard-working baby boomers settle into middle age and yearn for time to reflect and explore nonwork possibilities. These long leaves of absence help employees sort out personal concerns, recharge batteries, and even renew loyalty to their employer. Here are examples of company sabbaticals.

Wells Fargo Bank in San Francisco gives employees a three-month paid break for every ten years of employment. Remarks a bank spokesman, "It's worth ten times the investment, to have employees who feel they are appreciated."

At Tandem Computer Corporation, sabbaticals are considered essential. Explains president James Trebig: "We recognized early on that many of our employees were working flat out in the early days of the company and that they could not continue in this mode. Away from the day-to-day operations, employees have the time to reflect, to figure out ways to do things better in the future. And innovation, after all, is what the computer industry is all about."

McDonald's Corporation places few restrictions on its twelve-year-old program. Corporate employees get eight weeks at full pay for every ten years of full-time service, and 90 percent of those eligible take them.

According to Families and Work Institute, these are seven attitudes that stand in the way of becoming a family-friendly company:

- *Keep your personal problems at home*
- *Give them a inch and they will take a mile*
- *Equity means treating everyone the same*
- *Benefit programs are provided for long-term security and protection*
- *Benefit programs can only satisfy workers and make them happy; they cannot make people more productive*
- *Presence equals productivity*
- *Hours equal output*

Corporate Policies and Strategies

There is a fine line among paternalistic companies between those that are authoritarian and hidebound and those that are responsive and accommodating to employee needs, that is, family friendly. The latter institute policies and programs that enable people to integrate all facets of their personal and professional lives and respond to people's families across the lifespan—from prenatal care to retirement planning. For these companies, a focus on families is essential for recruiting and retaining the next generation of highly trained, committed employees.

A Gallup Poll commissioned by the Employee Benefit Research Institute found that almost 75 percent of Americans believe employers can do a lot more to help employees be both good workers and good parents.

There is extremely heavy competition for good people these days. One of the ways to get and keep them is to help them fulfill their family responsibilities.

MICHAEL J. CAREY
Vice-President, Human
Resources, J&J Personal
Products Co.

Too often, companies underestimate the importance of family life to their employees and the economic cost of this concern to their operations. Unhappy employees struggling with barely functional families are not good workers; they are distracted and, at times, angry and frustrated at their situation and their employer. For a company to become family friendly, attitudes must change, policies must change, and new programs must be put in place.

Policies and programs are changed a number of ways. Some companies hire outside consultants experienced in work and family problems. A capital investment may be necessary for any number of services: child-care referral, education programs, relocation materials, and extended coverage for maternity or paternity leave. While initial investment may run into the thousands, savings in terms of retained employees, less lost work time, and fewer stressed, unhealthy employees will far exceed program costs. Furthermore, companies offering programs have found ways to make them self-supporting by charging nominal fees, forming co-ops with other companies, or forming partnerships with community groups.

Lastly, these programs take time—not simply time to organize, but time for employees to understand and accept that family matters are important to their company and to feel free to seek help and support for family concerns from their employer. Similarly, executives and managers need time to adjust their thinking about employee priorities and their role in helping employees, and themselves, become fuller, more balanced people. Here are nine steps for building a family-friendly company:

1. DEVELOP A CORPORATE FAMILY POLICY. Companies must not only appear to be family friendly, they must also officially, publicly announce the importance of family values in policy statements and communications. They must let it be known that family concerns matter and that employees will not be penalized for wanting full, healthy family lives.

For example, Johnson & Johnson recently added this statement to its company credo: "We must be mindful of ways to help our employees fulfill their family responsibilities." And DuPont's mission statement declares, "[We are] making changes in the workplace and fostering changes in the community that are sensitive to the changing family unit and the increasingly diverse work force."

2. CREATE A WORK–FAMILY TASK FORCE. A company task force on work and family issues can help identify specific concerns or problem areas that need to be addressed and draft proposed solutions. The members of the task force should represent the widest possible variation in terms of employees.

Levi Strauss and Company formed a work–family task force to find out what issues were most important to employees. The eighteen-member force, comprised of staff from all levels in the company, collected information from written surveys and small group discussions. After assembling the information, it presented recommendations to senior management. CEO Robert Haas, who participated as a member of the group, explains the importance of diverse family viewpoints: "My family situation is about as traditional as it gets. I have a wife at home who looks after our daughter. What do I know about the problems of a sewing machine operator . . . expected to punch in at a certain time and punch out at another and with a half-hour lunch break? Or whose child's day-care arrangements fall through that morning?" Needless to say, Haas learned a lot from listening to his employees' families.

The corporate culture historically says that employees should keep their personal problems at home. This inhibits employees from revealing family problems to supervisors. Generally, top managers have not experienced the same complexity of work-family conflict because they have spouses at home. Thus, they remain removed from the problems of their workers.

The Conference Board, 1989

3. APPOINT A MANAGER FOR FAMILY AFFAIRS. Along with official company policy should be official support in the form of an influential manager who ensures that the family-friendly rhetoric is put into action. Designating someone in the company responsible for helping develop and publicize family programs reinforces a company's commitment and employee participation.

At the *St. Petersburg Times,* this person is called the work and family resource counselor. Even the military has begun to recognize the family; the Air Force has appointed a chief of Air Force family policy and research. And both Aetna and IBM have positions called manager of dependent care programs—individuals responsible for sharing information about company programs and helping employees coordinate their work–family activities with different departments in the company.

In some companies, the individual responsible for work and family issues handles a number of positions. At Lancaster Labs, a 370-person service bureau in Pennsylvania, manager Carol Miller supervises human resources, management training, employee assistance, and work–family issues.

4. EDUCATE EMPLOYEES TO BE FAMILY FRIENDLY. A company may have to take the lead in developing family-sensitive programs and policies, and a good place to start is in educating all its employees. Informing employees about company policy on what is available and what is permissible affirms family values. Here are some examples of how companies have done this:

The real issue rests in the way we raise our families. Companies can start to influence that. Employers should adopt a long-term strategy. Cost sharing needs to happen, but unless we change behavior, we'll never get costs under control.

MOLLY McCAULEY
Director of Health Promotion, AT&T

- PSFS Bank, Philadelphia, gives six-hour parenting seminars so people can describe the stresses and rewards of raising young children and how it affects their work.

- Oster/Sunbeam started a prenatal education program that is mandatory for all pregnant employees and open to spouses on a voluntary basis. After initiating the program, the company saw its maternity costs dive from a per-pregnancy average of $17,000 to just $3,500.

- Monthly lunchtime workshops, employee support groups, and a work–family newsletter are just a few of the many resources available at Time Inc. magazines.

- US Sprint Communications Company gives employees counseling and referral services in a variety of life-management areas, including child care, elder care, and marital conflicts.

5. DESIGN BENEFITS FOR ALL AGES. Company benefits should allow enough room for the needs of all employees. Flexible benefits, sometimes called comprehensive cafeteria plans, give employees the freedom to set their own personal priorities. Hewitt & Associates, a benefits consulting firm, estimates that 20 percent of employers have these plans, and 80 percent of those with such plans have flexible spending accounts. Under these plans, employees receive core benefits, then choose or purchase, using credits received from employer contributions, additional benefits that suit their needs. The following is a sampling of benefit programs.

The Seattle Times

- The Seattle Times officially opened its day-care center for employees in May of 1988. Employees can use flexible dependent-care spending accounts to pay for child care and a child-care referral service. A local hospital runs a satellite center for mildly ill children.

- The benefits policy at the Bureau of National Affairs, a Washington, D.C. publishing company, allows employees to take individual hours of sick leave in order to visit sick relatives.

- In Dallas, the Brock Hotel Corporation sponsors after-school clubs for six-to-twelve-year-olds in some of its Chuck E. Cheese Pizza Time Theater and Showbiz Pizza Palace franchises.

- Fel-Pro, Inc., an Illinois manufacturer and seller of automotive and industrial gaskets, offers its 2,000 employees a unique benefit: a summer camp for their children. The company picks up about 80 percent of the costs of Triple R Camp, which costs parents just $15 a week.

- Remington Products Inc., a Connecticut appliance maker, reimburses employees caring for elderly relatives for half the cost of hiring someone to come into their homes for a few hours while the employee runs errands.

- General Foods lets workers purchase long-term health-insurance coverage for their parents at affordable group rates.

- Original Copy Centers in Cleveland offers special benefits to the young, single employees that make up most of its work force. The company headquarters has a laundry room, a movie theater, a game room, and a kitchen.

Companies are learning that the "one size fits all" approach to benefit design is no longer valid. Benefits aren't just for protection and security but for everyday coping.

Employee Benefit News

6. EXPAND FAMILY LEAVE. The practice of giving parental leave is growing in the United States, although the nation still lags far behind other industrialized countries, as reported by the World Health Organization. Again the healthy companies are out front, offering segmented leave time—including maternity leave, paternity leave, and death-in-the-family leave—under an umbrella category called family leave, which is made available to employees for any family reason. Their policies include the following.

- Colgate-Palmolive allows up to three months' unpaid leave for salaried employees for birth, adoption, family illness, or elderly care.

■ The New York architectural design firm Perkins Geddis Eastman combines family leave with flextime so that new parents can work at home two days a week.

■ The Arthur Andersen Worldwide Organization, a leading professional services firm, has a plan for employees who want to make partner yet take time for their families. Managers are allowed to work part time for up to three years, with no loss of seniority or of consideration for advancement.

■ IBM has instituted a Work and Personal Life Balance Program that offers employees family leave, alternative work arrangements, individualized work schedules, work-at-home options, referral services, and family seminars. The program allows up to three years of unpaid absence, although employees must put in some time during those years to maintain their skills. When they return to full-time work, employees are guaranteed comparable jobs, though not necessarily at the same location.

I never use my personal sick days at work for myself, no matter how ill I become. That would be a luxury I can't afford. I am afraid that I will need them later in the year to be with my children when they get sick.

Mother quoted in *Working Mother*

Data Bank

A 1988 study by the Bureau of Labor Statistics found that companies with ten to forty-nine employees offer these benefits or policies:

Employer-sponsored day care: 1.9 percent

Assistance with child-care expenses: 2.4 percent

Child-care information or referral services: 4.3 percent

Counseling services: 3.8 percent

Flextime: 45.1 percent

Voluntary part-time schedules: 36.0 percent

Job sharing: 16.0 percent

Work at home: 9.2 percent

Flexible leave: 43.8 percent

7. OFFER ASSISTANCE FOR EMPLOYEE DEPENDENTS. Out of the nation's six million employers, only about 4,100 offer active child-care programs, and these companies tend to be large, with many female employees, non-union, young, fast growing, led by entrepreneurs, and experiencing labor shortages—in short, a special type of company. Yet experts agree that child care is quickly becoming essential for all kinds of companies. Declares Ellen Galinsky, co-president, Families and Work Institute "Couples seem to feel that child care is their problem alone. It's not. It's an institutional problem. Families have changed much faster than the institutions that the family relies on."

While on-site child care is the ideal for some companies, it is not the only option available. In some industries and in some parts of the country, child care has become so essential to attracting and keeping employees that few companies can afford to ignore the issue. So when they cannot afford a child-care center they devise other alternatives, including referral services, child-care subsidies, contracting for community child-care services, or implementing the government's Dependent Care Assistance Plan. Authorized by the IRS, the plan enables employees to use up to 5,000 pre-tax dollars a year to pay for child care. Sometimes a simple approach works best: increasing access to telephones so employees can make contact with their children during the day.

But dependent care today is not limited to children. A recent twist is the addition of aging dependent parents. Millions of baby boomers are finding themselves wedged between caring for children and for elderly relatives, becoming the so-called sandwich generation. To assist these employees, some companies are offering referrals for finding homes, nursing services, or live-in care for elderly relatives.

Some companies, such as Stride Rite Corporation, are already addressing both ends of the age spectrum. This Massachusetts-based shoe company has opened at its offices a combination child-care and elderly-care center. Its innovative intergenerational day-care center includes as many as sixty children, some as young as fifteen months, and as many as twenty-five elderly relatives of employees. The Stride Rite centers not only affirm the company's values but also improve its balance sheet. The company estimates it saves $22,000 per employee by enabling it to keep highly skilled people and avoid the cost of retraining.

Data Bank

- ■ *Twenty-six percent of nonworking mothers with young childen say they would work if they had reasonably priced child care.*

- ■ *Twelve percent of elementary-school children and 30 percent of middle-school children are latchkey kids, according to a 1987 Louis Harris poll.*

- ■ *Child-care expenditures are the fourth largest for families with children, trailing closely behind housing, food, and taxes.*

Surveys of Fortune 500 companies reveal that between 20 and 30 percent of employees regularly care for elderly parents.

ELLEN GALINSKY
Families and Work Institute

Honeywell

Child-Care Options

Companies are using an array of creative options to help employees solve child-care problems. Here is a sampling of what is being tried:

- On-site centers open to the entire community where parents drop off children before work, visit them during the day, and pick them up after work. In Cincinnati, Procter & Gamble runs two child-care facilities with three-fourths of the slots earmarked for employees' children and the remaining quarter open to the community.

- Off-site centers with many child-care services. Wang Computer established a facility for 235 children a few miles from its Lowell, Massachusetts headquarters that contains twenty-four classrooms, a cafeteria, and a gymnasium.

- Child-care support for the most needy employees. Employees at Polaroid must have a family income of less than $30,000 a year to qualify for its child-care support program. For these employees, Polaroid subsidizes up to 80 percent of child-care expenses. Subsidies are in the form of vouchers that can be used at independent child-care facilities.

- Child-care centers supported by a consortium of groups. Grieco Bros., Inc., a Massachusetts maker of men's clothing, joined with a nearby mill, the Amalgamated Clothing & Textile Workers Union, foundations, and the city council to construct a community day-care center to be managed independently.

- IBM established a referral service for its 237,000 employees and 33,000 retirees, and in its first month of operation, helped more than 4,000 employees asking for suggestions for caring for children and elderly parents.

- Child-care support for sick children. Honeywell, Inc., in Minneapolis, has refined its day-care program by covering 80 percent of the cost of caring for employees' sick children. The Unity Medical Center's Sick Care Program is a day-care center for mildly ill children, and TenderCare for Kids arranges for trained personnel to care for the severely sick child at the employee's home.

- The Washington, D.C. law firm of Wilmer, Cutler, and Pickering, with 250 lawyers and a total of 500 employees, saved 1,500 billable attorney hours by establishing an on-site emergency child-care facility in 1986.

8. MANAGE RELOCATION THE RIGHT WAY. Job transfers are a major event for everyone not only because of the change in homes, but also because they rupture family routines and ties. Some 20 percent of the U.S. population moves each year as a result of corporate relocation. Companies that ignore the family trauma that accompanies most moves may end up with unhappy, discontented employees. Companies need to include family considerations when making transfers and extend help beyond spouses to live-in partners, school-age children, and dependent relatives living nearby. Here are some suggestions:

A 1989 study of 280 companies by Merrill Lynch Relocation Management reports that 26 percent of "first-choice" candidates for transfer were reluctant or refused to move. The main reasons were cost of living and housing, adjustment problems for children, and spouses' career plans.

- Consider the disruption to working spouses and children in school when arranging relocation packages. They experience the most stress, and they are the ones who can sabotage a move.

- Communicate. Let employees know how they will be compensated, how long they will stay, and how they will be treated if they refuse to relocate. Follow up your communication after the transfer.

- Consider quality-of-life issues, such as cost-of-living increases, quality of schools, home buyback options, and job assistance for spouses.

Baxter Healthcare Corporation, Deerfield, Illinois, has a variety of relocation programs, including mortgage assistance, home-sale assistance, living differentials for moving to higher-cost cities, and help with house moving. And Corning Glass Works helps unmarried couples by paying the expenses of live-in partners who accompany employees on house-hunting trips. They also open orientation sessions to partners.

9. CATER TO OLDER WORKERS. As employers grapple with labor shortages, companies must turn toward America's elders to help fill the gap. It is now commonplace for people to work well into their senior years; according to research by Louis Harris & Associates, there are 1.9 million available workers between ages fifty and sixty-four. Yet many companies are still squeamish about the lingering questions of older workers' adaptability to new technology and the cost of their health insurance.

Older workers, for their part, often have a strong commitment to quality and dedication but want working arrangements that give them freedom and control to do a variety of things besides working. Explains *Age Wave* author Ken Dychtwald: "Older workers don't want to punch the clock, would like a better blend of work and play, usually want to collaborate with intergenerational teams, and want to be more appreciated for their unique skills and experience."

Here are examples of company programs aimed at maximizing the contributions of older workers. Many of them go beyond the usual financial planning offered by companies around retirement time.

- IBM has created a Retiree Education Assistance Program that pays up to $5,000 in tuition to employees and their spouses in the three years before retirement and two years after. People use the money for a variety of studies, from earning real-estate licenses to learning carpentry.

- Like a number of other firms, Polaroid Company in Cambridge, Massachusetts offers retirement rehearsals —trial periods when employees take a leave of absence from work and either return or decide to quit permanently. About half the Polaroid employees who use retirement rehearsals return to their jobs.

- Employees near retirement age at Varian Associates in Palo Alto, California can taper back to a four-day week for a year, then to a three-day week for another year before leaving.

- Aerospace Corporation uses retired former employees in its casual employment program. This allows people to work up to 1,000 hours a year (about half time) without losing pension benefits.

- Travelers Corporation in Hartford, Connecticut operates a job bank for retirees, functioning as an in-house temporary agency that provides a pool of skilled personnel to fill temporary vacancies. The retirees are consistently rated higher than other temps by their supervisors, and the company saves approximately $4 million a year by avoiding temporary-agency fees. Over 750 retirees are registered with the job bank.

American organizations have suffered under the syndrome of men and women wanting to "have it all," struggling to maintain a work and family life. Accepting personal limitations while retaining self-esteem and a sense of values will emerge as our greatest challenge. We will have no choice if we are to thrive as healthy, successful adults in the workplace of the 1990s.

SARAH BULLARD STECK
Healthy Companies

- Helping active employees ease into retirement is the goal of Kollmorgen Corporation's Rehearsal Retirement Program, open to full-time employees aged sixty-two and older who have at least ten years of service with the company. Through the program these employees can gradually substitute volunteer work at a local community agency for their normal work load at the company.

- Champion International Corporation, a paper and forest products manufacturer headquartered in Stamford, Connecticut, developed a Retired Employee Assistance Program that provides confidential counseling and referrals for retirees suffering from family care-giving responsibilities, loneliness, and bereavement.

HEALTHY FAMILIES, HEALTHY COMPANIES

Preoccupied by career pressures and family trade-offs, many employees live in a world of sacrifices and compromises. Nevertheless, they continue to search for the right combination of success that integrates career advancement into a broader vision of purpose in life.

The healthy company understands this dilemma. It knows that with one malfunctioning component, such as an employee with an unhappy, stressful family life, the entire company suffers. Managers can do much to help employees meet their work and family responsibilities. The family-friendly company is a major step in that direction.

On Rose Blumpkin, age ninety-four, chairperson of a division of Berkshire Hathaway: "She is clearly gathering speed and may well reach her full potential in another five or ten years. Therefore, I've persuaded the board to scrap our mandatory retirement at 100 policy. . . . It's about time. With every passing year, this policy has seemed sillier to me. . . . My God, good managers are so scarce I can't afford the luxury of letting them go just because they've added a year to their age!"

WARREN BUFFETT
Chairman, Berkshire
Hathaway

Final Thoughts

IMAGINE THAT EACH OF the principles and practices found in this book occurred in your company. If this sounds radical and idealistic, it shouldn't. Many of the companies cited here are already living proof that working conditions can be dramatically improved. When this is done well, all the stakeholders benefit—shareholders, customers, employees, and families. Healthy people do make healthy companies. And healthy companies are more likely, more often and over a longer period of time, to make healthy profits and to have healthy returns on their investments. By now, you probably are aware of the ways you can make a difference.

I began this book by sharing my own personal journey that led to the concept of the healthy company. This book is the culmination of that work, but it is just the beginning. In 1987, the MacArthur Foundation initiated a three-year development process to study the problems and opportunities facing employees and their organizations. A series of meetings with business, union, and academic scholars was conducted around the country. This planning process determined that the time was right for a new paradigm, for a major philosophic shift in the way institutions define and manage work and our relationships to our jobs, to each other, and to our organizations. Much as the industrial revolution predominated the 1900s and the information revolution captured the 1960s, the 1990s will be a time when the human-resource revolution takes center stage.

In January 1991, the MacArthur Foundation funded a multi-year, evolutionary program for the sole purpose of promoting a new model of healthy work for the year 2000—one that promotes human development, organizational effectiveness, and economic success. The program will involve a team of international business and academic experts and focus on the following activities:

Knowledge development. We will collect and analyze existing knowledge and create new research; build a common language and create new models of healthy organizations; identify and codify the best thinking; and create an international database of the best business practices from a broad base of people-oriented organizations.

Communication and dissemination. We will articulate a credible, independent voice on healthy organizations; identify, publicize, and celebrate leaders and leading organizations; and develop a national education strategy that legitimizes healthy organization practices at work.

Network development. We will build a community of business practitioners and academic researchers who share common values and vision about the new healthy organization, and create a membership organization of business practitioners who can learn new approaches and share successes with fellow colleagues around the world.

Ultimately, the goal of these activities will be to improve the health of individuals and families, the economic success of organizations, and the health of our society. We have ignored for too long the unassailable fact that individual values, workplace values, and societal values are intimately connected. Just as healthy people cannot survive in unhealthy organizations, healthy companies cannot prosper and thrive in sick societies.

Their success and failure depend on one another and we can do better.

The 1990s will be a very exciting time. As employees, managers, and companies join together to create new ways for working, we will build organizations that are true reflections of our healthy values and dreams. For I believe that the secrets to success are inside—inside us and inside our organizations. All we need to do is look.

WRITE TO US

The Healthy Company is a composite of the best minds, the best people, and the best companies. Send us your ideas, suggestions, and best management practices. We will pass them on to others.

For more information about Healthy Companies research, programs and products, contact:

Healthy Companies
P.O. Box 1648
Arlington, VA 22201

Bibliography

The Healthy Company is based on materials collected over the course of four years. Sources have included: newspapers, magazines, academic journals, books, company publications, research reports, speeches, testimony, television transcripts, government documents, unpublished research, newsletters, videotapes, and hundreds of interviews. Below is a listing of selected references for each chapter:

INTRODUCTION / THE ANATOMY OF A HEALTHY COMPANY

Alperson, M.; Marlin, A. T.; Schorsch, J.; and Will, R. 1991. *The Better World Investment Guide.* New York: Simon and Schuster.

Committee for Economic Development. Research and Policy Committee. 1990. *An America That Works: The Life-Cycle Approach to a Competitive Work Force.* New York: Committee for Economic Development.

Doyle, Frank P. 1989. *People Power: The Global Human Resource Challenge for the Nineties.* Paper presented at the World Management Congress.

Goldbeck, W. B. September 29, 1988. Testimony presented to United States Senate, Subcommittee on Education, Arts and Humanities. Senate Joint Resolution 368.

Healthy Companies. Newport Beach, CA: Foundation for Wellness, 1988. Television film.

Howard, R. 1990. Values Make the Company: An Interview with Robert Haas. *Harvard Business Review,* September-October, 134–44.

Kanter, R. M. 1983. *The Change Masters.* New York: Simon and Schuster.

Kravetz, D. J. 1988. *The Human Resources Revolution.* San Francisco: Jossey-Bass.

Levering, R. 1988. *A Great Place to Work.* New York: Random House.

Maccoby, M. 1988. *The Workplace and Matters of the Heart.* Washington, DC: Cathedral College of the Laity.

The New America. 1989. *Business Week,* September 25.

Polakoff, P.L., and O'Rourke, P. 1990. *Healthy Worker—Healthy Workplace: The Productivity Connection.* Sacramento, CA: California Legislature.

Schein, E., ed. 1987. *The Art of Managing Human Resources.* New York: Oxford University Press.

Seidman, W. L., and Skancke, S. L. 1990. *Productivity: The American Advantage.* New York: Simon and Schuster.

Workplace of the Future. 1990. *The Wall Street Journal Reports,* June 4.

CHAPTER 1 / THE POWER OF RESPECT IS
GREATER THAN THE POWER OF MONEY

Anderson, J. D., and Porter, E. A.
1989. *The Project on Moral Character and Development at Work: A Report.* Washington, DC: Cathedral
College of the Laity.

1989 Annual Report. Ben and Jerry's.

The Art of Loving. 1989. *Inc.,* May,
35–46.

The Boeing Company. *Business Conduct Guidelines.*

Carlzon, J. 1989. *Moments of Truth.*
New York: Harper and Row.

DePree, M. 1987. *Leadership Is an
Art.* New York: Doubleday.

Farnham, A. 1989. The Trust Gap.
Fortune, December 4.

Hanson, K. 1983. Ethics and Business: A Progress Report. *Stanford
GSB,* Spring, 10–14.

Horton, T. 1986. *"What Works for
Me": 16 CEOs Talk About Their Ca-
reers and Commitments.* New York:
Random House.

Kanter, D. 1989. *The Cynical Americans.* San Francisco: Jossey-Bass.

Kelly, M. 1989. A Poet and a President. *Business Ethics,* April-May.

Koestenbaum, P. 1987. *The Heart of
Business.* San Francisco: Saybrook
Publishing.

Levering, R. 1988. *A Great Place to
Work.* New York: Random House.

Louis Harris and Associates, 1989.
The Office Environment Index 1989.
Louis Harris and Associates.

National Center for Employee
Ownership. 1986. *The Employee
Ownership Casebook.* Oakland, CA:
National Center for Employee
Ownership.

CHAPTER 2 / WISE LEADERS KNOW HOW
TO FOLLOW

Bennis, W. 1989. *On Becoming a
Leader.* Reading, MA: Addison-
Wesley.

Being the Boss. 1990. *Inc.,* October,
49–65.

Block, P. 1988. *The Empowered
Manager.* San Francisco: Jossey-Bass.

Bowles, J. G. 1990. Advertising Supplement: The Human Side of
Quality. *Fortune,* September 24.

Brim, G. 1988. Losing and Winning.
Psychology Today, September,
48–52.

Dumaine, B. 1990. Who Needs a
Boss? *Fortune,* May 7, 52–60.

Gallagan, P. 1988. Donald E. Petersen: Chairman of Ford and Champion of its People. *Training and
Development Journal* 42. August.

Lawler III, E. E., and Ledford, Jr., G.E.
1989. *Employee Involvement in
America: A Study of Contemporary
Practice.* Houston, TX: American
Productivity and Quality Center.

Managing at Syntex. 1990 Syntex
company materials.

National Center for Employee
Ownership. 1986. *The Employee
Ownership Casebook.* Oakland, CA:
National Center for Employee
Ownership.

National Center for Employee
Ownership. 1987. *Beyond Taxes,
Managing an Employee Ownership
Company.* Oakland, CA: National
Center for Employee Ownership.

Pugh, M. 1990. Palms West Hospital:
We Are the Competition. *Palms West
Hospital Corporate Newsletter,* July.

Rosen, R. 1986. *Healthy Companies:
A Human Resources Approach.* New
York: American Management
Association.

Semler, R. 1989. Managing Without
Managers. *Harvard Business Review,*
September-October, 76–84.

Stayer, R. 1990. How I Learned to Let
My Workers Lead. *Harvard Business
Review,* November-December.

Walton, W. B. 1986. *The New Bottom
Line.* San Francisco: Harper and
Row.

CHAPTER 3 / IF YOU DON'T MANAGE
CHANGE, IT WILL MANAGE YOU

Fisher, A. B. 1988. The Downside of
Downsizing. *Fortune,* May 23.

Franzem, J. S. 1987. Easing the Pain.
Personnel Administrator, February.

Hamilton, M. M. 1989. New USAir Is
Off to a Flying Start. *Washington
Post Business,* August 7.

Henkoff. 1990. Cost Cutting: How to
Do It Right. *Fortune,* April 9.

Hipp, E. 1988. Surviving the
Shakeout. *HealthAction Managers,*
October 25.

Kanter, R. M. 1989. *When Giants
Learn to Dance.* New York: Simon
and Schuster.

Marks, M. 1988. The Disappearing
Company Man. *Psychology Today,*
September.

Mills, D. Q. 1988. *The IBM Lesson.*
New York: Times Books.

Scott, C., and Jaffe, D. 1988.
Managing Organizational Change.
Los Altos, CA: Crisp Publications.

Tomasko, R. M. 1988. *Downsizing.*
New York: Amacom.

Waterman, Jr., R. H. 1987. *The
Renewal Factor.* Toronto, Canada:
Bantam Books.

CHAPTER 4 / LIFETIME LEARNING PAYS
LIFELONG DIVIDENDS

Burlingham, B. O. 1990. This Woman
Has Changed Business Forever. *Inc.,*
June, 34.

Carnevale, A. P.; Gainer, L. J.; and Villet, J.; 1990. *Training in America: The Organization and Strategic Role of Training.* San Francisco: Jossey-Bass.

Committee for Economic Development. 1990. *An America That Works: The Life-Cycle Approach to a Competitive Work Force.* New York: Committee for Economic Development.

Hall, D. T. 1986. *Career Development in Organizations.* San Francisco: Jossey-Bass.

Howard, A., and Bray, D.W. 1988. *Managerial Lives in Transition.* New York: Guilford Press.

Kirkpatrick, D. 1990. Is Your Career on Track? *Fortune,* July.

Kuhn, S. E. 1990. How Business Helps Schools. *Fortune (Education Issue),* Spring, 91–94.

LaBier, D. 1986. *Modern Madness.* Reading, MA: Addison-Wesley.

McCall, Jr., M.; Lombardo, M.; and Morrison, A. 1988. *The Lessons of Experience: How Successful Executives Develop on the Job.* Lexington, MA: Lexington Books.

Perry, N. J. 1988. Saving the Schools: How Business Can Help. *Fortune,* November 7.

Senge, P.M. 1990. *The Fifth Discipline: The Art and Practice of the Learning Organization.* New York: Doubleday/Currency.

Therrien, L. 1988. Motorola Sends Its Workforce Back to School. *Business Week,* June 6, 80–81.

CHAPTER 5 / HEALTHY PEOPLE ARE APPRECIATING ASSETS

Alves, F. D., and Wood, M. W. 1988. *Wellness at Work: A Practical Guide for Health Promotion in Small Business.* Helena, MT: Montana Department of Health Incentives.

American Productivity and Quality Center. 1985. Case Study 44: Tenneco, Inc. Houston, TX: American Productivity and Quality Center.

Behrens, R., ed. 1985–89. *Worksite Wellness Series.* Washington, DC: Washington Business Group on Health.

Cataldo, M. F., and Coates, T. J. eds. 1986. *Health and Industry: A Behavioral Medicine Perspective.* New York: John Wiley.

Freuenheim, M. 1990. Assessing the Corporate Fitness Craze. *New York Times,* March 18.

Hyatt, J. 1987. Health Returns. *Inc.,* April, 80–86.

Jaffe, D. T., and Scott, C. D. 1984. *From Burnout to Balance: A Workbook for Peak Performance and Self-Renewal.* New York: McGraw-Hill.

Kets deFries, M. 1989. *Prisoners of Leadership.* New York: John Wiley.

Matteson, M. T., and Ivancevich, J. M. 1987. *Controlling Workstress: Effective Human Resource and Management Strategies.* San Francisco: Jossey-Bass.

Pelletier, K. R., ed. 1991. A Review and Analysis of the Health and Cost-Effective Outcome Studies of Comprehensive Health Promotion and Disease Prevention Programs. *American Journal of Health Promotion* 5, March/April.

Roberts, M., and Harris, T. G. 1989. Wellness at Work: How Corporations Help Employees Fight Stress and Stay Healthy. *Psychology Today,* May.

CHAPTER 6 / SICK JOBS SABOTAGE LONG-TERM INVESTMENTS

Barge, B. 1989. Study Identifies Excellence in Managing Workers' Compensation. *The Human Factor,* April. St. Paul, MN: The St. Paul Companies.

Carbine, M. E.; Schwartz, G. E.; and Watson, S. D. 1989. *Disability Intervention and Cost Management Strategies for the 1990's.* Report from the Second Annual National Disability Management Conference. Washington, DC: Washington Business Group on Health/Institute for Rehabilitation and Disability Management.

Dainoff, M. J. 1986. *People and Productivity: A Manager's Guide to Ergonomics in the Electronic Office.* Agincourt, Ontario: Gage Educational Publishing.

Equal to the Task II. 1990. Survey of Employment of People with Disabilities. Wilmington, DE: DuPont.

Ivancevich, J. M.; Matteson, M. T.; and Richards III, E. P. 1985. Who's Liable for Stress on the Job? *Harvard Business Review,* March-April.

Karasek, R., and Theorell, T. 1990. *Healthy Work: Stress, Productivity, and the Reconstruction of Working Life.* New York: Basic Books.

LaBar, G. 1990. Ergonomics: The Mazda Way. *Occupational Hazards,* April.

Mueller, J. 1990. *The Workplace Workbook: An Illustrated Guide to Job Accommodation and Assistive Technology.* Washington, DC: The Dole Foundation.

Overman, S. 1990. In Search of Prescriptions for a Healthier Office. *HRMagazine,* February.

Promoting Health and Productivity in the Computerized Office: Models of Successful Ergonomic Interventions. 1988. Conference sponsored by the National Institute for Occupational Safety and Health. Miami, FL: Center for Ergonomic Research, Miami University.

Walton, R. E., and Susman, G. I. 1987. People Policies for the New Machines. *Harvard Business Review*, March-April.

Westin, A. 1990. Organizational Culture and VDT Policies: A Case Study of the Federal Express Corporation. In *Promoting Health and Productivity in the Computerized Office: Models of Successful Ergonomic Interventions*, eds. Sauter, S. L.; Dainoff, M. J.; and Smith, M. J. London and New York: Taylor and Francis.

CHAPTER 7 / OUR STRENGTHS LIE IN CELEBRATING DIFFERENCES

Census '90. A Joint Report with American Demographics Magazine and The Wall Street Journal. *The Wall Street Journal*, March 9, 1990.

Copeland, L., and Griggs, L. 1988. Valuing Diversity Film Series. San Francisco: Copeland-Griggs.

Fierman, J. 1990. Why Women Still Don't Hit the Top. *Fortune*, July 30.

Loden, M., and Rosener, J. B. 1991. *Workforce America! Managing Employee Diversity as a Vital Resource*. Homewood, IL: Business One Irwin.

Nussbaum, B. 1988. Needed: Human Capital. *Business Week*, September 19.

Sandroff, R. 1988. Sexual Harassment in the Fortune 500. *Working Woman*, December, 69–73.

Singer, M. R. 1987. Intercultural Communication: A Perceptual Approach. Englewood Cliffs, N. J.: Prentice Hall.

Thomas, Jr., R. R. 1990. From Affirmative Action to Affirming Diversity. *Harvard Business Review*, March-April.

Towers Perrin, 1990. *Workforce 2000/Competing in a Seller's Market: Is Corporate America Prepared?* Indianapolis, IN: The Hudson Institute.

Will, R. B., and Lyndendberg, S. D. 1987. 20 Corporations That Listen to Women: A Ms./Council on Economic Priorities Survey, *Ms.*, November.

CHAPTER 8 / WORK AND FAMILY ARE PARTNERS FOR LIFE

American Association of Retired Persons. 1989. *Business and Older Workers: Current Perceptions and New Directions for the 1990's*. Washington, DC: American Association of Retired Persons.

Burden, D. S., and Googins, B. 1987. *The Boston University Balancing Job and Home Life Study: Managing Work and Family Stress in Corporations*. Boston, MA: Boston University.

Copeland, L. 1988. Learning to Manage a Multicultural Work Force. *Training*, May.

Cronin, C., and Hartman, R. 1989. *The Corporate Perspective on Material and Child Health*. Washington, DC: Washington Business Group on Health.

Maccoby, M. 1988. *Why Work?* New York: Simon and Schuster.

Dychtwald, K., and Flower, J. 1989. *Age Wave: The Challenges and Opportunities of an Aging America*. Los Angeles: Jeremy P. Tarcher.

Footlick, J. K. 1990. *What Happened to the Family?* San Francisco: Harper & Row.

Friedman, D., and Gray, W. 1989. *A Life Cycle Approach to Family Benefits and Policies*. New York: The Conference Board.

Friedman, D. E. 1989. *Productivity Impact of Work and Family Problems and Programs*. New York: The Conference Board.

Levin, R., and Weil, J. B., eds. 1989. Business and Aging. *Generations*, Summer.

Levin, R. C., ed. 1989. *Together on Aging*. Washington Business Group on Health, Fall.

Martinez, M. N. 1990. Making Room for Work/Family Positions. *HRMagazine*, August.

Rodgers, F. S., and Rodgers, C. 1989. Business and the Facts of Family Life. *Harvard Business Review*, 36–43.

Schaef, A. W., and Fassel, D. 1988. The Addictive Organization. *Healthy Companies*, Fall.

Schwartz, F. N. 1989. Management Women and the New Facts of Life. *Harvard Business Review*, January-February, 65–76.

Work and Personal Life Balance Programs. IBM Company Materials.

Index